THE KING'S
CHINESE

From Barber to Banker, the story of
Yeap Chor Ee and the Straits Chinese

The **Strategic Information and Research Development Centre (SIRD)** is an independent publishing house founded in January 2000 in Petaling Jaya, Malaysia. The SIRD list focuses on Malaysian and Southeast Asian studies, economics, gender studies, social sciences, politics and international relations. Our books address the scholarly community, students, the NGO and development communities, policymakers, activists and the wider public. SIRD also distributes titles (via its sister organisation, **GB Gerakbudaya Enterprise Sdn Bhd**) published by scholarly and institutional presses, NGOs and other independent publishers. We also organise seminars, forums and group discussions. All this, we believe, is conducive to the development and consolidation of the notions of civil liberty and democracy.

THE KING'S CHINESE

From Barber to Banker, the story of
Yeap Chor Ee and the Straits Chinese

Daryl Yeap

**Strategic
Information
and Research
Development Centre**

World Scientific

Published by

World Scientific Publishing Co. Pte. Ltd.
5 Toh Tuck Link, Singapore 596224
USA office: 27 Warren Street, Suite 401-402, Hackensack, NJ 07601
UK office: 57 Shelton Street, Covent Garden, London WC2H 9HE

British Library Cataloguing-in-Publication Data
A catalogue record for this book is available from the British Library.

Published by arrangement with Strategic Information and Research Development Centre.

THE KING'S CHINESE
From Barber to Banker, the story of Yeap Chor Ee and the Straits Chinese

ISBN 978-981-126-310-1 (hardcover)
ISBN 978-981-126-377-4 (paperback)

For any available supplementary material, please visit
https://www.worldscientific.com/worldscibooks/10.1142/13047#t=suppl

Desk Editor: Nicole Ong

Contents

To my parents and
to the memory of
my great-grandfather

Preface

Homestead was the home of my great-grandfather, Yeap Chor Ee. In 2006, when the decision was made to entrust it to an education foundation, we had to think of what to do with its contents. A family friend suggested a gallery paying tribute to Chor Ee and the philanthropic work done by his foundation. No. 4 Penang Street, a previous home to Chor Ee and his family, had been rented out ever since the 1930s. The interior had been altered several times through the years. My mother, being an architect, converted the interior to house most of the large pieces of furniture from Homestead. It was during the renovation process that I started the research that led to writing this book.

Without much to go on besides family anecdotes I engaged the historian Dr Wong Yee Tuan. While he searched the National Archives in Kuala Lumpur, I spent months sieving through records and scrolling through reels of microfiche in the libraries and archives in Singapore.

Sometime in the 1980s the National Archives of Singapore recorded an interview with Yap Siong Eu, which included details of how Chor Ee managed the day to day operations of his bank. In the archives of the ISEAS library I unearthed previously unknown private letters between Yeap Chor Ee and his wife Lee Cheng Kin, and other letters between Chor Ee and Tun Tan Cheng Lock.

In Kuala Lumpur Yee Tuan uncovered a number of articles and government records that were of particular value, including copies of minutes of meetings between the Financial Secretary, the Treasurer, and the Attorney General of the Settlements. There was also a petition from Ban Hin Lee Bank to Sir Henry Gurney, requesting the return of a very large sum of money confiscated by the Japanese during the occupation. No living family member knew about this dark episode of the bank's history. I sought the advice of several lawyers, but they concurred that since the event had taken took place almost seventy years earlier it would be complicated to trace the money. In any case this discovery prompted me to continue searching. Slowly but surely, pieces of information eventually came together, which is one of the reasons this book took almost twelve years to complete.

There were not many people left who had known or met Chor Ee. Most family members were too young to recall the details of his business and personal life, but they had plenty of memories of life at home and remembered stories passed down from Chor Ee's wife Lee Cheng Kin.

When I started my interviews, the oldest living family member was Chor Ee's adopted grandson Yeap Leong Sim. He was already in his early nineties, but despite being quite frail he was able to give descriptions of events from the 1930s onwards, including the Japanese occupation. Being a keen photographer he also had a decent collection of photographs, including photos of the family, Homestead, and the construction of the bank on Beach Street during the 1930s.

Another grandson, Dato' Seri Goh Eng Toon, whose father worked for Chor Ee in the 1930s, furnished information about Chor Ee's estates and oil mill businesses. Dato' Seri Goh had also worked in Ban Hin Lee Bank before becoming its chairman in the 1990s, so he had a good understanding of the bank's culture. It was he who kept the bank's old ledgers and minutes. Beautifully handwritten, they detailed acquisitions, loans, transactions, and information that would not normally be found in archives.

I was fortunate to be able to interview the late Tun Lim Chong Eu, who was Chief Minister of Penang for twenty-one years. Even in his late eighties, he had incredible presence. I must admit I was in awe of him. In response to my questions he would often talk at great length, taking diversions into unrelated topics. Not wanting to derail his thoughts, I let him speak freely. Years later, when I had a better grasp of the subject matter, I realised that this extraordinary man knew what I was going to write before I did myself. Although he did not know Chor Ee, he helped clarify my understanding of society, particularly in the Chinese community of that era.

My father was still a small child when his grandfather passed away. Like his sisters, he was mostly able to relate tales from his grandmother Cheng Kin, but he also described Chor Ee's philanthropic endeavours and the developments of his grandfather's key businesses.

A number of my interviews with family members were conducted using WhatsApp, which I found a particularly useful tool, since people who lived apart could be interviewed at the same time, each event recalled by one person aiding the recollection of the others.

My research also led me to several locations outside of Malaysia. In November 2006 I visited the site of the ancestral home in Lam Au, Amoy (Xiamen) and again in November 2012. A few old relatives, descendants of Chor Ee's older brothers, still lived there, but the original house was gone, replaced by a big courtyard styled stone house, built with money Chor Ee had provided sometime at the turn of the 20th century. While still in good condition, the house looked as if it had not changed much since it had been built. In the middle of the courtyard, in front of the main door, was an altar. The rooms in the house were mostly empty, as the majority of family members had moved out and built bigger homes close by. The few inhabitants left were friendly and welcoming, but I speak no Mandarin and it was difficult to understand their Hokkien dialect, which was different from the 'bastardised' version spoken in Penang. Despite the awkwardness in communication, seeing the surrounding countryside where my great grandfather had grown up, the ancestral home his money had built, and the faces of my distant relatives, I felt a deep sense of connection to the place.

In 2009, the Chinese Year of the Snake, I ventured further north, to the ancient capital of Henan, the cradle of Chinese civilisation and the birthplace of the Ye clan. Every twelve years, thousands of clansmen and clanswomen congregate to commemorate the birthday of Shen Zhuliang, the progenitor of the Ye clan, at his mausoleum in Pingdingshan. It was an unforgettable experience, which I describe in more detail later.

By 2011, I had collected enough material. I needed to decide on a narrative structure. There were already numerous books about the rags to riches stories of the self-made immigrants. Although Yeap Chor Ee was a fairly well-known figure to the older generation in Penang, a book solely about a young Chor Ee working his way from itinerant barber to captain of industry, would not garner much interest, except perhaps with family members, friends, and a few historians. The story had to be about more than Chor Ee.

Most of the people I interviewed and spoke to for this book were of Chinese descent. In fact Singapore and Malaysia between them are home to the largest overseas Chinese community in the world. But despite our common background, many of us have little or no idea about our families in China, or of how our forefathers came, why they came, what they brought with them, and how they started life in their new homes.

Certainly there are books already written about the *huiqiao* and mass migrations from China, but they are often academic in nature, not personal accounts of real people and stories of actual families. This is why I chose to place the story of Chor Ee within the context of all those who had joined the exodus.

At the end of 2012, I put together an exhibition at the gallery that included a detailed timeline, documents, photographs, infographics, animation, e-books, old footage, oral history recordings, and other objects that offered an insight into the lives of Chinese immigrants through Chor Ee's life.

It was from this exhibition that this book took its form, though it provides more detail on the social impact of this Chinese exodus, and the influence it had on Penang's cultural history. But like the exhibition, this book is not just about the life of one man. It echoes the shared experience of a community.

One noteworthy experience during the research for this book was meeting Mrs Lovy Tanner, the daughter of Oei Tiong Ham, the late Sugar King of Asia and one of Chor Ee's business partners. A chauffeur-driven car pulled up to the lobby of the Kian Gwan office near Bangkok's Lumpini Park. The ninety-seven year old Mrs Tanner stepped out of her car, light as a feather and impeccably dressed, holding a rather elegant walking stick. She was accompanied by her equally neatly-attired nurse.

Two of Tiong Ham's daughters married two of Chor Ee's sons and some of their offspring still live in Penang. Mrs Tanner had brought photographs of a family visit made sometime in the nineteen seventies, when they met the Penang side of the family. Although her memory flagged at times, she was able to relate memories of her childhood in Semarang and her charismatic mother, Lucy Ho (more about her later).

Meeting Mrs Tanner, daughter of Oei Tiong Ham, sister-in-law to my late grandfather and grand-uncle, and a lady who an hour earlier had been a complete stranger to me, suddenly brought to life everything I had worked on for the previous ten years. I was no longer just dealing with folders full of material, books, and historical archival records. All the people I only knew through family stories and research were just out of hand's reach, sitting in front of me in the form of this woman who had known so many of them personally. At the end of our meeting I gave her a hug, and she gave me a big smile with a little twinkle in her eye. I went back feeling the living connection between present and past.

Acknowledgements

There are many people I would like to thank for helping me write this book. First of all, my parents, who have been supportive of my efforts in completing this project and who have funded most of the research work, particularly in Singapore and China. I am also indebted to everyone who granted me an interview, in particular, my aunts, Jennifer, Natalie, and Janet, my uncle Dato' Seri Goh Eng Toon for having the sense to keep the bank's ledgers and minutes all these years, and the lovely Mrs Lovy Tanner.

This book required a vast amount of research and reading. To this end, I am grateful to Dr Wong Yee Tuan for being so thorough in digging up articles, documents, and records from the archives. A special word of appreciation to Ch'ng Kim See, chief librarian at ISEAS library, and Christine Khor, director at the National University of Singapore Centre for the Arts, for helping me extract material from ISEAS and the National Archives of Singapore that would otherwise have taken me a long time, and to Dr Cheah Jin Seng for allowing me to use images from his private collection for the book.

To Dr Loh Wei Leng and Louise Goss-Custard who kindly read the manuscript, offered useful comments, and ensured cohesion. I am also indebted to my sister Peta, for working on the front cover of the book; Marc de Faoite for his thorough assistance and thoughtful advice throughout the editing process, Kwoh Shoo Chen for being patiently helpful with my constant questions on Chinese words and terms. I am also grateful to Shoo Chen and her team for their dedication and hard work on tracing our family genealogy, a project which took four years to complete. Finally to friends who have offered advice, put me in touch with key people, helped source information, and granted me permission to use their images in this book.

A big thank you to you all.

List of Figures

Timeline of Key Events

531 BCE	Shen Zhuliang, progenitor of the Yeap surname was born.
947 AD	Xue Yu, the first descendant of Shen Zhuliang migrated from Northern China to Lam-oa (Nan'an) province.
1368	Founding of the Ming dynasty.
Early 1400s	The great Admiral Zheng He launched and commanded seven major expeditions across the globe to cultivate trade and display Chinese supremacy.
1636	Founding of the Qing dynasty, which ruled China from 1644 to 1912.
Mid-1600s	China's population steadily rose from sixty million to about one hundred and fifty million.
1786	Francis Light founded Penang.
1760-1820	British Industrial Revolution.
1826	Formation of the Straits Settlements, a group of British territories in Southeast Asia comprising of Singapore, Malacca, Penang, and Dindings.
Early 1800s	China's population tripled, bringing its population close to four hundred and thirty million.
1810-1849	China's four famines led to nearly 45 million deaths.
1840	First Opium War begins.
1840	Opening of Chinese treaty ports to foreign trade.
1850-1864	Taiping Rebellion, led by Hong Xiquan, ravaged China and led to millions of deaths.
1856-1860	France and Britain defeat China in the Second Opium War.
Mid-1800s	Beginning of the first wave of Chinese diaspora, known as *Huaqiao*. (Between 1850-1950, millions fled China.)
1860	Official withdrawal of emigration ban by Qing government.
1868	Yeap Chor Ee was born in Lam-oa, Amoy.
1869	Opening of the Suez Canal, which offered vessels a shorter journey between the North Atlantic and Indian oceans.
1876-1879	The Great North China Famine led to the deaths of 9.5–13 million people.

xvi   The King's Chinese

1870s	Four Malay states, Selangor, Perak, Negri Sembilan, and Pahang, came under British protection.
1877	Establishment of a Chinese Protectorate in the Straits Settlements.
Early 1880s	Beginning of large scale development by the colonial administration in Penang.
1885	Yeap Chor Ee set sail to Penang as a young illiterate migrant.
1890	Chor Ee set up a provisions store named Chop Ban Hin Lee.
1890s	Oei Tiong Ham, took over his father's trading company, Kian Gwan.
1890s	Chor Ee returned to China to take his first wife.
1894	Travel restrictions on emigration for women were lifted in China.
1897	Lee Cheng Kin was born.
1900	Tiong Ham and Chor Ee entered into a business relationship trading sugar.
1900	Boxer rebellion, followed by the Allied Nations' occupation of Beijing.
Early 1900s	Chor Ee became a millionaire. To mark the occasion he bought a Daimler. Around the same time, he took a second wife in Penang.
1911	Qing dynasty overthrown by revolutionists led by Sun Yat Sen.
1912	Most Chinese men cut off their queues.
Mid-1910s	Chor Ee married his third wife, and shortly after that, his fourth wife, Lee Cheng Kin.
1913-1914	Chor Ee purchased No. 4 Penang Street from Khaw Joo Keat's family and made it his official residence.
1914-1918	World War 1.
1918	Chor Ee set up an informal banking operation within Chop Ban Hin Lee.
1919	Southeast Asian rice crisis as a result of poor harvest. Speculative buying led to rice shortages in the region.
1919	Lim Mah Chye commissioned the construction of Homestead, Penang's grandest mansion, on Northam Road.
1920-1930s	Chor Ee commissioned Messrs Stark & McNeil to design a complex of offices and godowns along China Street Ghaut to house his growing businesses.
1929	Beginning of the Great Depression, one of the worst worldwide economic downturns.

1932	Chor Ee purchased Homestead from Lim Chin Guan, son of Lim Mah Chye.
1933	Affected by the depression, three Chinese banks — the Ho Hong Bank, the Chinese Commercial Bank, and the Oversea-Chinese Bank — were merged to form Overseas-Chinese Banking Corporation Ltd.
1933	Marriage of Yeap Hock Hoe and Ida Oei. The marriage took place in Homestead.
1935	Chor Ee incorporated his banking business and renamed his company Ban Hin Lee Bank, Ltd. At the same time, he bought into a rice mill in Burma and an oil mill in Penang.
1938	Ban Hin Lee Bank, Ltd moved into its new headquarters on Beach Street.
1940	To raise funding for the war efforts, estate duty in Malaya was raised from 20 per cent to 60 per cent, before settling at 40 per cent.
1941-1945	Japanese occupation of Malaya.
1941	Bombing of Pearl Harbour.
1945	Japanese surrender. Reoccupation of Malaya by the British.
1949	Inauguration of Malaya's first university, University of Malaya.
1952	Chor Ee passed away, aged 83.
1952	Marriage Ordinance was introduced in Malaya.
1957	Women in Malaya got to vote.
1957	Malaya gained Independence.

A Note on Names

The romanisation of Chinese names currently follows the pinyin format, which can cause much confusion, particularly when dealing with historical subjects and when quoting from original Western sources. Further adding to the word muddle are the various dialects used by the sub-ethnic Chinese groups, as well as the assortment of foreign loanwords adopted by people living in the Straits Settlements. For the sake of consistency and simplicity, I have used pinyin to refer to proper nouns and personal names of people or items found in China, such as *kang* for bed, and Shen Zhuliang, the name of the progenitor of the Yeap clan.

Chinese place names, villages, and everything else outside of China mentioned in the text are generally in the old style, as they appear in the sources, with current pinyin romanisation in parenthesis at first appearance. Using pinyin romanisation would turn familiar places in Penang such as the Kwangtung Public Cemetery into the Guangdong Public Cemetery and Amoy Lane into Xiamen Lane, neither of which exist on the island.

Since the Chinese community in Penang is mainly Hokkien speaking, Hokkien terms and names are generally used throughout the book. Similarly, period spellings are also used for other ethnic groups such as Manilamen (Filipinos) and Boyanese (Baweanese). They are kept in their original form to reflect the speech patterns and culture of that era, with the English meaning in parentheses following the first mention. Unless otherwise stated, all currency values are quoted in Straits Dollars. A glossary of non-English terms is included towards the end of the book to help readers with local terms.

Chinese Conventional Place Names
Amoy (Xiamen)
Canton (Guangzhou)
Chuan Chew (Quanzhou)
Hai-nan (Hainan)
Honan (Henan)
Kwangtung (Guangdong)
Lam-oa (Nan'an)
Macao (Macau)

P'ing-ting Shan (Pingdingshan)
Shangtung (Shangdong)
Soochow (Suzhou)
Swatow (Shantou)
Yangtze (Yangzi)
Yeh-ch'eng Province (Ye Province)
Zeitun/ Zayton (Quanzhou)

Other Conventional Place Names
Acheen (Aceh)
Dindings (Pangkor Island)
Sourabaya (Surabaya)
Billiton (Belitung)
Malacca (Melaka)
Burma (Myanmar)
Nanyang (Southeast Asia)
Boyan (Bawean)
Annam (Vietnam)
Siam (Thailand)
Ceylon (Sri Lanka)
United Provinces (Uttar Pradesh and Uttarakhand)

Chinese sub-ethnic groups
Hokkien (Minnan)
Cantonese (Guangdong)
Teochew (Chaozhou)
Khek (Hakka)
Hylam (Hainanese)

Other ethnic groups
Achinese (Achenese)
Anamese (Vietnamese)
Boyanese (Baweanese)
Burmese (Burmese)
Chitties/ Chettis (descendants of South Indian traders)
Chulier/ Chulia (Indians from Chola Kingdom, Tamil Nadu)
Hindoo (Hindu)

Kling/ Keling (Indian or Overseas Indian — now considered a derogatory term.)
Manilamen (Filipino)
Parsee (Parsi)
Siamese (Thai)
Singhalese/ Sinhalese (Sri Lankan)

The Yeap Family Tree

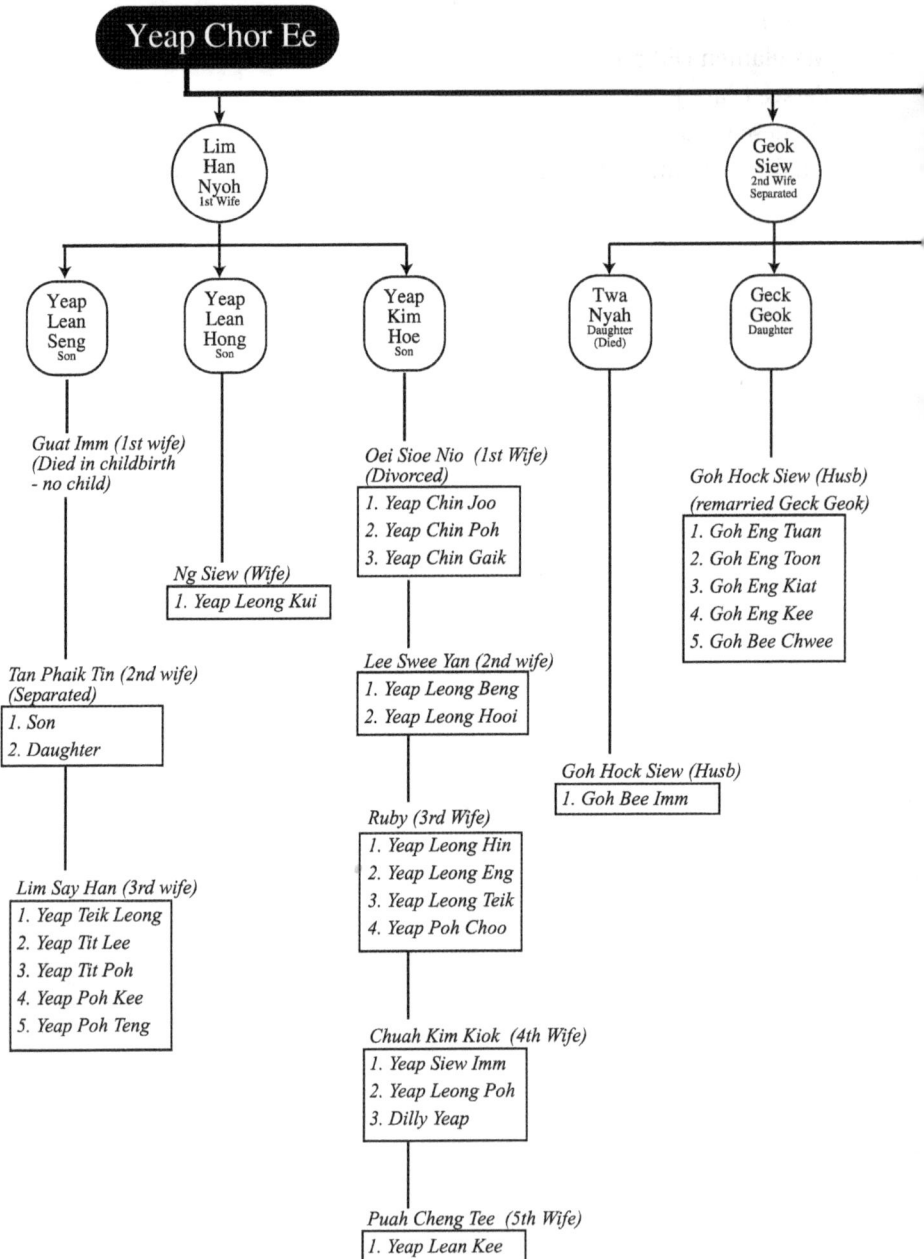

Yeap Chor Ee

- Lim Han Nyoh — *1st Wife*
- Geok Siew — *2nd Wife, Separated*

Children of Lim Han Nyoh:

- Yeap Lean Seng — *Son*
- Yeap Lean Hong — *Son*
- Yeap Kim Hoe — *Son*

Children of Geok Siew:

- Twa Nyah — *Daughter (Died)*
- Geck Geok — *Daughter*

Yeap Lean Seng (Son)

Guat Imm (1st wife)
(Died in childbirth
- no child)

Tan Phaik Tin (2nd wife)
(Separated)
1. Son
2. Daughter

Lim Say Han (3rd wife)
1. Yeap Teik Leong
2. Yeap Tit Lee
3. Yeap Tit Poh
4. Yeap Poh Kee
5. Yeap Poh Teng

Yeap Lean Hong (Son)

Ng Siew (Wife)
1. Yeap Leong Kui

Yeap Kim Hoe (Son)

Oei Sioe Nio (1st Wife)
(Divorced)
1. Yeap Chin Joo
2. Yeap Chin Poh
3. Yeap Chin Gaik

Lee Swee Yan (2nd wife)
1. Yeap Leong Beng
2. Yeap Leong Hooi

Ruby (3rd Wife)
1. Yeap Leong Hin
2. Yeap Leong Eng
3. Yeap Leong Teik
4. Yeap Poh Choo

Chuah Kim Kiok (4th Wife)
1. Yeap Siew Imm
2. Yeap Leong Poh
3. Dilly Yeap

Puah Cheng Tee (5th Wife)
1. Yeap Lean Kee

Twa Nyah — Daughter (Died)

Goh Hock Siew (Husb)
1. Goh Bee Imm

Geck Geok — Daughter

Goh Hock Siew (Husb)
(remarried Geck Geok)
1. Goh Eng Tuan
2. Goh Eng Toon
3. Goh Eng Kiat
4. Goh Eng Kee
5. Goh Bee Chwee

Chor Ee's wife.............. ◯
Chor Ee's child............ ◯
Chor Ee's grandchild..... ▭

Three generations of the Yeap family

A simple chart depicting Chor Ee's wives, his children, their spouses and the grandchildren.

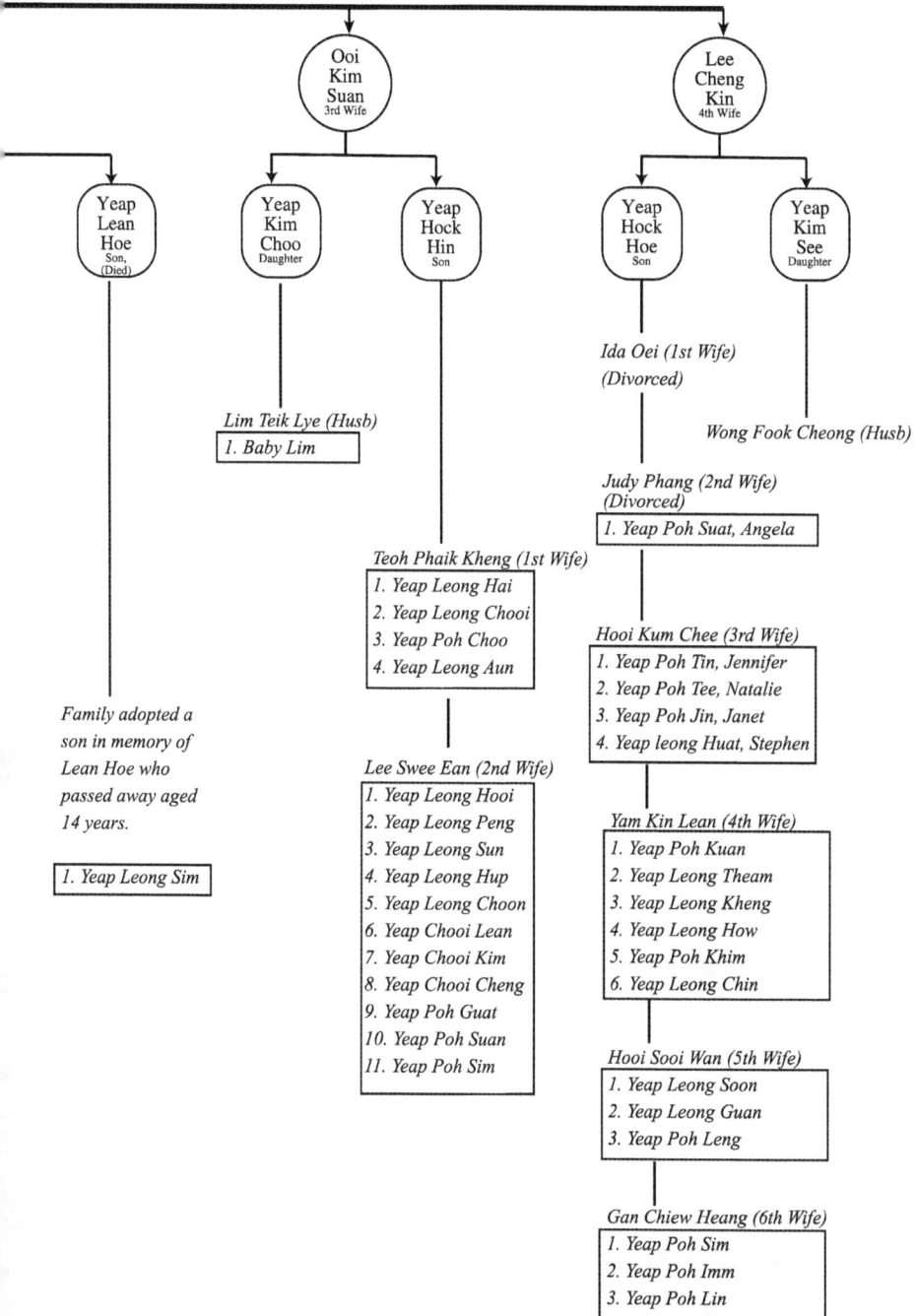

Ooi Kim Suan (3rd Wife)

Lee Cheng Kin (4th Wife)

Yeap Lean Hoe — Son, (Died)

Yeap Kim Choo — Daughter

Yeap Hock Hin — Son

Yeap Hock Hoe — Son

Yeap Kim See — Daughter

Family adopted a son in memory of Lean Hoe who passed away aged 14 years.

1. Yeap Leong Sim

Lim Teik Lye (Husb)
1. Baby Lim

Teoh Phaik Kheng (1st Wife)
1. Yeap Leong Hai
2. Yeap Leong Chooi
3. Yeap Poh Choo
4. Yeap Leong Aun

Lee Swee Ean (2nd Wife)
1. Yeap Leong Hooi
2. Yeap Leong Peng
3. Yeap Leong Sun
4. Yeap Leong Hup
5. Yeap Leong Choon
6. Yeap Chooi Lean
7. Yeap Chooi Kim
8. Yeap Chooi Cheng
9. Yeap Poh Guat
10. Yeap Poh Suan
11. Yeap Poh Sim

Ida Oei (1st Wife)
(Divorced)

Judy Phang (2nd Wife)
(Divorced)
1. Yeap Poh Suat, Angela

Hooi Kum Chee (3rd Wife)
1. Yeap Poh Tin, Jennifer
2. Yeap Poh Tee, Natalie
3. Yeap Poh Jin, Janet
4. Yeap leong Huat, Stephen

Yam Kin Lean (4th Wife)
1. Yeap Poh Kuan
2. Yeap Leong Theam
3. Yeap Leong Kheng
4. Yeap Leong How
5. Yeap Poh Khim
6. Yeap Leong Chin

Hooi Sooi Wan (5th Wife)
1. Yeap Leong Soon
2. Yeap Leong Guan
3. Yeap Poh Leng

Gan Chiew Heang (6th Wife)
1. Yeap Poh Sim
2. Yeap Poh Imm
3. Yeap Poh Lin

Wong Fook Cheong (Husb)

Chapter 1

The Hungry Years

China, summer of 1849.

Villagers looked to the sky, desperate for signs of rain. The air was dry. The soil parched. For the second year, the summer monsoons that brought life to the autumn harvest never came. When it did rain, it was sparse, the droplets blown away by dusty winds. China experienced another cruel drought. Wheat planted by farmers failed again. Even the hardy millet and sorghum withered till there was nothing left to harvest. Without grain, there was no food and fodder. Without stalks, there was no fuel to keep the kitchen stoves burning or warm the houses. Desperation set in. Winter clothes were pawned for food and seed. Furniture, doors, house beams were sold. Unbearable hunger drove half-starved villagers to eat leaves, weeds, tree bark, sometimes mixed with ground clay just to fill empty stomachs. As winter drew near, typhoid fever, dysentery, and typhus spread through the villages. By the time the famine had ended, millions had perished, mostly the rural poor. The disaster that struck in the summer of 1849 was just one in a litany of droughts in China. Three more occurred in the first half of 19th century. They were known as China's four famines. The number of people who died is estimated at over forty-five million.

Roughly six hundred and fifty years ago China was ruled by the ethnic Han Chinese under the Ming Dynasty (1368–1644). Its people lived in relative peace and stability. Under Emperor Hongwu (1368–1398), the unpopular policies of the Mongols (also known as the Yuan Dynasty 1269–1368) were reversed and land reforms distributed plots of land to farmers and peasants, protecting them from greedy landlords. The clever Emperor ordered the planting of fifty million trees around Nanjing, reconstructed canals, repaired dykes, improved irrigation, provided tax exemptions, and relocated southerners to the north to repopulate the region. They introduced technological advancement in agriculture, which enabled farmers and peasants to thrive. Commercial plantations appeared on the country's landscape for the first time, each region producing crops that were suitable to weather and soil conditions. Architecture flourished. Literacy levels rose.

It was also a period when Chinese maritime expeditions burgeoned. In the early 15th Century, the great Admiral Zheng He launched and commanded seven major expeditions across the globe to cultivate trade and display Chinese supremacy. By the mid-17th Century, China's population had risen steadily from just sixty million to about one hundred and fifty million people. When the Qings (1644–1912) arrived in 1636 (The Manchus established the Qing Dynasty in 1636 but only began to rule China properly in 1644), they implemented a form of government similar to that of Ming Dynasty. They continued contact with the West and introduced several new crops — corn, sweet potatoes, and better strains of rice. Improved yields and efficiency triggered a population explosion after two hundred years of economic progress, the number of people almost tripled, bringing China's population close to four hundred and thirty million by the 19th century.

Eventually this long period of uninterrupted growth began to take its toll. Extensive farming in certain parts of China led to deforestation and soil degradation, which accelerated erosion and ultimately led to flooding. At the same time, arable land became limited, leaving only a handful of regions capable of absorbing internal migration. Inevitably, flooding, land shortages, and overpopulation, coupled with a decline in bureaucratic efficiency, created significant strains on China's ability to feed her people. Its citizens became preoccupied with their subsistence and fell deep into a sense of hopelessness.

In the midst of these adversities came a curious man named Hong Xiuquan, an unorthodox Christian convert who successfully recruited millions of famine-stricken peasants to stage an uprising against the ruling regime. Even more peculiar was their acceptance of Xiuquan's claim that he was the younger brother of Jesus. Anyone with an inkling of knowledge of Chinese culture would realise how preposterous this idea might be. Firstly, due to their long history of cultural isolation, the Chinese people generally disdained anything foreign. Secondly, the major Chinese belief systems of Confucianism, Taoism, and Buddhism did not embrace the monotheistic idea of a singular omnipotent god as in Christianity or Islam. But incredibly even the most narrow-minded and insular proletarians were indoctrinated by Xiuquan's preaching. Unlike other peasant uprisings in China's conflicted past, the uprising of the winter of 1850 grew to be the most radical and the most colossal. Sown from the seeds of oppression, and considered one of the bloodiest civil wars in the world, Xiuquan led his army into a fourteen-year war, known to us today as the Taiping Rebellion. Over six hundred Chinese cities were destroyed. Twenty million people died. Many historians view it as the precursor to communism, laying the foundations for the rise of the people against the imperial forces. In many ways, it was to be the beginning of China's awakening.

At first, things were not so bizarre. All Xiuquan wanted in life was to be part of the establishment and the prestigious elite. He genuinely wanted what was best for his country. A village school teacher by profession, Xiuquan immersed himself in books of the teachings of Confucius, and sat the imperial civil service exam, only to flunk again and again. His continual failures drove him into a state of deep depression, rendering him delirious for days. Upon recovery, he claimed to have seen a vision of the Christian God calling on him to annihilate the devils on earth, namely the Qing dynasty. For the next ten years, Xiuquan studied Christian texts and began to preach his own version of the Christian doctrine. His followers were initially a small Hakka community in Southern China. The Hakkas, who had traditionally been a discriminated and marginalised sub-ethnic group of Chinese Han, immediately took to Xiuquan's political and religious teachings. With great enthusiasm and confidence, they named their cult Taiping or 'Great Peace', which stood for a simple goal: to fight for equality and shared land ownership. From this small cult, Xiuquan recruited more followers, and eventually had a formidable army large enough to concern the imperial administration.

Although Xiuquan's crude army of untrained peasants was severely factionalised, its sheer magnitude bulldozed its way out of Southern China, up the Yangtze (Yangzi) valley, capturing Nanjing as their capital. Against the Qing regime's opium-smoking and increasingly inept troops, Xiuquan's forces extended their range across large parts of China, conquering city after city with nothing more than primitive weaponry, relying on swords, spears, traps, improvised grenades, and the firearms they occasionally bought from foreigners or looted from the Qing armoury. The imperial forces retaliated by savagely killing, with unimaginable cruelty, all who came before them, including civilians, since they believed them to be supporters of the rebellion. Eyewitness accounts spoke of rotting corpses strewn across the Yangtze valley and wild animals feeding off the dead. China was in a state of disorder and turmoil.

The British and French colonial powers quietly observed the revolt unfold from their treaty port of Shanghai. A weak empire suited them. Having the upper hand, with trading privileges and autonomous concessions over opium, was very good for these colonial masters. But when Xiuquan's men prepared to march towards Shanghai in 1860 things took a turn. Only then did the colonials decide that this Christian fundamentalist was a threat to business. Subsequently, the British joined forces with the Qing army, and using modern artillery, fought the rebels. By 1864, the imperial forces, with the help of their colonial allies, crushed the revolt, ending the deadly war. By then, China was left vulnerable. Millions died. Large tracts of land were left in ruins. Villages disappeared. Cities lay desolate. The once fertile and prosperous Yangtze Delta and other rich provinces could no longer contribute the same amount of taxes to government coffers. The Qing imperial administration won, but at a great cost, and it soon became clear that they no longer held the power of control.

But China's misfortunes did not end with the war. Eight years into this state of gloom, yet another famine — the Great Famine of 1876 - struck Northern China. Lasting three years, it was the most catastrophic, with between nine-and-a-half million to thirteen million deaths recorded. Corpses were piled into what were called "ten-thousand man holes" — gigantic mass graves for the deceased. As the famine grew more severe, starving families sold their farms and their children, turning to slavery and murder just to survive. Stories of cannibalism surfaced. It became the first Chinese famine to receive international attention, and China obtained relief assistance from the West.

Against this backdrop of enormous death, that cursed China for decades, a weak imperial government, and the chaotic state of China's domestic economy, millions abandoned their homes and undertook the dangerous voyage across oceans to unfamiliar countries. Coming from a Confucian-centric culture, it was a tough decision for many. Their primary attachment was to the family, the ancestral home, and the spirits of the dead required rituals to be observed by living descendants. Many regarded the Middle Kingdom as the centre of civilisation and all other countries as savage nations. Leaving the homeland then, was truly a last resort. The exodus was accelerated by the opening of Chinese treaty ports to foreign trade in the early 1840s, and the official withdrawal of the emigration ban by the Qing government in 1860.[1]

---

1   Although migration from China had occurred before the mid-nineteenth century, emigration was never officially encouraged and there were periods under the Qing when it was banned totally.

Across the globe, another drama was unfolding. The 19th century, it must be remembered, was a decidedly transformative and prosperous age. Thanks to the Industrial Revolution, it was a period rich in technological and manufacturing innovation. Together with the opening of the Suez Canal in 1869, these developments boosted trade relations between Europe and Asia and spelled enhanced importance for the two continents, with Asia serving as a both a market for manufactured goods and a source of raw materials.

Colonies required labourers to work tin mines, rubber plantations, and sugar fields. Around the same time, steamships began to take over the bulk of passenger traffic, making transit easier. Elsewhere in the world, discoveries of gold mines and the emancipation of slaves in the Americas and other countries created a demand for cheap labour. The combination of these events paved the way for waves of migration from China that lasted almost a century. It was the beginning of the Chinese diaspora, known as *huaqiao* (Chinese sojourners or overseas Chinese), and the most widespread series of exoduses by one nation the world had ever seen. Within a span of a hundred years from 1850 to 1950, millions fled China.

Nowhere would the surge in immigrants have such an important impact as Nanyang (South Seas), notably the Straits Settlements. Established in 1826, as part of the territories controlled by the British East India Company, the Settlements was a group of British territories made up of Malacca, Dindings (Pangkor Island), Penang, and Singapore.

Our story begins here, notably on the island of Penang towards the final two decades of the 19th century. What attracted these young immigrants to converge on the island was not Penang's beautiful golden beaches or coconut trees, but its capital, George Town, which was about to begin a major transformation.

Chapter 2

Cinderella of the Straits Settlements

From its very beginning as a settlement, Penang was a trading post for the British in the Far East. Cotton and opium from the Indian subcontinent, pepper and betel nut from Aceh, tin from Phuket, Burmese rice, Sumatran tobacco, and Japanese copper all crisscrossed the Indian Ocean and the South China Sea since as far back as the 17th century. Drawn to Penang's free port status, merchants from neighbouring lands came to trade and redistribute goods to the rest of the region. Much of Penang's initial success as a trading port was due to its sheltered harbour, which provided safe anchorage for vessels, and its strategic location in the northern reaches of the Straits of Malacca. Penang was also the first British settlement in the region, and the base for the East India Company, whose fortunes would establish the course of British settlements around the region. Backed by its own army and navy, the East India Company expanded from this base and secured commercial hegemony in the Malay-archipelago, eventually ending Dutch influence on the peninsula.

Despite these credentials Penang was often regarded as the Cinderella of the Straits Settlements. It was once on a par with Madras, Bombay, and Bengal, being counted as an Indian Presidency before being relegated to a Colonial Governorship, then a Lieutenant-Governorship, and finally, further downgraded to the status of a mere Resident Councillorship. Compared to Singapore, which came into British possession thirty-three years later, government spending on Penang's infrastructure was paltry, despite the island's contribution to the treasury. Penang's people resented being denied a voice in the affairs and management of the colony and often complained of their demands for improvements being ignored while Penang's revenue went to further the embellishment of the capital — Singapore.[2] One newspaper report read, "it cannot be that the older Settlement must starve in order that the younger one may fatten, the one to pinch herself and grovel in the mud so that the other may pride herself upon possessing a skyscraper post office."[3] Even Sir John Coode, a British Civil Engineer appointed to look into improvement works of Penang Harbour, detected the biased handling of the colony. In his report on Penang's revenue and military contribution, he noted mockingly that the audit office often manipulated figures so as to make it appear that all of Penang's revenue was spent in Penang when in fact it often was not. He wrote, "Penang which is undefended, which derives no benefit from the presence of troops and which is well known, will be left absolutely unprotected in case of war, is in this delightful statement, debited with four-tenths of the military arrears."[4]

In the 1850s, eighty years after Captain Francis Light, founder of the settlement, stepped ashore, George Town continued to remain a relatively small town, with a collection of a few dozen streets laid out on the grid Light designed. It had about forty thousand inhabitants. According to Robert Van Someren (doyen of the Malayan Bar, who was born in Penang, and whose father was the town's coroner in the 1850s) there was just one government administrative office located on a street later renamed Downing Street. Unlike Singapore, Penang had just one godown, owned by Messrs Reverly & Co., and only one jetty on its harbour. Beach Street, the main commercial thoroughfare on the island, had a string of buildings whose occupants included a number of English and European merchants who had established themselves in Singapore before trickling to Penang — Schmidt, Kusterman, Mathieu & Co, Boustead & Co, Fraser & Co, and Lorraine & Sandilands, to name a few. A handful of these firms were also from the days of the early settlers. Among them was Brown & Co. Initially named Scott & Co. the company was started by James Scott, Light's shipmate, and later trading partner, who arrived in Penang in 1786 to make his fortune. Being so close to Light, Scott quickly secured a monopoly over trade and became the largest landowner on the island. After his death, his estate was left to his son who had to sell off his assets to pay creditors from a number of failed ventures. In came David Brown, another fellow Scotsman, who was also

2   'Penang Notes', *The Singapore Free Press and Mercantile Advertiser* (*Weekly*), 28 June 1906.
3   'The Crying Needs of Penang', *The Singapore Free Press and Mercantile Advertiser*, 7 February 1927.
4   'The Origin, Growth and Progress of the Penang Agitation', *Straits Times Weekly Issue*, 28 March 1893.

a partner of Scott & Co. Brown took over the ailing company and changed its name to Brown & Co. Brown married four local wives and had nine children. Interestingly, he was also godfather to Ku Hung-Ming[5] (Gu Hongming), the Penang-born English-educated intellectual and cultural critic, who later served as advisor to the Chinese Imperial Foreign Ministry in the late 19th Century.

Like Brown's relationships with the locals, there didn't appear to be much territorial division within the town's commercial space. Interspersed between the Western merchants were a number of Chinese-owned businesses — general merchants, ship-chandlers, and naval contractors. There was only one bank, the

Early drawing of Penang Harbour with Fort Cornwallis in view. *Penang Museum.*

[5] Hung-Ming ended up a staunch monarchist and an advocate of Confucian values, preferring to keep his queue even after the overthrow of the Qing Dynasty.

Mercantile Bank of India, London and China, and a handful of legal offices on Beach Street. At the junction of Beach Street and Church Street was a Chinese bakery, while the only other bakery, which was also the only butcher in town, was on Penang Street. The town received its news from the *Pinang Gazette*, edited by James Logan, a lawyer who came to Penang with his brother Abraham in 1839. They had their press and office on Union Street. The other source of news was the *Penang Argus*, owned by Blackburn. Both papers were published twice or thrice a week. Aimed primarily at merchants, their pages featured lists of ship arrivals and departures, current wholesale prices, and advertisements placed by wholesalers and retailers. They also contained accounts of events in the community — births, deaths, and marriages — and extracts from political speeches from the homeland. Government notices were printed in the *Straits Gazette* by the Indian Government, which was governing the Straits Settlements at the time.

The maintenance of law and order depended on the town's police force. Headed by Mr Robertson, the police court buildings were located further down Beach Street, close to Union Street. The police force was also responsible for managing the town's water supply, registering births, and taking charge of jail duties. They were also the Settlement's firemen.

Water for the town was supplied from two storage tanks raised ten feet above ground, one located opposite the Esplanade and the other on Love Lane. In turn, water was brought down to the tanks by pipes from the waterfall. The town folks also relied on wells for drinking water, but during dry seasons, when the wells and tanks ran dry, they had to buy from water carts. To alleviate the water woes, pipes were ordered for Penang sometime in 1840s, but instead, they were "carried off" to Singapore "for use in a project which did not materialise."[6]

The Esplanade, where Captain Light first landed, was much smaller in the 1850s than it is today. The section facing the sea was reclaimed much later. There were two bungalows overlooking the Esplanade, where the current municipal buildings stand. Mrs Wright, widow of Captain Wright, who was the previous Master Attendant, had her residence there. Next to her was Essex Lodge, the residence of Alex Rodyk, who worked as the Registrar of the Supreme Court. Behind them was a nutmeg plantation belonging to George Scott, who also owned Ayer Rajah Estate. The Resident Councillor, William Thomas Lewis, had

---

6   Khoo Salma Nasution, *The Chulia in Penang: Patronage and Place-Making around the Kapitan Keling Mosque 1786-1957*, Penang: Areca Books, 2014, p. 216.

his residence at the site of the current E&O hotel's main building. The bungalow had a big garden facing the sea. Beyond that was the old cemetery where Captain Light was buried. The town's boundary was beyond the old cemetery and demarcated by a ditch that is presently Transfer Road. The ditch ran through Burma Road and up to the Prangin Road and was so wide and deep that junks could sail in during high-tide.

As for the inhabitants of Penang, they were a motley lot. The few Europeans living there were connected somewhat, either by marriage or distant relatives. The rest were mainly Malays, Chinese, and an assortment of Siamese, Javanese, Achinese, Armenians, Jews, Indians, Arabs, Bugis, and Persians. About the only thing they had in common was that nearly everyone was there to trade. Children on the island went to one of five missionary schools. Boys either went to Free School, St Xavier's, or the Mission school facing the old cemetery on Northam Road. Girls, on the other hand, went to either Convent Light Street or a school run by the wife of a Free School Master, John Clarke.

Things took a turn upwards and by the last two decades of the 19th century Penang was about to undergo a construction boom. The Suez Canal and the introduction of steam power transformed the shipping industry and shortened travel time. It brought about a new era in trade between East and West. Asia was suddenly more commercially accessible to the West. Nor was the shipping business the only industry to be transformed. Tin mines underwent comparable changes, as did agriculture and the rubber industry. As trade grew, so did the size and tempo of Penang's waterfront. By 1871, there were tell-tale signs that Penang's harbour could not cope and desperately needed an overhaul.[7] Merchants longed for deep draft vessels to ship goods across thousands of sea miles.

"If Penang were to keep her trade," noted the colonial secretary, William Maxwell, "her harbour facilities should be in keeping with modern requirements, and they now scarcely exceed those of a purely native port." Between 1882 and 1888, Penang's trade increased by eighty-seven per cent, whereas Singapore for the same period registered a forty-four per cent increase. Shipping passage was often obstructed because George Town's coastline was mudflats that constantly silted. Storage facilities also became visibly insufficient. Not surprisingly, a number of trades, such as tobacco, were diverted to Singapore.

---

[7] 'Meeting of the Legislative Council', *Straits Times Weekly Issue*, 18 February 1890, p. 10.

   At about the same time, and as if by some inexplicable coincidence, the imperial government took measures to consolidate its political foothold in the Malay Peninsula. Britain then, only had control of the Straits Settlements — Penang, Singapore, and Malacca. The Malay Peninsula was comprised of seven other Malay federated states which were ruled by their respective Sultans. By the mid-1870s, the four Malay states of Selangor, Perak, Negri Sembilan, and Pahang came under British protection. Johor followed shortly after, when it relinquished its foreign affairs to the British. Having this position secured paved way for the British to create new markets and to inject new capital into infrastructure.

   By the early 1880s, after a hundred years as a crown colony, the colonial administration decided to promote larger scale settlement in Penang, developing Penang's harbour and the commercial area along Beach Street. From a single jetty previously, a dozen new piers and jetties sprouted along Weld Quay, a reclaimed landmass named after Sir Frederick Aloysius Weld, Governor of the Straits Settlements (1883-1889). The most important new facility, a deep-water wharf capable of servicing large ocean-going vessels, was built north of the quay, towards the old fort. After almost twenty years of representation, and despite

Headquarters of the British East India Company. Late 19th century. *Courtesy of Dr Cheah Jin Seng.*

grouses from sceptics, the scheme finally advanced. When completed in 1906, it included godowns and storage facilities that had been in shortage not long before. To handle the increased demand for goods, a tramway line was laid from the quay to the hinterlands (Ayer Itam) and used for carting raw materials and farm produce to and from the port. The improvement in port facilities pulled in plenty of large-scale merchant houses with networks in the West and regional headquarters in Singapore. In addition to the firms that Van Someren recalled in the 1850s, a number of big European merchants, including Behn Meyer & Co, Straits Trading Co, MacAlister & Co, Paterson, Simon & Co, and Guthrie & Co, began erecting imposing offices and godowns of uniform elevation facing Beach Street and the waterfront. Two new foreign banks established branches along the commercial street to promote trade with their respective countries. Hongkong and Shanghai Bank set up base on Beach Street, shortly followed by the Dutch Nederlandsche Handel Maatschappij Bank.

In these same years came the construction of government buildings to replace the small administrative office along the fittingly named Downing Street: the General Post Office, the Telegraphy Office and the Telephone Exchange, the Governor's Office, the Resident Councillor's Office, the Audit Office, the Public Works Department, the Land Office, and the Marine Department. Not too far off Downing Street, a town hall (where Mrs Wright had her residence) and a new supreme court were constructed. A new home for the Resident Councillor was commissioned, moving it from the site of the E&O Hotel to its current location west of town near the polo grounds. Set on a twenty-six-acre plot, the Residency, as it is called, was completed in 1890 and cost the public works department over $80,000. Other new government buildings included a convalescent bungalow on Penang Hill, the reconstruction of the bungalow on Government Hill, a new administration block for the police station, and government staff quarters.

Soon, George Town resembled a boomtown. Communities built schools, clan houses, and places of worship. Rich towkays (Chinese bosses) erected shop-houses. Hundreds, if not thousands, of these shop-houses sprouted and expanded away from Captain Light's grid and the waterfront, pushing the town's boundary further westward. The physical appearance of these shop-houses gradually evolved from being uncomplicatedly straightforward to having more height, width, and a bit more flair. To accommodate the town's expansion, the buildings grew outwards and upwards, sometimes up to three floors, decorated with pilasters with Corinthian capitals and European neo-classical motifs.

However, they all functioned the same — shops on the ground floor and residential accommodation or tenement housing on the upper floors. China Street and King Street, the two-key nuclei of Chinese settlement, were bursting to the seams with migrants sorting themselves according to dialect groups: Hokkien, Cantonese, Teochew, and Hakka. Next to the Chinese settlement was the Indian enclave towards Chulier Street (now known as Chulia Street) where the Kapitan Keling Mosque formed the centre of society for the Indian Muslim community and the Sri Mahamariamman Temple for the Hindus. Further south was the Malay town, which evolved between Prangin River and the southern portion of Chulier Street, with the Acheen Malay Mosque as its community centre.

Light Street, Penang. Late 19th century. *Penang Museum.*

Next came the public utilities. Improvements were carried out on the town's drainage and waterworks, including the construction of another reservoir capable of holding about five million gallons of water, which was completed in 1894 to pipe freshwater down to the town and the harbour. No longer was the town only dependent on the water tanks located at the Esplanade and Love Lane. Incinerators, abattoirs, markets, and bridges were built and erected.[8] The

---

[8]   'Municipal Loans', *The Singapore Free Press and Mercantile Advertiser*, 21 June 1899, p. 3.

George Town's Fire Brigade and Horse Drawn Fire Engine. Late 19th century. *Penang Museum.*

private sector also fostered development of the town by donating funds and land to build hospitals and schools. The public works department levelled, graded, and laid out macadamised streets (broken stones), a job that used to be done by convict labourers in the 1860s. By the turn of the 20th century, these were replaced with tarred roads, while electric street lighting replaced paraffin street lamps.[9] Angsana trees were uniformly planted along the streets to give it shade and a touch of civility. George Town was transforming into a city.

The expansion of government offices, mercantile firms, and godowns magnified the number of clerks, storekeepers, and bookkeepers. Below the ranks of these semi-skilled employees were battalions of Chinese, and to an extent, Indian immigrants, who powered Penang's busy port with the raw strength of their muscles. They were in steady demand as *twakow* (lighter) coolies and stevedores who loaded and unloaded sacks, bales, and barrels to and from the vessels. There was also a big demand for bullock cart drivers, rickshaw pullers, and general coolies to lumber goods through crowded streets. And not to forget, the thousands of bricklayers, carpenters, plasterers, and manual labourers who built the town.

---

[9]   'Penang Electric Lighting', *The Straits Times*, 18 April 1903, p. 5.

From a population of about 40,000 in 1850, the number of Penang's inhabitants gradually climbed to about 90,000 in 1881. Between 1884 and 1885, over 80,000 Chinese migrants landed in Penang, almost doubling the island's population. It was as if a new town had superimposed itself on the old.

Not all the newcomers became permanent residents. Some departed immediately to work in tin mines and plantations, while others moved on after a few years. However, a large percentage did stay. Among them, and soon to make an indelible mark on Penang, was seventeen-year old Yeap Chor Ee. Initially earning a living as a barber, Chor Ee eventually climbed his way into the town's upper and middling ranks, first as a merchant, then moving into finance and banking. It was young men like him who helped change and shape life in the Settlements — its religion, cuisine, employment, architecture, language, laws, culture, trade and industries. Against this backdrop of social change a new nation began to emerge.

Through the prism of Chor Ee's life, the remaining chapters of this book tell the story of the long migration of the Chinese who fled their motherland in search of a better life.

Chapter 3

A Not So Fortunate Beginning

Before achieving colossal success in his new home of George Town, Chor Ee led a largely desolate life. He entered a world that was short of people and strove to keep those it had. Born four years after the Taiping rebellion on 18th October 1868, Chor Ee was delivered in a county called Lam-oa (Nan'an) in Fukien Province. During the war years, deaths outnumbered births. When at last the war ended, millions had perished throughout the country. Chuan Chew (Quanzhou), the nearest city to Lam-oa, was left with only two hundred thousand inhabitants compared to a million before the rebellion. Lam-oa itself had a relatively small population of just a few thousand by the time Chor Ee was born. The village was built on an open plain that used to have miles of farmland. But the soil was poor. The long-drawn war and over-farming had crippled the economy and cut rice and crop production to abysmal levels.

One of the peculiarities of Lam-oa was that it was made up of families with the surname Ye or Yeap. This arrangement, known as the "greater-family" not only applied to Lam-oa but most villages throughout China. There could be a few hundred or a few thousand relatives living in the village. Chor Ee's father, Tong Mei, was a Yeap. His mother Ching Niang was from the Chen clan. Not much is known about his parents except that they were both farmers. They farmed and lived off the produce of their land. In better years, they grew rice, sugar cane, wheat, bamboo, and sweet potato. They kept pigs and chickens when they had enough to feed the animals. As a result of generations of subdivision of land from father to sons, farms in China were often fragmented. Tong Mei and Ching Niang's farm was not very large, just enough to feed their family and sell excess crops in the village market. If the season was a poor one, and the crops became parched from too much sun or swamped by too much rainfall, they would likely have had to resort to the merciless village moneylender for help. To avoid having to pay back extraordinary sums, Tong Mei and Ching Niang slogged away and became beasts of burden, extracting as much as they could from their land.

The couple had two other sons before Chor Ee. The convention at that time was that the mother gave birth at home, with the delivery assisted by a "birth granny" or a mid-wife. Because of the lack of proper medical support, birth was a dangerous affair for both mother and child. If the labour was complicated and things went wrong, there was little the mid-wife could do. For this reason, infant mortality was a common occurrence. When Chor Ee came out healthy and a boy, there was a muffled cry of joy in the household. Although his birth meant another mouth to feed, Chor Ee was a son who would one day mourn alongside his father's coffin and carry on the family name. But the person most comforted by the sex of the healthy newborn was Chor Ee's mother, Ching Niang. For months, she was anxious about the birth. Her heart pounded with uneasiness for fear that the child might be a girl. Exhausted from the delivery, she managed a little smile, but deep down she felt an extreme sense of relief that only a Chinese mother could know. She would not have to endure the humiliation to the family of bearing a baby girl. Nor would she have to sob and weep for weeks when the neighbours shunned her for producing a worthless girl. By giving birth to a son, her position in the family and the village was assured — her mother-in-law's overbearing manner and her husband's affections were once again placated and satisfied. She could walk down the village street and be looked upon by the other wives and women with an air of respectability.

Oblivious to the conditions that made life challenging, Chor Ee's first few months on earth were rather blissful. He was a sweet-faced baby with large black eyes and a round fat face. Wrapped in several layers of clothing to protect him from the cold winter, he suckled at his mother's bosom and slept by her side. But no more than three months after his birth, his parents tragically died. We don't know exactly how they died or what caused their deaths. The only certainty we possess for this early period of Chor Ee's childhood was that his grandmother took over his care. She strapped him on her back with a cloth and lulled him to sleep while she attended to her chores during the day. At night, she would put him to sleep in her bed next to her. His older brothers, Zhu Zhou and Zhu Quan, were of little comfort to him. They were much older than Chor Ee, and although they took over much of the farm work after the death of their parents, they probably understood little about being a role model for young Chor Ee. There was no emotional intimacy, very little empathy, and certainly no affection shown towards their youngest brother.

Just like the other children in their village, Chor Ee grew up in the shadow of the rebellion. The children knew nothing but hardship and fear and that, to them, was normality. Chor Ee, like many children in his village, never went to school. This was not for the lack of desire to learn. Quite the opposite. The Chinese have a strong faith in education thanks to the great Chinese sage, Confucius, who valued education and learning. Scholars in Chinese culture were regarded as the top echelon of society. No matter how remote a village, communities from different districts pooled resources to set up a school, or what they called a Confucius Shop. But by the 19th century, constant uprisings and rebellions ceased much of that. Schools being prime targets for attacks, were often the first public spaces to be disrupted. For fear of their lives, teachers abandoned their posts and parents stopped sending children to school because of what might happen to them along the way. In Chor Ee's days a staggering proportion, or ninety-nine per cent of China's population was illiterate. Even its powerful ruler, the Empress Dowager Cixi, who governed the country from behind a screen, was semi-illiterate. After the Taiping rebellion China's education system took many years to rebuild and as a consequence several generations of the populace grew up illiterate.

In 1875, when Chor Ee was not quite seven, his grandmother passed away. His older brothers took charge of his welfare, and his carefree days of being a child were again disrupted. They piled chores on him, more than expected of someone his age. In those days, when a child reaches a suitable age, they would be taught the jobs of their parents. It was for this reason inherited occupations in China were common. If he was the son of a farmer, he would be trained in that role — tending animals, planting rice, hoeing the earth for the new crops. If the father was a tailor, the child would help with sewing or spinning yarn. But being physically frail as a young boy, Chor Ee was not able to ease his brother's load by working the land, so they banished him to the kitchen and assigned him the grimy tasks of disposing of the night soil and collecting manure from the pig pen. Without any knowledge of modern day farming techniques, the family, like most farming families, relied heavily on manure and night soil to fertilise the crops. It was cheap and plentiful and it was young Chor Ee's duty to collect and feed it to the crops. Day after day, he followed

Yeap Chor Ee's ancestral house in Lam-Oa, Amoy, China. Built sometime at the turn of the 20th century with remittances from Chor Ee. 2006

the same routine with very few words of complaint. Rice planting season was in April and again in August, while the harvest was July and November. Regardless of the seasons, he hardly had any time for play.

Chor Ee's family home, set among the paddy fields, was a simple dwelling made of bricks of moulded soil, wood, and thatch. Inside the house was a large communal space with no rooms. Practically everything was done there — they ate, dressed, and slept in that open space. Strewn about in the cheerless and gloomy interior were a few pieces of furniture, some wobbly stools and a well-used table. The family cooked over an earthen furnace inside the house. Kitchen utensils were few and simple — an iron-wok for stewing and frying and two or three different shaped pots for boiling water and vegetables. Even though food was scarce, eating was an important affair for the family. If everyone is able to eat, then everyone is well. And if everyone is well, everything is well, or so the saying goes. Eating was so important it was customary to greet a friend on the street by *"Lu chiak-pah liau boay?"* or "Have you eaten rice already?" There was a hierarchy and protocol to meal times, no matter how poor the family. At every seating, following a ranking order, the youngest at the table had to "invite" the elders to eat before he or she was allowed to tuck in. Chor Ee, being the youngest, ranked lowest in the pecking order. The food was simple and just enough to fill the stomach. Most of the time, the family subsisted on rice or sweet potato, supplemented with salted cabbage or turnip and duck eggs as condiments. On special occasions, a meat dish of stewed pork was served.

The world was painfully dim when Chor Ee was growing up. The family had no electricity or running water. Lighting was by oil lamps, but that didn't bother anyone as no one had any consciousness of the house being dark at night. What drove Chor Ee to bed early was not boredom but tiredness. When it was time to go for bed, sleeping arrangements tended to be informal – they rolled out heavily patched quilts on the *kang* (bed) made of earthen bricks and straw, then clambered over each other and slept side by side. Privacy was a much different concept back then, and life tended to be more communal and exposed than today. The only problem with this type of bedding arrangement was that it had to be performed together with the troublesome task of sexual intercourse. Somehow, they managed. Being the youngest, Chor Ee had to make his bed on the floor. Sometimes, he would spread his clothes over his quilted mattress to add an additional layer of warmth during winter months. When winter came, the house was heated by a set of flues which channelled smoke from the furnace under the *kang*. To make heat, they depended on whatever that came from land for fuel, including dry manure. As ingenious as they are, most Chinese houses had no chimney. Instead, thick smoke circulated within, choking the interior when the windows were shut. Chor Ee's family house was always cold in winter, hot in summer and smoky all year round.

There wasn't a great deal of comfort in Chor Ee's early childhood. Daily life was devoted to simply surviving. Life started at sunrise and ended at night when there was no more light. Day in day out, each member of the family followed the same routine, just as their forefathers had before them. They farmed the fields in the same way, they went to the same markets in the same order, they bought, sold, and wore the same things, and after a hard day of work, they sat and told the same stories as if for the first time. Such was the monotony of village life.

It was certainly this austere upbringing and stark childhood that consequently developed Chor Ee's character, thought, and ingenuity. His resilience was toughened by toiling on the farm from young, his wit and resourcefulness fostered from the struggles with life and nature.

Chapter 4

People of Bushy Eyebrows

The Yeaps were descendants of a noble Hokkien family that lived during the Spring Autumn Period (770–476 BCE) of the Zhou Dynasty (1045–221 BCE). According to clan history, Chor Ee's great ancestor, Shen Zhuliang, a nobleman from the ruling house, fathered the first line of Yeap descendants.

Zhuliang was a general commander in Emperor Chu Zhuangwang's (d 591 BCE) army. During this period, China was rife with rivalry and bloodshed. The ruling Zhou court was on the decline and individual states began to wage wars among themselves. Territories were divided into many fiefdoms and kingdoms. The Chu state was a warmongering state which began small but eventually developed into a large kingdom. Zhuliang's father, Shen Yin Shu, was a minister of the Chu court. After Yin Shu died in battle, the emperor awarded his son Zhuliang a fiefdom known as the Yeh-ch'eng (Yè) Province in gratitude of his father's service. Zhuliang's position was also elevated to that of a duke. From there he adopted the name of Yè Gong (Duke of Yè). What became of him then is unknown — yet there is a story which says the old emperor gave his blessing for Zhuliang to marry one of the emperor's daughters. Settled in the fertile new territory, the newly-weds adopted the surname Yè, or Yeap. Zhuliang's descendants carried on the family name, and the tradition, established centuries earlier, of recording each birth and death in the book of generations. Through the passage of time, many of these families changed the spelling and pronunciation of the original name. It appears from the records that there are at least nine different variations of Yè: Yeap, Yip, Yeh, Yee, Ee, Ip, Yap, Diep, and Yo. Today, an estimated six million Chinese share one of these surnames.

Etching of Shen Zuliang. Shen Zhuliang's mausoleum in P'ing-ting Shan, Honan, China. 2009

It seems Zhuliang was also a friend of the great Chinese sage, Confucius. Though it was an age of turmoil, and although many had been massacred, the Spring Autumn period was also known as the golden age of Chinese philosophy. It was a time when knowledge and religion flourished. The existence of many small states and fiefdoms with their own language, culture, and beliefs encouraged discussion, free thought, and intellectual expansion. As a result, several schools of thoughts emerged — the two foremost being, Confucianism and Taoism. Confucius hailed from the neighbouring province of Shandong and his conversations with Zhuliang were recorded in Confucius's Analects.

Around the tenth century, between the great Tang and Song eras, when China was again going through a period of political disorder, several branches of the Yè family migrated to Southern China, where they subsequently proliferated. One of these migrants was Xue Yu, or San Weng as he was generally known. Born in the year 947, during the Wu Dai Dynasty, San Weng was the first of Zhuliang's descendants to move south to Lam-oa, where he lived until his death in 1001. San Weng is honored as the founding ancestor of the Yè people in Lam-oa. Chor Ee was a descendent of San Weng's line, a hundred and thirty-three generations after Zhuliang. By then, Chor Ee's family's status had been reduced. His father, Tong Mei, was a farmer, as was Chor Ee's grandfather, Cheng Zhao. By venturing out of his village, Chor Ee was the first in his family to break that chain.

Shen Zuliang's tomb. P'ing-ting Shan, Honan, China. 2009

Of San Weng's progeny, the most celebrated was Hui Ze Zhun Wang, an eleventh generation Yeap. Born in 1189 to a middle-class family, Wei Shen, as he was originally named, grew up an ordinary farm boy. There was nothing exceptional about his family, nor about Wei Shen, until the summer of his nineteenth year, when he entered a deep meditative trance from which he never emerged. Many villagers believed he became immortal and achieved sainthood. From then on, he was revered by his followers. Emperor Ningzong of the Song Dynasty later awarded him the title Wei Wu Hui Ze Zhun Wang, meaning the "powerful one". In modern-day Penang, he is known as Chor Ong. His acolytes maintain temples in his honour and dedicate much of their time and money to propagating the belief of his sainthood and immortality. Once, during a clan celebration in Penang, Chor Ong's statue was brought from China to grace the event. Clansmen from Penang arranged a business-class flight for the statue and an attendant. Such was the perceived greatness of Chor Ong, and the faithful practice of ancestor worship, that when the plane landed, hundreds of eagerly awaiting devotees, some in their eighties, fell to their knees in unison on the blazing tarmac, bowing three times as a mark of respect for their ancestral god.

Ancestor worship constitutes the core of the Chinese way of life. It is more a form of reverent ceremony rather than a superstitious cult. Children are obligated to respect their parents in life, to remember them after their death, and to ensure the continuity of the family bloodline through future generations. In the family hierarchy, ancestors rank at the top, followed by the most senior living family member, and so on, down to the youngest. For the average family there are two main rituals related to the practice. Once a year in April, most Chinese families make a pilgrimage to their ancestral graves for Cheng Beng, or tomb sweeping day, to pay homage to their departed ancestors. They tidy the graves, offer incense, food, and wine, burn ghost money, and pay respects. The second custom is keeping an altar to house ancestral tablets at home. Varnished in red, the tablets are made of oblong pieces of wood with inscriptions about the ancestors in gold. Incense, wine, or teas are offered throughout the year. For the unfamiliar, it may seem cult-like when graveyards, offerings, and departed ancestors' spirits are involved, but it is no different from the veneration of the dead in many major religions. The whole idea of the pilgrimage and offerings is to conciliate the spirit of the ancestors in return for blessings and good fortune for the living. Generally speaking, when a Chinese person dies, he or she becomes either a *shen* (good spirit of deity) or a *kwei* (evil spirit). A *shen* is canonised and is believed to bless the living. A *kwei* is dreaded for its malignant spirit and is supposed to wreak vengeance on mankind. Evil spirits are pacified during the seventh moon festival (Ghost month). The idea is to appease the dead if the ancestors have become malignant spirits and to pray for blessing if the ancestors have been deified.

With little to go on in way of hard facts about Zhuliang's early life, I visited his mausoleum in the spring of 2009 to see if I could gather more information about the family line. Now declared a national heritage site by the Chinese Government, Zhuliang's mausoleum is situated at P'ing-ting Shan (Pingdingshan) in Honan (Henan). The province is also known as the birth place of Chinese civilisation. It is also the birth place of almost two thirds of common Chinese surnames. My trip was part of a commemorative event arranged by the World Yeap Association in honour of Zhuliang's birth year. Held every twelve years, in the year of the snake, thousands of Yè descendants from across the globe congregate in P'ing-ting Shan. Most of us spent a night in this small mining town before making our way to Zhuliang's mausoleum the next morning. After hours of travel through some of the oldest landscapes within Chinese civilisation, and passing through acres of wheat fields and agricultural land, we arrived at the main entrance of the mausoleum. There, we were greeted by a school brass band fully attired in faded uniforms that seemed to have been passed down over the years. Villagers waving flags lined the dusty road, while looking rather bemused to see foreigners who shared the same surname streaming in by the busload.

After manoeuvring back and forth, our bus driver finally found a parking spot among hundreds of other vehicles. I had hoped to stretch my legs when we got off the bus, meet the curious villagers, and explore the surrounding area for a bit. But within a split second of exiting the bus, we were herded like cattle through the rather imposing entrance of the mausoleum. Erected next to the entrance was a mural etched on a black stone wall of Zhuliang in his armour bearing a sword and commanding his army from a galloping horse. This was the first image of Zhuliang I had come across. In fact, it would have been the first image of Zhuliang anyone had seen. The mural appeared recent which begs the question — how would its maker know what a man who lived two thousand five hundred years ago looked like? Wisps of smoke from burning joss sticks drifted through the courtyards as we entered. Preparations had already begun on the main square in front of the ancestral hall. At the doorway of the hall a sacrificial goat and pig lay flat on a table, each with a token red ribbon tied around their lifeless necks. Next to these offerings, a huge black urn of joss paper, or ghost money — probably worth millions in heavenly dollars — burnt furiously, puffing out thick clouds of black smoke. Piles of joss sticks were placed at the other side of the doorway in anticipation of our arrival.

Pandemonium struck at the sight of a massive golden statue of a seated Zhuliang in the hall. It was as though the crowd saw the man himself. They jostled, shoved, and elbowed to get through the door for a closer look at the statue, creating a state of utter chaos, as hundreds scrambled to get in. Beleaguered mausoleum guides attempted to control the over-excited mob, but no one paid them any notice. Finally, a very agitated man, presumably the curator of the mausoleum, got hold of a loud-speaker and told everyone to step back and remain calm. The crowd settled down and somehow assembled together into their respective country groups. Feeling less irritated, the curator spoke for a bit, and at his call, every man, woman, and child respectfully took three bows towards the twenty-foot-high gold-clad statue of Zhuliang. With a bit more composure, the curator invited each respective country group to enter the hall, and one by one we traipsed in like obedient schoolchildren.

While waiting, I couldn't help but notice the eyebrows of my fellow kinsmen. On one of our visits to the family home in Lam-oa, my father flippantly commented about the eyebrows of our distant relatives, and that the one distinct physical characteristic shared among Yeaps is bushy eyebrows. Even with my eyes burning and tears from the smoky air blurring my sight, I saw what he meant. The average eyebrow for the male Yeap is short and thick. Some were not bothered about grooming; instead allowing the occasional rogue hairs to extend beyond the brow line to flop over. The older generations tended to wear their eyebrows with a flick, almost like the waxed moustache of an Indian colonel. The female Yeaps' eyebrows were less characteristic, probably because they had been plucked or heavily tattooed. When I found myself counting the number of bushy eyebrows I thought it was time for me to make other, more meaningful, observations.

I snuck out of the hall and took a look around Zhuliang's ancient tomb before the large crowds descended. Grass and a few fir trees grew on top of a large mound that spanned at least seventy feet across. Supporting all that mass was a foundation of bricks, discoloured by the years. Every twenty feet or so, small air-vents, the size of a man's fist, were set into the brick structure. I took a peep in, but only darkness and the eerie sound of hollowness pervaded. Chinese tombs in ancient times were an inner palace for the deceased and contained the daily comforts of their past life, such as clay replicas of their servants, pets, animals, ceremonial pots, copper coins, and sometimes concubines. With a tomb that size, I suspected Zhuliang was not alone in his peaceful rest.

After the mausoleum visit, we drove to another town for lunch, followed by a whole afternoon of dreary speeches and memento presentations. I checked out. The single most apparent thing I observed from the mausoleum experience was the strong sense of filial piety and kinship expressed by the devoted crowd. For many, it was a pilgrimage to honour and pay respect to our great ancestor. For some, including myself, it was the feeling of coming back to the home we had never known.

Wooden carved figure of Chor Ong, ancestral God of the Yeap clan. 2012

Chapter 5

Consulting the Gods

Though Chor Ee was descended from nobility dating back some 2,500 years, his immediate family were simple farmers living in an intensely feudal and harsh environment. Yet somehow in a relatively short time he rose above these arduous conditions to become a notable success in a distant land.

During long winter evenings when he was growing up, Chor Ee and his friends in the village would have heard stories from recruitment agents or sojourners who had returned from their travels. The men sat around a fire, smoking hand-rolled cigarettes, recounting tales of the treacherous sea journey and life in the land of opportunity called Nanyang (Southeast Asia). The green villagers gathered and listened, captivated by the words of these worldly men. The stories excited them and nurtured in their minds the prospect of seeking out these adventures for themselves. As a young boy, the thought of migrating was half-exhilarating and half-terrifying. To think of going to Nanyang in those days would mean a fifty-fifty chance of life or death. Chor Ee was approaching manhood and knew he must go, but how?

The year was 1885 and he was about to turn seventeen. Today's travellers turn to the internet and social media for travel advice, but Chor Ee's generation, and the generations before him, relied instead on supernatural forces for guidance. For any important decision, villagers sought the help of higher powers. Before breaking the soil for sowing grain, the farmer asked a priest to read prayers and conciliate the local deity that presided over the ground. When a young couple was to be married, they consulted the gods for an auspicious wedding date. Fortune tellers were consulted to determine the right day for a child to start attending school. Chor Ee must have had countless sleepless nights, thinking of his family and what they would do without him, wondering how he would find the passage money and what he would do when he reached his destination. The dangers of the sea journey must have crossed his mind. Would he survive? The only way to find out was to make enquiries with the spirit world.

In the autumn of that year, during the Nine Emperor Gods procession in his village, Chor Ee received his answer. On the first and the ninth day of the ninth moon every year, villagers followed vegetarian diets and made a pilgrimage to the temple. Nine Emperor God, a sea spirit who is both revered and feared, is believed to be generous to those who worship him. Any wish asked for would be fulfilled. During these nine days, séances were held at the temple. At each séance, a *kee-tong* (medium) entered a trance to the beats of drum and cymbals and the burning of incense and joss-stick. The spirit entered the kee-tong's body and he took on the voice of the God. Favours and fortunes were asked of him. When it came to Chor Ee's turn, the *kee-tong* told him to "go south to seek your destiny."

Excited and restless, Chor Ee made a promise to the God that if he could show him a safe passage and guide his vision, Chor Ee would show his gratitude with rice and money upon his return. That night, he had a dream. He dreamt of a road to a temple set amongst the hills. There waiting for him was the statue of Kuan Imm, the Goddess of Mercy, the greatest figure in Chinese Mythology. Chor Ee woke the next morning feeling that the Nine Emperor Gods had answered his prayers.

Chor Ee began to prepare for his journey. His first duty was to pay respects to his deceased ancestors and make offerings, including joss money and food to cover his long absence abroad. With the help of his family, he stripped dry bamboo leaves near his house, cut them into little square blocks and covered them with markings to look like paper money. Little garments and other symbolic gifts for the spirits were also made from the bamboo leaves. Chor Ee spent days and weeks making enough of these provisions to cover the time when he would be away. In the following days, he packed his belongings and said his final goodbyes to his friends. On the day of departure, he woke from a restless night and shared his last breakfast with the family. There were hardly any tears as he exchanged farewells. Barely knowing the written characters of his own language and never having left his village, Chor Ee headed towards the city of Amoy by foot, a walk of over a hundred kilometres.

There were no roads in southern China in those days, just narrow footpaths winding and twisting between the paddy fields and through the valleys and hills. The journey would have taken at least three or four days. Somewhere along the way, Chor Ee came across the temple which had appeared in his dream. An abbot had anticipated his arrival, for, as the story goes, the old abbot had a similar dream of a young man calling upon him on his travels. The abbot fed a very hungry Chor Ee, blessed him a safe journey, and presented him with a figure of Kuan Imm. To this day, Chor Ee's Kuan Imm presides in our family home and continues to be cherished by the family. Intricately carved, Kuan Imm sits leisurely on what appears to be a dragon whose head points toward the sky. In front of her are two small figures of mortal beings — men. She wears a beautiful smile.

Continuing his journey southeast, Chor Ee had another unforgettable experience. A tiger crossed his path. Tigers are native to southern China and used to roam in abundance, feeding on wildlife, but today are close to extinction. Hearing Chor Ee's approach through the thick undergrowth, the tiger turned its head, and both man and beast stared at each other for what felt like forever. Chor Ee considered for a moment that his plans for a future life in Nanyang would all come to an end here. But instead of attacking him, the tiger turned away and continued on its own path, as disinterested in Chor Ee as if he were invisible. To most readers in the twenty-first century, the fact that the tiger didn't pounce on him could have been because it was not hard-pressed for food, but to those who heard the tale back then, it was a good omen, a clear sign that the carving of Kuan Imm that Chor Ee carried had protected him from harm.

Amoy (modern-day Xiamen) gave Chor Ee his first sights of the world that lay beyond China. In the 1880s Amoy was China's commercial port, the home of seamen, the emigration hub of Fukien, and the most colourful coastal city of its age. In the fourteen-century, long before Amoy became a major port, the nearby city of Zeitun, or Zayton (now Quanzhou), was famous for its extensive trade with India, Arabia, and Western Asia. It must have been one of the greatest, if not the greatest commercial hubs of the world at that time. Precious stones, pearls, silks, satins, and spices were exported in immense quantities. It was also from this ancient city that Marco Polo set sail.

In 1885, the year Chor Ee left China, approximately one hundred and twenty-five thousand people fled for the Straits Settlements from the four ports of Amoy (Xiamen), Swatow (Shantou), Hong Kong, and Hai-nan (Hainan). They first sailed on crammed decks to Singapore, which was the port of call for sailing vessels. It was also a mandatory stop for Chinese migrants. In that year, a steamer dropped anchor off Singapore every other day, each carrying between two hundred and fifty and three hundred and fifty Chinese passengers. A staggering ninety-eight per cent of them were men. Until the 1920s, few Chinese women, other than those destined for prostitution, left China. Of the men and women who left, over half settled in Singapore. From Singapore, a few hundred went to places around the region, including Batavia,

Bangkok, Semarang, Sourabaya (Surabaya), Billiton (Belitung), Malacca (Melaka), and as far as Australia and Mauritius. The rest, or about slightly over a third, sailed onwards from Singapore to Penang.

Chor Ee managed to board a junk bound for Singapore, working his passage as a kitchen hand, since he didn't have much money. The shipmasters were bent on maximising profits. The junk was overcrowded, with sixty to eighty men packed like sardines in a can for a fee of $5 to $8 Straits dollars per head, more than a month's wage for the average coolie. With an overloaded boat, fresh water and food were in short supply. In that two-week journey, men lived in squalid and unsanitary conditions, without basic comfort or much in the way of medical care. Disease was widespread.

In addition to the appalling shipboard conditions, the men faced the terror of the unknown, being frequently storm-battered in the South China Sea — the sea of sickness and typhoons. Because of its shoal draft, and often overloaded weight above deck, the top-heavy Chinese junks were prone to capsizing. During stormy nights, the vessels tossed about precariously, apt to be engulfed by a giant wave at any moment. If you can't swim, like most Chinese of that era, being out at sea when it is angry is a severe test for anyone's nerve and stamina. Thoughts of drowning in this big expanse of ocean probably made them wish they had never left Amoy and dry land. They clung to their belongings and prayed for the storm to pass. At the break of day, when all was calm once again, fear deserted them. Feeling safe once more, they continued to dream of a new life in Nanyang and the wealth they intended to amass in that promised land. On clear nights, when the stars were intensely bright, the men sang the *Keh-huan-gua*, or rhymes about their journey. Those on-board who had travelled to the Straits Settlements before gave unsolicited advice to the greenhorns, warning them of devious recruiters who would mislead them for their own profit, and about wealthy merchants in Singapore with their great houses in the country. When the sea was too calm, and there was no wind, anxiousness struck again, for they had heard stories of cannibalism on board when the boats ran out of food. They pretended to be so ill that their contaminated flesh would be unsafe for consumption, to avoid being eaten by their fellow shipmates. But for most of the journey the junk meandered along, unhurried and silent except for the sound of hemp squeaking through wooden masts. They got to know each other, and often made life-long friends, pledging to look after each other and their families for the rest of eternity.

Chapter 6

In the Land of Eternal Summer

The junk almost keeled over when the men first caught sight of land. Excited and overjoyed to finally reach Pin-Lan-Su (Penang), they rushed to the starboard side of the vessel for a better view of the lush island as it emerged from the horizon. Their sea-weary eyes opened wide in awe at this foreign land soon to be their home. The shipmaster hollered from the helm for them to get back into position, but few paid any attention. As they approached the harbour, months of anxiety and trepidation dissipated. They felt like new men. And befitting of new men in the land of eternal summer, they were now called *sinkhek*, or the new guests from the Celestial Empire.

To ensure things were in order, and that passengers had not been overcharged, all junks were required to report to the Chinese protectorate upon arrival. Prior to 1933, the immigration laws of the Straits Settlements were quite relaxed, and foreigners could come and go with little restriction. But in the wake of the great depression the regulations changed to control admissions. After 1933, any foreigner who entered the colony had to have a landing permit, obtainable at the immigration office near the wharf at a cost of $5, or almost the rate of a good monthly wage for an unskilled coolie. The landing permit only allowed for one landing and could be exchanged for an admission certificate at the local Chinese protectorate for an extended stay. Once cleared, *sinkehs* who paid their own passage were free to go ashore. Unpaid passengers were detained on the vessel until their services were engaged by local employers looking for coolies. These indentured labourers were usually sent to the tin mines of Perak and Selangor, where they worked off their debt. Before 1877, a large proportion of migrants from China came in through the indentured or credit ticket system. It was essentially a masked slave trade which became a dark chapter in Malaya's history. A recruiter or broker enlisted men, promising them employment. In return, the men mortgaged their labour until their passage was fully paid. But often they were kept confined, cheated of their money, and forced to accept employment at low wages. Until the debt was paid off, the broker had a hold on the worker's services. The establishment of a Chinese protectorate in 1877, curtailed much of the abusive practices of the slave trade, but human temptations persisted. Despite the protectorate's efforts, brokers continued using secret societies to pressure ignorant migrants to accept employment at below market rates. In the year Chor Ee made his way to Penang, sixteen per cent of those who went with him were under the indentured system. It wasn't until the 1920s that this practice was completely abolished. Seventeen-year-old Chor Ee was fortunate not to have arrived in Penang under the credit ticket system, or his destiny might have been very different.

Chinese Protectorate building on the far right and Hongkong and Shanghai Bank Building on the far left hand side. Early 20th century. *Courtesy of Dr Cheah Jin Seng.*

Everywhere they turned in their new home Chor Ee and his brethren were confronted with experiences and objects they had never come across before. For a start, the weather was sweltering and humid. It was not the sweetness but the thickness of air that gave them the first impression of their new home. Sng Choon Yee, a migrant who came to Penang in 1906 and worked as a student interpreter for the Chinese protectorate, said, "it was so hot that if you left a fresh crab out in the morning, it will be good to eat by afternoon."[10] The decomposed crab probably wouldn't make an appetizing meal but his analogy gives a vivid impression of how these new arrivals perceived the weather. The Chinese were not the only ones bothered by the weather. The Europeans found the heat and humidity unbearable too, particularly those on their first posting to the tropics. They took weeks, if not months, to acclimatise to the "deadly climate" and believed the heat induced certain conditions such as anaemia, liver abscesses, and sunstroke.[11] The British had hill stations built to escape from the heat and recover from tropical diseases. Not only were Penang's residents required to adapt to the weather, but fixtures, buildings, and fashion too. Furniture used generous amounts of local wood, such as teak. Architects broke away from traditional practices and adapted designs to suit the tropics. Courtyards with air wells that opened to the sky, borrowed from the Chinese, helped with ventilation, while deep verandas and lofty high-ceilinged rooms were a feature of large bungalows. Arcade-like covered passageways called five-foot-ways,[12] sheltered Penang's pedestrians from the sun and rain. Clothing also had to be adapted to the weather, and nowhere were the changes more visible than the evolving fashion of the Europeans. Their practice of wearing thick tweed, flannel, dark coloured clothing, collared shirts, and ties, rapidly fell out of favour, replaced by light tropical suits, short trousers, or knickerbockers.

Another striking difference between the Celestial Empire and this tropical island was almost everything carried a price tag. Peddlers of all description plied nosily through the streets. This was a totally unaccustomed practice in rural China where most people were self-sufficient. In the villages of China, most wore shoes made of towels with sewn buttons, but in their new home, cotton shoes could be bought for a price. Chinese villagers made their own soaps from ashes and firewood, but in Penang bars of soaps were available for sale. If they wanted food before, they grew it on their farms, but in their new home, they had to buy it from bazaars. Beef cost $0.10 per pound, eggs cost about $0.01 each, a dozen whole chickens cost $1.65, and good quality fish was only $0.10 per *catty*

---

[10] Oral History interview of Sng Choon Yee, a Chinese migrant who arrived in Singapore in 1907, National Archives of Singapore.

[11] 'The Possibility of Acclimatization of Europeans in Tropical Countries', *British Medical Journal*, 19 March 1898.

[12] Five-footways were first introduced in Singapore with Raffles explicitly including this feature in his Singapore Town Plan of 1822. Eventually, five-foot ways became integral in building designs in other parts of the Settlements.

(one *catty* = approximately 600 grammes). Sugar was incredibly expensive by today's standard. Priced at $0.09 per *catty* it cost almost the same price as fish. This was because sugar was still considered "white gold", a food that nobody needed, but one which everybody craved. Even buying a common nail was a novelty for these *sinkheks*. Back where they came from, most farmers used cut bamboo, and tongue and groove joinery to fasten pieces of wood together. Hardly anyone wasted money on something as insignificant as nails. Perhaps the height of extravagance was having to pay for firewood, which cost $0.60 for one hundred pieces — totally incomprehensible for a *sinkhek* when manure could do the same job at the cost of absolutely nothing.

As they meandered through the streets, Chor Ee and the new arrivals were drawn to the cries of peddlers, which at first seemed confusing and senseless, each man screaming above the other. The labouring classes seldom cooked their food, preferring to have meals prepared by hawkers. From early morning till night, hundreds of men on the street sold single product items, ranging from

Chinese men and vendors standing outside an eating house. Late 19th century. *National Archives of Malaysia.*

food to goods and services. As the new arrivals drew closer, the vendors' calls became decipherable. Dozens of smells drifted through the afternoon air — the sulfuric odour of onions and garlic in musty jute bags, the fiery fumes of dried chili, and the briny tang of dried anchovies festering under the hot sun. The stench of raw sewage from open drains gave the town an overpowering scent which even the most enticing smell of roadside cooking could not mask.

"*May up tan. Sit up tan,*" cried the egg man, with his tray of shelled hard-boiled eggs soaked in bean sauce and chili. The cry of "*ark-tau*" announced the approach of the duck broth seller. "*Tok-tok mee,*" yelled the wan-ton noodle man, knocking on a wooden block to echo the tok-tok sound of his call. "*Bua-kar nar,*" called a Teochew peddler with a woven bamboo tray of preserved olives, the tray darkened by years of use. Around the corner the old porcelain and pan mender who pieced broken china together with brass cleats like stained glass, sang out "*por-tiah, ting wur*" (repair saucepans, mend bowls), his tools and wares scattered all around him. "*Roti-roti,*" hollered the Indian bread man, "come buy them while they are fresh." Even the soft-spoken Javanese *satay* man had to call out if he were to get any attention. The cloth peddler was popular with the women and eager to share his ideas on the latest colours and designs. But the king of all hawkers was the candy seller, who traded small trays of sweets for pieces of iron, brass, clothing, and other junk. He was always surrounded by children and older folks, entertaining them with funny stories and the latest news about town.

Starkly obvious was the lack of women. Almost seventy per cent of the island's population were men. Of the women on the island, the Malays were the only race with a relatively balanced male to female ratio. The other nationalities had far fewer women among them; there were only three women to every ten Chinese men, and even fewer for the Europeans, with slightly over one woman to ten men. Of the Chinese women, most were born in Penang (Peranakans), while the rest had been brought in to work as prostitutes and servants. There were various reasons for this disproportionate pattern. One was the restrictive immigration laws that kept Chinese women from emigrating. Under the Qing government in China, prior to 1860 Chinese women were not allowed to emigrate. In 1894, the restrictions on emigration were finally lifted for women. Another reason for the disproportionate ratio was because of China's patriarchal society, where women were required to remain in China to look after their parents-in-law and take care of ancestral worship rites while their husbands travelled abroad to work.

But it was the diversity of races and the assortment of languages and mannerisms of the different nationalities on the island that made the strongest impression on Chor Ee and his friends. For generations, the Chinese were confined to their own country. Rooted to the motherland, most had never ventured from their own villages, let alone China. They looked upon foreigners with suspicion and it wouldn't have been surprising if they felt apprehensive. Penang was a melting pot of nationalities. Half the population on the island was Chinese. Malays made up slightly under a quarter, while Tamils made up sixteen per cent. Europeans, who controlled most of the island's trade and administration, made up less than one per cent of the total. The rest were a smattering of nationalities, most from around the region, with others from further afield — Achinese, Jawi Peranakan, Armenians, Eurasians, Africans, Boyanese, Bugis, Burmese, Japanese, Javanese, Jews, Parsees, Manilamen, Arabs, Anamese, Siamese, Sinhalese all congregated in Penang to trade. They spoke their own languages, and some a smattering of Malay or English. The Chinese themselves were divided by the different dialect groups. If someone like Chor Ee hadn't come from the same village, he would have had little comprehension of what his fellow countrymen were saying. This was one of the main reasons they tended to flock together. Of the Chinese dialect groups, Hokkiens dominated, with slightly over a third (31 per cent), followed by the Cantonese (22 per cent). The proportion of Teochews (12 per cent) and Hakka (10 per cent) were roughly the same, while the smallest dialect group was the Hainanese (5 per cent). The remaining twenty per cent were local-born Chinese.[13] Presumably, these local born Baba and Nyonya spoke Hokkien and Malay.

After clearing immigration, Chor Ee and the new arrivals headed to China Street to find a *khek-pang* (boarding house), taking in the sights of the diverse people around them. There were turban-wearing Sikhs in white cotton, Sinhalese women wearing colourful sarongs and tortoise-shell combs tucked neatly in their hair buns. There were Arabs in long flowing robes, dark-skinned Tamils driving bullock carts, Parsees wearing black phetas on their heads, similar to the songkoks worn by the Malays. There were Malay women dressed in kebayas, their hair decorated with sweet-scented jasmine flowers. Neat and striking Siamese gentlemen wore white stockings and white *bajus* matched with luscious yellow silk sarongs. There were Chitties, many working as moneylenders, always dressed in white and baring shaved heads. The Japanese wore dyed indigo

---

[13] 'Straits Settlement', *Blue Book of The Straits Settlement*, 1881, Singapore.

tunics, while scantily clothed Chinese coolies with pigtails rushed about in a hurry. Rich Chinese merchants rode horse-drawn gharries, shading themselves from the harsh sun with paper umbrellas in striking colours of red and purple. Tall European men dressed in linen suits, the women in summer dresses, their golden hair partially concealed by straw hats and veils. Fresh off the boat, the *sinkheks* stood out like sore thumbs in their black buttoned-up coats and hats. But as soon as they settled in, they quickly shed their heavy clothing, not because they wanted a tan or to show off their supple bodies, but to better cope with the relentless scorching heat.

China Street — Penang's original Chinatown, 1890. *Courtesy of Dr Cheah Jin Seng.*

China Street was one of the oldest streets in Penang, laid out around the same time as Light Street and Beach Street. Second only to Beach Street it was also one of the young town's main commercial thoroughfares. From this nucleus, *sinkheks* spread in almost every direction, looking for room and board. Though the Hokkiens were quite spread out in town, Pitt Street and China Street were predominantly their territory. Market Street, Queen Street and King Street had a high concentration of Hakka migrants, while the Cantonese speakers were commonly found in Chulier Street, Love Lane, Penang Street, Bishop Street and Church Street. The Teochews tended to congregate around Carnarvon Street and Kimberley Streets. The earliest Malay settlement was around Acheen Street. Malabari Indians occupied Kampung Kaka, while early Eurasians gathered around Cintra Street. The small community of Europeans lived mostly around Light Street and Farquhar Street.

Most workers opted to live in town, since that was where the work was. The boarding houses were usually cramped, often with twenty to thirty men living in a space of not more than two thousand square feet. Landlords sub-divided shophouses with makeshift partitions, jamming men into cubicles measuring only a few feet across. Poorly paid labourers who could not afford the rent shared cubicles with others to defray the cost. In some housing, beds or sleeping spaces were rented out for an eight or twelve-hour period.

Having just arrived, and without much money to spare, Chor Ee would have initially rented the cheapest cubicle he could find, paying around $0.30 to $0.50 per month to the principal tenant who also lived in the premises. His fellow kinsmen who had more money might have paid up to $1.00 for a larger space in the boarding house. With little light or ventilation, and even less provision for sanitary requirements, such crowding magnified the dangers of disease and fire. Given the limitations, many preferred to squat in wooden houses built on stilts along the jetties on the periphery of town. Even the housing there was organised according to different clans — Chew, Lim, Lee, Yeoh, and so on.

Living together meant associating with men of similar backgrounds, and many *sinkheks* soon found themselves drawn into secret societies. Sometime in 1870s, before Chor Ee arrived, around a third of the Chinese population in Penang belonged to a secret society. Of those who joined, more than half were members of Ghee Hin Kongsi, a Chinese group which was an offshoot of the Ang-mooi (Tiandihui, or Heaven and Earth Society) formed in the 1700s in Fukien to overthrown the Qing government. Modelled after the family system, these societies provided protection against harassment and generally kept peace in the community. They also offered their members camaraderie, identity, and a sense of being in control of their own destinies. These secret societies were territorial, each guarding particular pockets of town. At one stage, they dominated the lucrative immigrant traffic, as well as opium and prostitution. In the early years, the British government regulated the affairs of the Chinese through these societies, but when the number of members surged towards the latter half of 1800s, they became too powerful and dangerous to be used as instruments of indirect rule.

Typical Layout of Tenement Housing in Penang

GROUND FLOOR

FIRST FLOOR

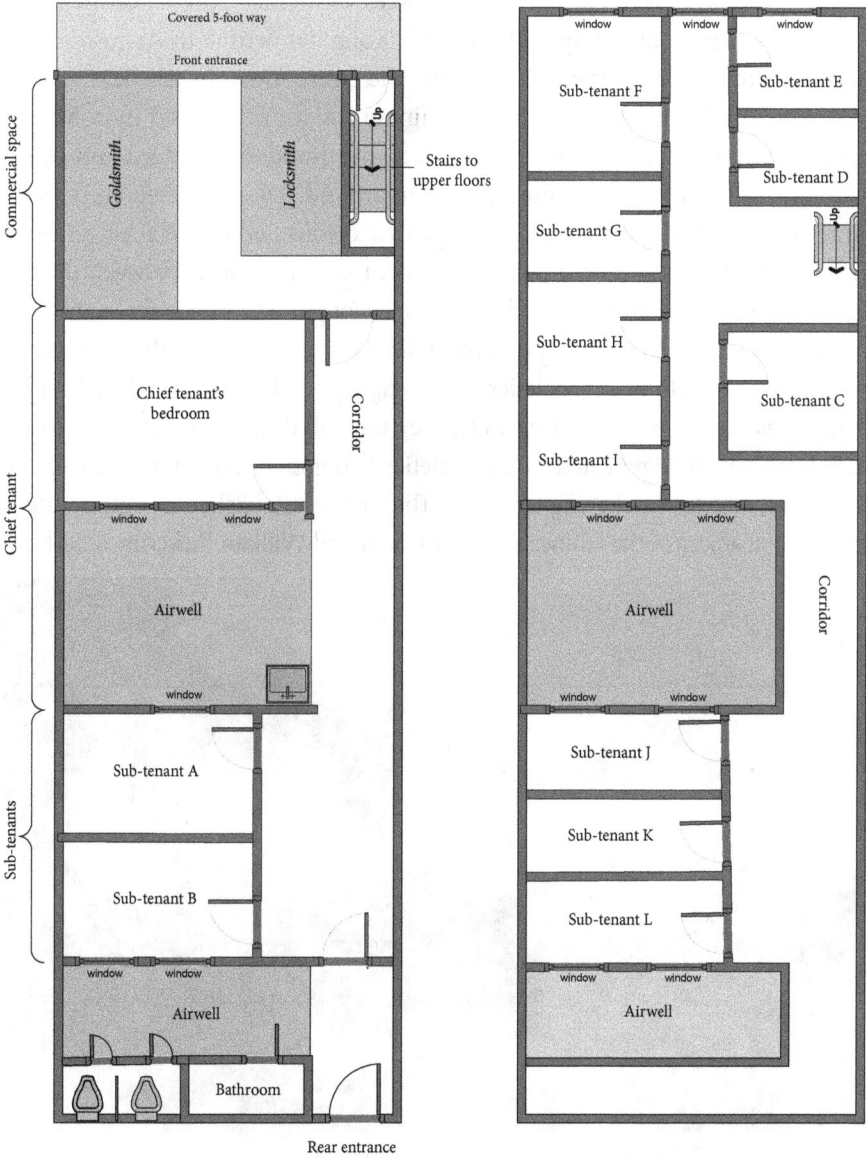

Typical Layout of Tenement Housing in Penang

Rivalry between these fiercely proud and intensely masculine groups led to regular scuffles. The most long-drawn conflict was one that erupted between the Hokkien Kian Teik (Tua Peh Kong society) and the Cantonese-based Ghee Hin Society, over the control of opium farms. The combat drew in others. The Malay White Flag secret society joined forces with Ghee Hin, while the Malay Red Flag society teamed up with Tua Peh Kong. Sometime in August 1867, a nasty confrontation took place, crippling the entire town for ten days. Half of Penang's population, thirty thousand Chinese and four thousand Indo-Malays, battled with each other. When it was over, five hundred lay dead and over a thousand houses had been burned to the ground. Despite Ghee Hin's much larger size, the Kien Tek alliance emerged victorious because of their powerful armaments. After the riot, a peace agreement was negotiated between the two factions. But the British had had just about enough. The police force chastised the secret societies for creating too much disorder and misery in the Settlements, subsequently labelling six societies, including Ghee Hin and Toh Peh Kong in Penang, as "dangerous"[14] and by 1890, they were all declared illegal. The August days were not to be repeated — the societies had gotten too big, too unruly, too organised, and too menacing to police. The British established a protectorate to manage the affairs of the Chinese with a man named William Pickering at its head.

Toa Pek Kong Chingay Procession, Penang. 1924. *Courtesy of Dr Cheah Jin Seng.*

---

[14] 'Statistics of Secret Societies', *Straits Times*, 11 November 1876.

The only son of a family of eight, Pickering was born in Eastwood, Nottinghamshire. At the age of sixteen Pickering apprenticed aboard a vessel that sailed to ports in China and parts of Asia. He developed a curiosity for all things Chinese, picking up several Chinese dialects. Such was his fluency that when someone was needed to head the Chinese Protectorate, Pickering was chosen.

The British were convinced the key reason newcomers flocked together, forming gangs and joining secret societies, was an ingrained distrust of their colonial masters. According to the British, the *sinkhek's* inability to speak English was "the greatest obstacle," and "ignorance of the language has operated heavily against the authorities here."[15] Being the only European man in the Settlements who could speak Chinese, it was Pickering's responsibility to talk to these immigrants and advise them of the government's role. Pickering was also a Freemason, which gave him an added edge to understanding the workings of secret societies. He soon realised that not everything about these gangs was negative and that there was a compassionate side to their existence. Societies took the role of an informal family, forming the closest to blood ties these men had in Penang. If a fellow member died, his relatives in China were informed and his body was taken care of according to traditional customs. Realising how futile it was to ban them, Pickering proposed a new ordinance prohibiting secret societies, but encouraging the formation of clan associations (*kongsi*). Clan associations could carry on the work of promoting kinsmanship, but not engage in illicit activities, breathing a new lease of life into these associations.

By the time Chor Ee arrived, secret societies had had their wings clipped and in their place, an assortment of sub-ethnic *kongsi* had emerged, a number of which lodged themselves along King Street. The principal aim of the kongsi was to find employment and accommodation for *sinkhek* when they first arrived. By the 1950s the number of *kongsi* in Penang swelled from a few dozen to about four hundred. There are no records of Chor Ee joining any societies in his early years in Penang, but he did sign up as a member of the Yap clan association sometime in the early 1920s, and at the same time donated a piece of land on Pitt Street, which became the site of the *kongsi* new clan house.

---

[15] 'Chinese Secret Societies', *The Straits Times*, 11 November 1876.

Chapter 7

Men and Women at Work

In the 1880s George Town's economy was controlled by different nationalities. The Europeans dominated the professional occupations, working as barristers, government administrators, auctioneers, chemists and druggists, engineers, architects and surveyors, missionaries, priests, nuns, physicians, surgeons, dentists, schoolmasters, police and military men, merchants, brokers and agents. The Malays were predominantly paddy planters, attap makers, mat and basket weavers, seamen and fishermen. They also entered the police and military force. The Indians were labourers, money changers, cloth hawkers, carriage owners, general dealers, cattle keepers, and tailors. They sold grass, curry, and milk. The Chinese broke into particular occupations depending on their skills and specialised in three major classes: the industrial class, as labourers, carpenters, masons and bricklayers, ship and boat builders, water carriers, firewood sellers, oil manufacturers, contractors and builders, coffin makers, boot and shoemakers, blacksmiths, barbers, and bakers; the commercial class, as boarding and lodging-house keepers, butchers and pork sellers, cake vendors, charcoal merchants, fishmongers, fruit sellers, hawkers, opium shop keepers, pawnbrokers, pig dealers, Ship-chandlers, shopkeepers, timber dealers, and vegetable sellers; and the agricultural class, where they dominated as fruit cultivators, gambier and pepper planters, and managers of estates. Some moved into the professional class as well, but only in a few professions, such as actors and musicians, clerks, chemists, physicians, dentists, and schoolmasters. A very small proportion became government civil servants.

For all these different occupations, the great majority of *sinkhehs* wound up working in manual labour and as domestic servants. Combined, they made up thirty-four per cent of the island's entire workforce. They earned as little as

$0.20 a day, or just $6 a month if they worked a seven-day week. At the other end of the spectrum, and above these battalions of unskilled labourers, lay a small minority whose monthly income far exceeded what a *sinkhek* could ever dream of making in a lifetime. The highest paying job on the island — aside from merchants who hardly ever disclosed their net worth — was the Supreme Court Chief Justice, who earned $1000 a month, sixty-seven per cent more than the second highest paying job, the Resident Councillor at $600 a month. The Attorney General's salary was on a par with the Resident Councillor, with a monthly pay packet of $600. The chaplain earned more ($315) than both the harbour master and the colonial surgeon ($250). A European police constable earned four times more ($40) than a Malay constable ($9). In today's worth, the current minimum wage would be two hundred and fifty times more, while the current basic salary of a Chief Justice is just twenty times more than in late 19th Century. Depending on how you see it — life for a coolie back then was much harder than that of a labourer today. It might also well be that the Chief Justice today is worse off than his predecessor of a hundred and forty years ago.

Still, the average *sinkhek* was content with a $6 monthly salary. For many of them, life in boom time George Town was a marked improvement on their former conditions in the villages of China. If the *sinkhek* was careful he would

Coolies unloading goods from a boat. Weld Quay. 1940. *Courtesy of Dr Cheah Jin Seng.*

Chinese itinerant vendor. *National Archives of Malaysia.*

Fortune tellers. Early 20th century. *National Archives of Malaysia.*

spend roughly $0.09 a day on food, or $2.70 a month. Minus all his other expenses of rent ($0.30), shaving and washing ($0.30), water and tobacco ($0.45), and contingencies ($0.05), he would still end up with one third of his income saved at the end of the month. Not too bad considering he came with nothing and couldn't possibly have made that sort of living in China. But, if he was hapless and succumbed to the habit of smoking opium, his life in George Town might turn out quite differently.

The Chinese community monopolised some trades by virtue of specialised skills. Back in the early 1880s they dominated the coffin making and tomb building trades, and were the only undertakers in Penang. The Chinese were also in great demand in the timber industry as sawyers, wood carvers, and coopers. They were the only pawnbrokers, cutlers, and sellers of charcoal in town. Paddy farming was an important activity in the Federated Malay States, but the nine rice mills that produced and sold rice in Penang in the early 1880s were all owned by the Chinese. They were also the only rice merchants in town.

One of the most controversial trades they once specialised in, but no longer reigned, was the production and distribution of opium. Introduced by the British as a counter-attack on the Chinese prohibition wars in the 1800s, opium became a social problem for over a century. The Straits Settlements played a key role for the British in distributing the drug around the region. Through a powerful agency called an Opium Farm, which held a monopoly procured from the government, raw opium was imported from the United Provinces and Bengal in India, then refined, packaged, and retailed to consumers in the colonies and elsewhere. Opium dens sprouted up everywhere in the settlements, and towns were awash with the drug. The system allowed the government to shift their moral responsibilities to the private sector, but at the same time derive significant revenues from three main sources — licensing fees from the cultivators in Bengal and the United Provinces, concession fees from the opium farms, and a hefty export levy from native states that cultivated opium. In 1890, more than half the government revenue from the settlements was derived from the opium trade ($2,044,185). The rest came from other sources, including land revenue, stamp duty, and spirit revenue.

Opium farms in Penang were controlled by a syndicate of Chinese towkays who also monopolised the lease of the Kedah Opium Farm. They kept a large force of detective police and a small fleet of revenue cruisers to ensure their goods were not smuggled by their own staff. Most of their workers were

Chinese opium smokers. Penang. 1900. *Courtesy of Dr Cheah Jin Seng.*

Chinese and all employees were prohibited from smoking the drug. William Shellabear, a pioneer scholar and missionary in British Malaya, estimated local consumption of opium in the Straits Settlements in 1891 at about thirteen per cent of the Chinese population. On average, a smoker spent $100 a year on the drug, or basically seventy-five per cent of his salary.[16] The rest of the opium produced was exported from Penang around the region to Perak, West Siam, and Sumatra. From Malacca, the drug was sold to Sungei Ujong, and from Singapore it was exported to China, East Siam, Selangor, Hong Kong, Saigon, Dutch India, Java, Rio, and Australia. The Straits Settlements became an important opium redistribution centre for the British and unsurprisingly, supporting the trade became a central imperative of British trade policy. Addiction reached epidemic proportions by the 1930s, yet the British government, bent on maintaining an immigrant work force, did not curtail it until years later.

From the sordid world of opium, it was a short step to the seedy world of prostitution. This, unfortunately, was one of the primary professions for young girls and women in the settlements. The earliest mention of the word 'brothel' in the colony dates back to October 1855, when a new bill for regulating the police of Calcutta, Madras, Bombay, and the Straits Settlements was read

---

[16] 'Mr W G Shellabear on "The Opium Curse"', *Straits Times Weekly Issue*, 10 October 1893.

out. The bill sought to establish a uniform code of conduct for the colonies. Taverns were to be licensed by the commissioner of police, and brothel keepers were to be punished if they allowed drunkenness or "prostitutes" to congregate in their premises. If there were three or more complaints by their neighbours, they would have had their business licence confiscated.[17] In all likelihood, prostitution, like drinking, existed in the Straits Settlements long before the police bill was issued. Prostitution was not outlawed, but the police could make arrests if there were objections made.

The brothels were mostly controlled by the Chinese secret societies. They exploited sex workers, known as *mui tsai*, sourcing them from poor villages in Canton and supplying them to the influx of young male immigrants who sought the comfort of these girls to escape the loneliness and strain of work. Girls as young as ten were abducted, or even sold by their parents into the trade, then brought to the colony to be resold at a higher price to a brothel-keeper. Many of these girls were trafficked as far as America. Like the Cantonese girls, they were sold at a price dependent on their beauty and virginity. When irate neighbours filed complaints against rowdy men frequenting the brothels, the girls were quickly herded to another location to avoid being caught. By end of the 19th century the sex trade became deeply entrenched in the colonies, particularly after the travel ban for women was lifted. Despite efforts to control the trade, prostitution proved irrepressible because the town's males supported it and brothel-keepers profited from it.

Feeble attempts to protect these girls and women were made in 1888 when the Women and Girls Protection Ordinance was introduced. The law set the age of consent at the tender age of ten. Three years later, it was raised to twelve. The law also required brothels and prostitutes to register with the authorities. By 1891 there were nine hundred and fifty-eight registered prostitutes in Penang. Without even counting the "sly prostitutes" and "clandestine houses", these working girls made up more than the colony's entire police force, schoolmasters and schoolmistresses, and merchants put together. Working conditions were appalling. The girls and women were deprived of freedom, repeatedly raped, and if they didn't earn their keep, beaten by the brothel-keepers. Lack of hygiene and precautions were common. As a result, venereal diseases became rampant. In 1899, the government responded to the alarming rise in cases of sexually transmitted diseases by introducing a penalty on

---

[17] 'Untitled', *The Straits Times*, 17 October 1855.

brothel keepers who allowed girls with contagious diseases to continue working. Unperturbed by the new law, simply because demand was so great, and with absolutely no regard for the welfare of the girls, these callous men brazenly remonstrated. Hoping their customers would retaliate against the authorities, they decided to go on strike by collectively closing all the brothels in town. Their protest was short-lived. After a visit by the Chinese protectorate the following evening, their dens of infamy were reopened for business as usual.

There were many pockets of the town where brothels thrived, their form varying with the local clientele. Coolies and rickshaw pullers frequented the dingy dens around Rope Walk and Kuala Kangsar Road. A mixed clientele went to the brothels along Cintra Street where the Karayuki-san held sway. Campbell Street was Penang's main red-light district, catering to higher-end clients, where at sunset a rickshaw parade with girls in *cheongsams* and heavily powdered faces went on display. Prostitution was also masked in various forms. In 1891, the Penang Independent reported of a "coffee-shop" business which appeared to have gained footing in Penang. The first such establishment was on Leith Street, conveniently located close to the Merchant's Club, a gentlemen's club for affluent Chinese men. The clever little enterprise involved a young woman from Singapore who started the business selling cold drinks and snacks. According to the paper, her refreshment venture was nothing but a front for selling "warm embraces." The paper also noted that so long as she remained single and only operated by herself, her venture was considered legal. But the moment a helpmate of the same sex assisted her, the whole enterprise could spell trouble and should be put to a stop. One of the quirks of the ordinance was that "a single woman trading in this way is considered an honest matron and, may be, a benefactress to mankind, whereas two would be set down as prostitutes and a nuisance."[18]

Another guise of prostitution took the form of sing-song girls, many of whom hailed from Soochow, a sleepy conservative walled-town near Shanghai. They were equivalent to the geishas of Japan. Recruited from villages, these young girls were put through a series of singing and etiquette lessons before they were sent to sing-song houses and opium and gambling dens that combined music, drink, drugs, and sex. The girls sang in high-pitched voices, often accompanied by screechy fiddles, or sometimes a band. Between acts, some served tables, while others solicited for sex in private rooms upstairs.

---

[18] 'A Cry from Penang', *Daily Advertiser*, 28 April 1891.

Those with poise and beauty were treasured. Aside from their physical assets, they were also distinct from the other girls by the way they dressed. They wore fitted *cheongsams* with silk hosiery and dainty embroidered shoes; their lips and cheeks lightly brushed with *poudre de riz*; their hair adorned with pins and combs, and their arms, ears, and necks graced with diamonds and jade jewellery. A number of them ended up becoming *seh-ee* (secondary wives) to wealthy Chinese men. They had no official status, like a concubine, and by the time of marriage, a number would have been pregnant. If they were smart,

Japanese dancing girls. Penang. 1910. *Courtesy of Dr Cheah Jin Seng.*

they could cover up so that no one knew who the father of the child was. This was a hidden secret in Penang for many years and rumour has it a number of children from respectable homes in Penang were fathered this way.

While the men in town leeched off sex workers, another trade the Chinese could not do without was the humble barber. Before 1912, barbers were a common sight and an essential part of society. Every Chinese man had to wear a *towchang* (queue) from the day of birth. When the Manchu Tartars (Qing) seized the imperial Chinese throne in the 17th century, the Emperor issued a decree ordering all Han Chinese to shave their heads and adopt the *towchang*. It was a compulsory hairstyle for males and the penalty for not wearing it was execution. "Lose your hair or lose your head," was a phrase commonly employed. The decree initially provoked bitter opposition from the Han, who saw it as a mark of suppression. Records even prove that the law drove many Chinese to emigrate to Japan. For a time, there was much resistance, but the clever Tartar Emperor resorted to using reverse psychology. Instead of coercion, he issued a further decree prohibiting criminals and convicts from wearing the *towchang*. Knowing full well the intense devotion of the Chinese to filial piety, the Emperor further forbade persons mourning the loss of a parent to shave or have his hair combed for a period of one hundred days. No matter how unkempt his appearance was, the hair must not be touched. Thus, with just two strokes of a pen, the wily Emperor made the *towchang* a mark of respect and an object of reverence. From then onwards, Chinese men wore it with dignity and honour.

By around 1912, after Sun Yat Sen overthrew the Manchu government, most Chinese men cut their *towchang*, but some continued to wear it even in the 1920s. It was no different when they travelled and lived abroad. The *towchang* had to be worn, and consequently the men's peculiar appearance was subject to immense ridicule and even persecution, particularly by those in the West unacquainted with the tradition.

Chor Ee's first bid for independence in Penang was by becoming an itinerant barber. A colony census completed in 1881 fixed the population of Penang Island at just over ninety-one thousand, about thirty-four thousand of whom were Chinese men. Of that, slightly over one per cent, or three hundred and fifty-seven, worked as barbers. On any given week, the humble barber roamed street to street, selling his services to at least a hundred customers. Since a price of a shave was fixed at $0.07, a barber could have easily accumulated a tidy monthly income of $28, or roughly four and a half times the paltry $6 earned by the unskilled coolie. In the year Chor Ee arrived, over forty-three thousand men came to Penang. Some may have gone to work in the hinterlands, but a great majority stayed on and laboured in the massive development taking shape in booming George Town. Thanks to a constant influx of new immigrants and the mandatory requirement for Chinese men to wear a *towchang*, barbering was a lucrative trade. And since Penang was principally a male-dominated society of able-bodied Chinese men, barbers reigned supreme.

With his tools on his back, Chor Ee peddled his services along the streets of Weld Quay towards the Prangin Canal. This was where most of his clients congregated. Once a week, his customers sought his service to have their heads shaved and hair plaited.

Seating his customer on a wooden triangular stool, Chor Ee set to work, grabbing hold of a towel hanging from his bamboo pole, he dipped it in boiling water, partially wrung it, then rubbed the towel over the customer's head to open the pores and soften the hair. With a sharpened razor and graceful motions, he worked his way from top to bottom until the crown was cleanly shaven. No soap was used. After a quick trim of the eyebrows, the ears were cleaned with a bamboo pick. With his deft hands, Chor Ee neatly re-plaited the *towchang*, the strands of hair drawn tight and snug, and bound with a black silk cord. Finally, a quick spine and shoulder massage was given to complete the half-hour process. Chor Ee soon built a long list of regular customers who knew him as Thi-Thau Ee (Barber Ee), a nickname that was linked to his trade.

He was earning a small fortune each month and could not possibly have imagined the prospect of accumulating so much wealth back in China. But he didn't intend to shave heads for the rest of his life. As an ambitious young man, Chor Ee had long decided that he wanted to be a man of enterprise. Engaging in trade was an obsession with the Hokkiens, but without capital it was next to impossible.

Hard cash, of which there was never enough, was difficult to obtain, even in a boomtown like George Town. There were only two banks in Penang, both set up to finance trade within the European community. None served the local community. Kwong Yik Banking Company Limited, the first local Chinese bank was only established in 1903. Even then, it was based in Singapore, with no branches elsewhere. European banks generally avoided Chinese enterprises pre-comprador days, let alone migrants like Chor Ee with no track record. In short, there was a gap in the market.

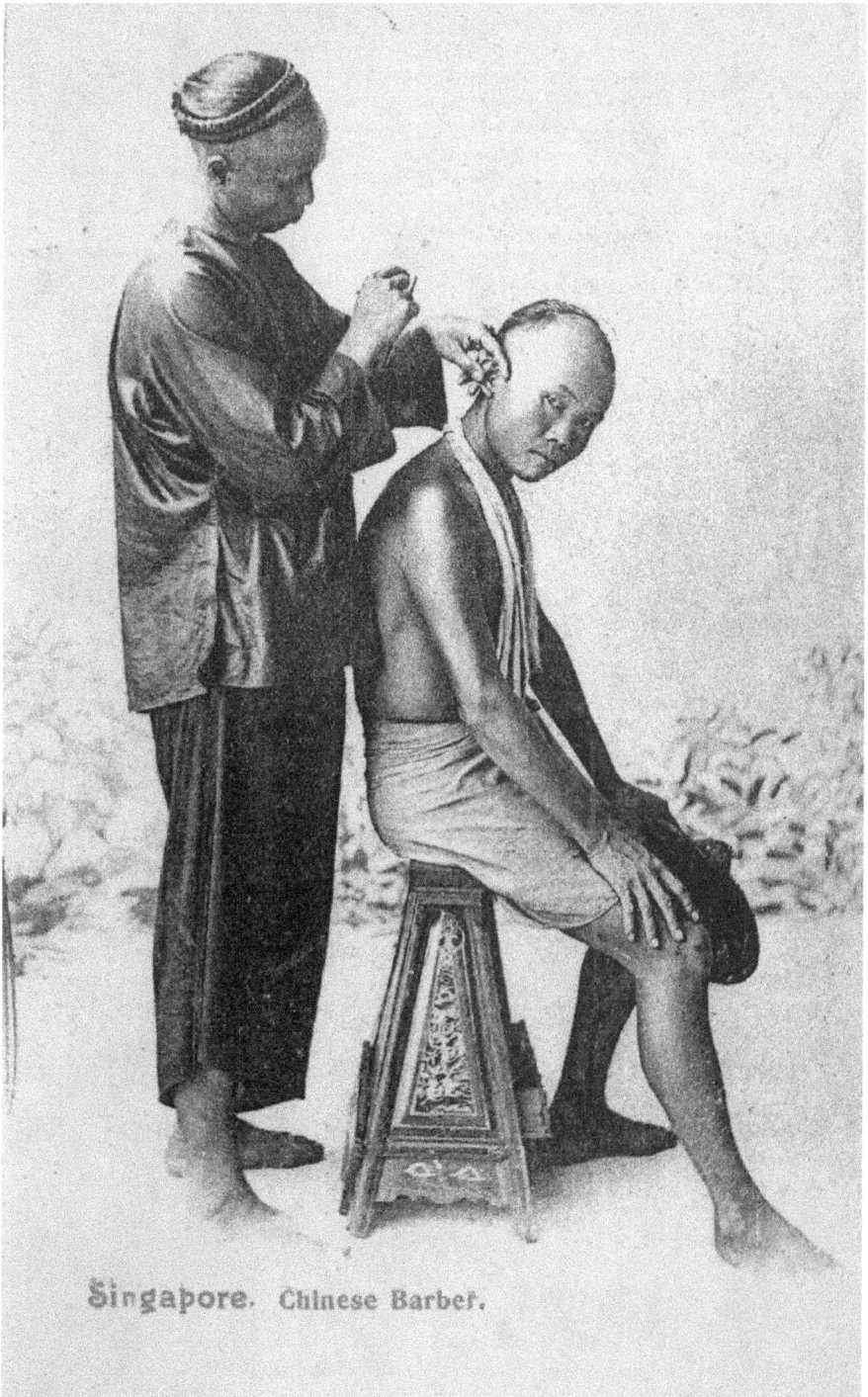

Singapore. Chinese Barber.

Chinese barber. Late 19th century. *National Archives of Malaysia.*

Chapter 8

A Chop for a Shop

I

Chor Ee worked hard for the next few years, shaving heads and plaiting *towchang*, saving for a business. Apart from capital, another prerequisite of setting up shop was a chop.

Chop was an important word in the colony back then. Firstly, it meant the stamp or seal that the Chinese used as a form of identification in lieu of a signature, in fact for the Chinese, putting a chop on a document was far more important than a signature. A man of importance would have his own private chop. He may have had a family chop too, as well as a separate chop for each of his businesses. To some extent this practice still continues. Secondly, the word chop is also used to denote a Chinese business or a *kongsi* (partnership), and there were a lot of them back then. Penang afforded its aspiring entrepreneurs a huge advantage: rapid population growth with an insatiable demand for basic needs. As a result, hundreds of small retailers, mostly immigrants, worked their way up from peddling to opening their own independent chops or *kongsi*.

Penang was a Crown Colony, ruled by a governor under the administration of the Colonial Office in London. All its residents, regardless of race, were British subjects. But Penang remained a collection of disparate parts due to its laissez-faire economy. Before World War II, there were no uniform laws regarding how businesses operated. Beyond establishing public order and extending the rule of law, legislative councillors left the economy much to its own accord, allowing free trade to flourish and businesses to form without much intervention and regulation. Penang's success owed much to the entrepreneurial boldness of its businessmen, who were prepared to take risks in the quest for profit. Market systems and business practices adopted and evolved through centuries of trade around the region, continued pretty much unchanged. This was very apparent in the assortment of measurement systems used in the market place: the popular *tahil* and *catty* from China, which is still in use in Penang, *pikuls* from Java, the Dutch standard *koyan*, and the British Imperial pounds and pints, to name a few. Some measurements were only applied to specific products. The Malaya *chupak* and *gantang* were only used for weighing unhusked rice. The *tahil*, used to buy and sell gold, and the Chinese *tee*, *hoon*, and *chee*, for measuring opium.

As chaotic as that may seem, no one batted an eyelid. Nor were people confused by the multitude of currencies used as mediums of exchange. Money too was an aspect of colony life that did not become standardised until later. In fact, no other country had seen such a profusion of copper coins and silver currencies used in trade as in the Settlements. Government offices kept their accounts in pounds, shillings, and pence, while businesses had their own system of accounting. But they accepted whatever tender that came to hand — from the Spanish Carolus dollar, which was mostly used in the pepper trade with Aceh, to the Mexican Eagle dollar, the American Trade Dollar, the Hong Kong Dollar, Peruvian and Bolivian Dollars, and the Japanese Dragon Yen. Added to this hodgepodge of currencies were copper coins from Kedah called Duit Ayam, the Dutch Duit Padang, and the Terengganu lead cent with a hole in the centre. It wasn't until after the turn of the 20th century that the colony finally issued its own currency, fittingly named the Straits Settlements Dollar. The move largely came about because the British thought it humiliating to have Japanese money circulating in a colony governed under the English flag.

Notably absent in the colony's freewheeling noninterventionist economy was income tax. No one was saddled with the burden of paying the government a part of their hard-earned income. But it was not for lack of trying on the government's part. The suggestion of imposing a tax on income was first broached as far back as 1860 by the secretary of state for the colonies, but it was met with much opposition from the business communities, on the grounds that the finances of the colony did not render it necessary. The Settlements' chief source of income came from opium concessions, and that revenue was more than sufficient to cover government expenses. Another reason voiced by the chamber of commerce was that such an "inquisitorial" tax would be detrimental to the economy of the settlements in view of the migratory nature of the population. No further action was taken after that. Half a century later, in 1911, the Government brought up the idea again, and again it was heavily opposed on much the same grounds. Over the years, as revenues from opium began to dwindle, the colonial office found other forms of taxes to help finance its way out of a global depression, and later, fund Britain's war efforts in Europe. The hostilities of World War I prompted an outpouring of fear, and the British and Asian communities of the Settlements showed a streak of patriotism by offering to help the empire with its war efforts, proposing to contribute to a war tax based on their income. It was understood by the business community that such a tax would only be levied with the special purpose of raising money to help the British government during war and pledges to that effect were given by the then governor. On 8 January 1917, he remarked, "From what was told to me by the members who formed the deputation which represented the various communities that it is now clear that their wish is for income tax — they put it by another name, a War tax based on income — merely for the reason that they are of opinion that it should be shown that it is to be a temporary tax."

The rate was set on a progressive scale ranging from two to six per cent. But instead of being temporary, the tax continued to be levied after the war, despite protest and much to the annoyance of the inhabitants of the Settlements. From then onwards, Chor Ee and the rest of the working population started paying income taxes. As we shall see in later chapters, such taxes had a huge impact on the decision making process of wealthy merchants like Chor Ee, and most certainly, Oei Tiong Ham, an influential businessman from the Dutch East Indies.

By the end of the 19th century, even as Penang prospered, cracks in the commercial system began to emerge. At issue, and a point of conflict between local Chinese and European businesses, was their attitude towards the relationship and the identity of business partners. For as long as anyone could remember, a typical Chinese partnership was governed by the concept of *guanxi*, derived primarily from the kinship system where trust was established through a web of social relationships. You build trust first, only then do you conduct business. On the other end of the commercial spectrum, Western firms tended to enter into business deals based on watertight contracts, backed by a stable legal system. Since there were no such laws requiring the registration of *kongsi* or businesses, European creditors often found it difficult to trace the identity of a Chinese debtor. A "Chinese Chop's Who's Who would be godsend to British traders," noted the journalist G. E. Raine. Because birth registries did not exist either at that time, a Chinese man could go by two or three different names, further adding another layer of anonymity to any transaction. The number of failures, and the troubles afterwards in finding the partners of the insolvent firms, caused a great degree of anxiety among the business communities.

Such concerns inevitably called for action. The first effort to pass a bill to get businesses registered was in the year 1888 following a "depression of trade" that swept over Asia. A number of smaller Chinese firms went down "like nine-pins" but "whenever they have done so, it has been ascertained that no rich Chinaman is a partner."[19] Legislators argued and deliberated, but since the proposed bill did not receive unanimous support from the business communities, it went into hibernation. Dozens of similar bills were proposed over the years. Proponents for such laws, the majority of whom were from the European community, felt they could boost trade within the colony. They argued: "In the abstract everybody agrees that registration will conduce to honest business, and will eliminate such courses as the putting up of men of straw to stand the brunt of insolvency while the undeclared partners who have been making a good thing out of their transactions for years, vanish into thin air when it comes to be a case of settling liabilities."[20] Its opponents, namely the Chinese community, strongly objected, claiming compulsory registration could lead to fraud, because most Chinese traders were not proficient in the English language: "there is nothing to prevent persons residents in the Colony from registering as partners in China. Such person might not be a partner at all, but if he had property in the Colony, his property might be seized in bankruptcy."[21]

Compulsory registration only came into effect in 1947. For a while, Chinese businesses kept pretty much to themselves.

II

It took Chor Ee five years to save up for his chop. In 1890, he opened a provisions store, named Chop Ban Hin Lee (Ten Thousand Prosperity), and employed a handful of staff. It wouldn't have taken much for him to start his

---

[19] 'Chinese partnerships', *Straits Times Weekly*, 2 December 1891.
[20] 'Registration of Partnerships', *The Singapore Free Press and Mercantile Advertiser*, 1 September 1910.
[21] 'The Registration of Partnerships', *The Eastern Daily Mail*, 3 December 1906.

enterprise. Based on bankruptcy court hearings of the late 19th century, all that was required to start a provisions shop was capital of between \$500 and \$3,700. He could easily have saved that much from shaving heads if he lived frugally. After consulting a fortune teller for a propitious opening date, Chop Ban Hin Lee started life on Prangin Road, the part of town where *sinkheks* mostly congregated. The road joins Beach Street, the main commercial district of the island. Despite being a poorer neighbour to the more upmarket Beach Street, Prangin Road itself was constantly bustling with activities. Peddlers jockeyed for position along the five-foot-ways, while shopkeepers served the community as key tenants. Small merchants, provision stores, agents, brokers, blacksmiths, silversmiths, locksmiths, carpenters, and eating houses, all elbowed their way into the rows of shop-houses further north, close to the junction of China Street, which was the epicentre of Chinese mercantile transactions. The farther north they went, the higher the rent and the pricier the real estate became. It was certain that Chor Ee commenced at the less salubrious end of town in the early years, but what is not certain is whether he purchased or rented his premises. A standard shop-house measuring twelve feet by sixty feet could be purchased in that area for a few thousand dollars. Moving towards China Street prices become steeper. In any case, with so many immigrants arriving each year, Prangin Road was a good place to do business for someone with modest means and just starting out.

Prangin Market, locally known as "Sia Boey" (end of town), where most of the *Sinkheks* congregated when they first arrived in Penang. 1910. *Courtesy of Dr Cheah Jin Seng.*

Beach Street. Chor Ee started Chop Ban Hin Lee around this end of Beach Street where the shop-houses a smaller. 1900. *Courtesy of Dr Cheah Jin Seng.*

If we were to go back in time to a shop-house in Chor Ee's day, it would not have changed that much from the shop-houses we see today in Penang. Chop Ban Hin Lee had an open shop front, with a signboard carved with the characters "Ban Hin Lee" hanging vertically, and another signboard under the five-foot way announcing the products sold. A wooden counter faced the unpaved street and goods were displayed in earthenware pots and gunny sacks stocked with provisions. Because of its deep and narrow structure, the interior was quite dark, except the air well where shafts of natural light peered through the stockpiled provisions. A long narrow staircase led to Chor Ee's living quarters on the upper floor, which he shared with his staff. Chor Ee's customers were mainly ship-chandlers and the labouring classes. He would typically have carried a range of basic goods, such as sugar, rice, flour, salt, oil, and tea. All that was required to do his trade were weighing scales and an abacus. Provision stores were basically all-purpose general traders catering to the town-dwellers' household needs. The inhabitants of George Town also shopped at the municipal wet markets, of which there were a few in town, selling fresh produce such as meat and fish and vegetables. Unlike their villages in China, no one had time to grow or make things. The transients that arrived, came for one purpose and that was to earn a living. They didn't have their wives, mothers, or sisters with them to produce soaps and candles, or dry the fish they caught from the pond. They had no time to grow and preserve vegetables, nor could they find a moment to weave cloth or sew clothes. Most things had to be bought.

In time, as the volume of business grew, more of these general-purpose stores evolved, becoming more specialised, concentrating on handling just a few lines of goods (dry goods, oil, hardware) or one kind of trade (retail or wholesale, import or export). Chor Ee focused predominantly on brown sugar sourced from Province Wellesley, the strip of mainland across the sea from Penang Island. Before the introduction of rubber, sugar was once king in Malaya. Lured by the richness of the soil, the availability of water, and the cheapness of fire wood, the Chinese started cultivating sugar in Province Wellesley in 1820. By 1858, there were eleven estates, with a total acreage of 10,720 acres. These estates produced four thousand tons of sugar and two hundred thousand gallons of rum. A major reason for the rapid and sustained development of the sugar industry in the Province — compared with its failure in Singapore — was the peculiar fact that the Imperial Government admitted sugar and rum of Province Wellesley into the home market at reduced colonial duties, while similar products from Singapore were charged foreign duties. We don't know why that was the case but that was how the Province's sugar estates managed to defray the large capital outlay required to set up sugar mills. But by the beginning of the 20th century, Province Wellesley saw a switch from sugar to rubber production. From eleven, the number of estates dropped to four, and eventually to none.

Brown sugar was not the only commodity to transform Chor Ee's life and business. Sometime in the late 1890s he had the good fortune of meeting Oei Tiong Ham, a man who hailed from Semarang in Java. Through his firm, Kian Gwan Kongsi, Tiong Ham had ventured into the production of white sugar in Java and was looking to expand his market. Oei Tiong Ham's name is perhaps no longer as well-known as it once was, but at the turn of the 20th century he was dubbed the Sugar King, the wealthiest and most powerful man in Southeast Asia. Tiong Ham was a first generation Chinese-Indonesian, son of an established merchant in Semarang. His father, Oei Tjie Sien, came from the district of Tong-An in China, not far from where Chor Ee was born. Like many others, Tjie Sien left the country in 1858, fleeing the repressive rule of the Manchus, settling in Semarang, which at that time was the largest commercial city in Java. Semarang was a good place for the Chinese to settle. It had a major harbour where native goods such as gambier and sugar could be exported, and imported foreign products could be distributed in the city and the hinterlands. In 1863, after several years of work, Tjie Sien set up a trading company called Kian Gwan. It initially traded in Chinese goods (teas, herbs, incense, silks), and then local products like rice, sugar, tobacco, and gambier. Tjie Sien's success saw him making a number of acquisitions, including large tracts of estate land in Simongan, Tjandi, and Randoesari in Semarang. He got married and had seven children, one of whom was Tiong Ham, his eldest son.

Tiong Ham went to a local Chinese school in Semarang. When he came of age his father took him under his wing and taught him the family business. In 1890 Tiong Ham took over Kian Gwan and oversaw the trading side of the business, while his brother looked after the land holdings. Not long after, Tiong Ham acquired his first sugar mill and estate called Pakkies. His timing was impeccable. Java was already a major producer in the global sugar trade, but historically lagged behind Cuba. When Tiong Ham came onto the scene, Cuba's industry had suffered a collapse caused by the island's war of independence. From just about a third in 1850, Java's sugar production in 1900 exceeded that of Cuba by over 250 per cent.[22] At 744,000 tons, Java commanded 14 per cent of world sugar production. Meanwhile, a new wave of technological innovation in sugar production emerged in the late 1880s. Owing to the recession that almost halted their operations, many existing sugar mills could not afford to replace outdated machinery. Quick to capitalise on this, and with fresh capital and determination, Tiong Ham built everything newer and better to improve the speed and capacity of production. The success of his first mill led him to procure other sugar estates.

How Tiong Ham conducted business and managed his operations took on a newly organised quality as well, partly because the estates and mills he took over were located in an area that was once under the control of the Netherlands Trading Society. Tiong Ham was mostly dealing with a number of European firms, hence needed to take on a "Western" approach to running his operations. Discriminative laws also made life difficult for the Chinese in

---

[22]   Ulbe Bosma & Jonathan Curry-Machado, 'Two Islands, One Commodity: Cuba, Java, and The Global Sugar Trade (1790-1930)', *New West Indian Guide / Nieuwe West-Indische Gids*, vol. 86, no. 3-4, 2012.

Java. He armed himself with the best legal mind he could find in Java, a Dutch nobleman by the name of Baron Van Heeckeren. He relied on Van Heeckeren to structure air-tight contracts to execute deals, rather than depend on the traditional kinship networks and family ties. He took the steps necessary to incorporate Kian Gwan as a limited liability company, and injected substantial amounts of capital to back its operations. This business model was contrary to how Chinese *kongsis* were usually structured. Tiong Ham recruited and built his organisation based on merit rather than nepotism. Professional managers replaced relatives in key management roles. Even his sense of dress took on a different flair. Twelve years ahead of most Chinese men he replaced his *towchang* and *samfoo* with a stylish European hairstyle and tailor-made Western suit. The Chinese community in Semarang rubbed their eyes at his defiance of traditions. His Elders were fuming. But Tiong Ham went ahead and looked the part of a young urbane gentleman. With his limited Dutch vocabulary, he cultivated cordial relations with Dutch officers and wined and dined the European fraternity. All in all, what appeared as a defiance of traditional norms was his determination to transform Kian Gwan from a Chinese *kongsi* into a modern business conglomerate. If he wanted a slice of the world he knew he had to move away from the past, and from the confines of a domestic community tucked away in obscurity. Under him, Kian Gwan thrived, transforming from a small import/export trading house to a business empire that extended across the Pacific, and as far as New York and mainland Europe.

There are several different accounts of how Chor Ee met Tiong Ham and how they dealt with each other in business — but every version of the story emphasises that it was Chor Ee's success in dealing with Tiong Ham in the sugar trade that counted for his economic rise. Both men were almost the same age and shared similar ambitions and entrepreneurial spirit. In other respects, however, they were as different as could be, not least in their upbringing and lifestyle. Tiong Ham came from a relatively well-to-do family. He was heavily influenced by modernity and the Western way of life, while Chor Ee was more comfortable with age-old customs and the traditional way of doing things, particularly in his business approach.

The first account of how they met went back to when Chor Ee was still a barber. Tiong Ham was his client and found him trustworthy and encouraged Chor Ee to start his own business. Allegedly it was Tiong Ham who suggested the name Ban Hin Lee, the firm of 'ten thousand prosperity.' Coincidentally, the Oeis used a similar term as good luck inscriptions during every Chinese New Year celebration. Painted on red paper, and posted throughout the house as decorations, the inscription read "ten thousand generations and long duration."

Another account has a more intriguing spin. Chor Ee had purchased crude sugar from Caledonia Estate in Province Wellesley, which he sent to Tiong Ham's refineries in Java for processing, before shipping the end product back to Penang, where he sold it at a huge profit. Sensing that Chor Ee might one day pose a threat to his own business, Tiong Ham decided to test his competitor's business acumen by delaying his invoices. By presenting him with a monstrous bill after an extended period of time Tiong Ham hoped to derail Chor Ee's cash flow. But much to his surprise, when the bill accumulated to two million dollars, Chor Ee not only paid in full, but paid promptly. Tiong Ham was so impressed with his honesty and reliability that he made a trip to Penang to meet his rival, and a friendship was quickly established between the two men.

Caledonia Sugar Estate, Province Wellesley. 1869. *Penang Museum.*

The third account of how they met is possibly connected to the first and second version of the story. Chor Ee, who had developed an eye for opportunity, saw the need to change sugar suppliers, since the demand was as strong as ever, but the estates in Wellesley Province were showing signs of a slowdown. He entered into a business arrangement with Tiong Ham sometime in 1900. Since credit was difficult to obtain, a common way to fund working capital was a type of private finance based on a person's reputation and creditworthiness, otherwise known as the consignment trade. Kian Gwan consigned sugar to Ban Hin Lee and at the end of month Ban Hin Lee paid for what was sold. This arrangement principally enabled Chor Ee to do business of value well above the total of his own capital, and formed the basis of his entire trading structure in the early years. The initial consignments were small enough for Chor Ee to quickly sell, replenish, and pay the amount owing to Tiong Ham. The consignment trade also benefitted the consignor as it was unnecessary for merchants to travel back and forth to sell their own goods. The distance between Java and Penang was at least a few days by sea. Competition was intense in a market crowded with numerous small businesses, subject to fluctuations in prices, and was almost completely unregulated. Chor Ee was soon competing with business rivals that not only included Chinese, but European import-export agents such as Behn Myer & Co, G.H. Slot & Co, Chop Bean Seng, Chop Sin Joo Seng, and Chop Yeo Chip Moh. Over the next five years, Ban Hin Lee, the little firm Chor Ee established only a decade earlier, became Tiong Ham's largest sugar distributor, and dominated the business in Chor Ee's part of the world. Chor Ee's sugar consignment was as large as eight thousand five hundred piculs, or about four hundred and fifty thousand kilos per shipment, enough to make about eleven million cans of soft drinks in today's calculations. Penang had never seen such huge quantities of sugar entering its port.

Chor Ee was still in his early thirties, operating in a bourgeoning economy, with an astute and enterprising business associate in Tiong Ham. The future looked promising for this ambitious young man. Within a decade of dealing in white sugar, Chor Ee was able to lay the foundation of his fortune. From white sugar, he diversified into rice, rubber, tapioca, tin, and other commodities. The ready availability of commodities, and overall surge in population and wealth in the region, suggested to Chor Ee that by geographically spreading his trading base, he could reap far greater profits than by just concentrating on Penang. Ban Hin Lee branches were set up to capitalise on the vibrant

Singapore and Burma trade. At first, he bought space on Rangoon-bound *twakows* (lighter crafts) owned by other merchants, shipping sugar and other local commodities to Rangoon and bringing back rice on the return voyage. Shipments came in almost every other day. He consigned these goods to local merchants and agents for reshipment elsewhere. Eventually, he opted to lower costs by investing in his own fleet of twakows and building his own rice mill in Burma. Alongside development in his rice trade, Chor Ee also ventured into the manufacturing of coconut oil by acquiring an oil mill from Bean Wan Lee in 1935. Located on the mouth of the Sungei Pinang in Penang with its own jetty, the oil mill was an ideal site for *twakows* to load and unload goods. Chor Ee refitted the factory with the latest machinery, including a powerful 350hp Deutz Diesel Engine to drive the milling process. Copra was procured from the coconut plantations on the island, milled and sold at different grades — branded one fish, two fish, and three fish — to make soaps, candles, and as cooking oil.

Chor Ee prospered so rapidly that by the second decade of the 20th century, he was known as the merchant prince of Penang, with warehouses, production plants, employees, and agents in the key trading ports of Southeast Asia. His ascent subsequently led his venture into banking. Penang's migrant residents were infamously cash-poor, often buying goods from shopkeepers on credit, who in turn procured their supply from wholesalers, like Ban Hin Lee, also on credit. This sequence of financing was good for business, but it also left creditors waiting for payment, usually for thirty days or more. Although there were a number of moneylenders in town, there were still no local banks to serve the non-European community. At the same time, the expansion of trade, domestically and around the region, created a demand for more credit. This prompted Chor Ee to set up an informal banking business in 1918. He initially lent to his customers and eventually, as his capital grew, he began to lend to a broader base of clientele. By then, he had about ten key administrative staff working for him –Yeap Lean Seng, who was his son, Yeap Chong Eng, Lee Gua Hum, Teh Chong Chee, Tan An Teng, Goh Puay Khoon, Chan Ewe Chiang, Chee Eow Kim, and Yeap Kwa Tiat, who were all either distant relatives or people from the same province in China. Chor Ee also had a contingent of labourers to help haul cargo off ships, around the port and warehouses, and onto customers' bullock-carts. The first bank account opened was his own, with the account bearing the numbers: 0/02/0001/69. But more about his foray into banking later.

Those who have heard of Chor Ee often ask how he could have grasped the complexities of banking and finance if he couldn't read or write. How could he have understood contracts and agreements without some knowledge of the law? Chor Ee's only known handwriting was his signature, written in angled, childlike strokes. The older he got, the more wavering the strokes became. Illiteracy was common in 19th century China, and most *sinkhek* who landed in Penang could not read or write. Although illiterate, Chor Ee was not innumerate, and certainly not unintelligent. He had an innate understanding of numbers and of people, and a sense of duty and pride in a job well done. He watched his accounts religiously, taking time to scrutinise his books, taking his bearings so he always knew precisely what his position was financially and how much stock he had left. He was as methodical and regular as a clock, always adhering to the principles of fair trade. He would have honed his survival instincts at an early age and it wouldn't have been surprising that he picked up vital commercial information and formed a relatively extensive network during his stint as a barber. Unlike the ignorant coolie who worked under the employment of one towkay, his continual presence along the commercial enclave of Prangin Road enabled him to hear what was going on in town. He would have heard about the sabotage of Sin Joon Seng's rubber plantation because the callous man had not paid his employees well. He would

have heard about the clerk at Chop Heap Leong Hin who was meddling with supplies, or about trivial matters such as who was hosting dinner on the fifteenth day of the eight moon. Chor Ee started off as a greenhorn in Penang, but armed himself with a fairly precise knowledge of the standing and affairs of the people he would be dealing with.

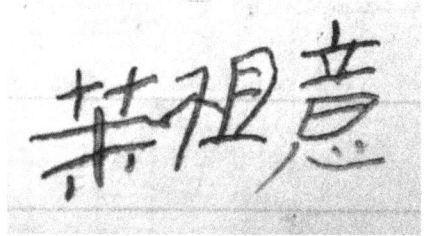

Chor Ee's only known handwriting — his signature. 1940s. In fact the first two characters were written incorrectly.

In an interview conducted in 1934, at age sixty-seven, and by then a multi-millionaire, Chor Ee credited his success to thriftiness, hard work, and honesty. In today's sophisticated business environment, these might seem like clichés, but back in those days it would have taken a combination of those three attributes for him to survive and thrive in an unfettered business environment. His old-fashioned ways prevailed primarily because businesses were largely driven by the consignment trade. To add to that, legal contracts among the local Chinese business community were not commonly used. It was consequently vital to uphold one's reputation as an honourable merchant and be creditworthy in the eyes of others. The system also gave advantages to wealthier merchants over smaller competitors. Because they could buy in bulk, instead of collecting from many small merchants, the consignor need only to chase after one consignee, and if the consignee was honourable, payment would be prompt and in-full. Chor Ee's reputation for being reliable and trustworthy was well-known and led to his swift economic ascent, but when it came to a food crisis and empty stomachs, reputation no matter how sound, unfortunately took a back seat.

In the wake of the rice crisis in 1919, Ban Hin Lee was accused of profiteering from rice. A poor harvest and speculative buying led to rice shortages in Southeast Asia, resulting in the imposition of controls on the Burmese rice industry — then the world's largest exporter of rice. Since rice was a staple diet in Malaya, with approximately two thirds imported, the shortage led to much discontentment in Penang and Singapore. In early 1919, the Government set a fixed price for Burmese rice. A week or so later, Chor Ee's clerk sold some old stock to a buyer who took Chor Ee to court because the buyer had paid four per cent above the fixed price. In Chor Ee's defence, his lawyer Mr Hogan, argued that the notice applied to rice stocks for the current year and not from previous years. He also maintained that the price the buyer paid was below Chor Ee's cost and that Ban Hin Lee had in fact, made a loss on the sale. But the courts disregarded the defence and slapped Chor Ee with a fine of $1000 to serve as an example to all. Believing they could do a better job in managing the crisis, all importation and internal distribution of rice was later brought under government control. Needless to say, the government profited on the transaction, but still made a mess of it. An article published in *The Straits Times* in December 1919 stated, "The government is endeavouring to conduct very large commercial transactions through officers who have no commercial experience. It is not the fault of these officers if they fail. Put commercial men in lawyer's offices and they would fail also. It is simply a case of every man to his trade."

Burmese rice was sold at controlled prices, but because of its acute shortage, opportunistic merchants doubled the prices for rice from Siam and Saigon. By the middle of the year spiralling rice prices led to outraged mobs demonstrating. Over eight thousand Chinese men of the "coolie class" attacked premises, smashed windows, and defied orders from the law. City authorities attempted to manage the situation, but failed to assert control. Mobs roamed the streets, robbing and intimidating innocent citizens. Looters had a field day. Ban Hin Lee was lumped together with other rice merchants, despite being a sole government-approved Burmese rice importer who had to abide by fixed prices. Chor Ee's plantation in Green Lane, miles away from town, was ransacked. Eighty angry men looted the property, taking twelve bags of rice kept for the coolies who worked there. So frenzied were the men, they accused Chor Ee of being a Japanese national, an allegation he later refuted by putting a notice in the Chinese newspaper stating that if he was indeed Japanese he would not have been admitted to the committee of the Chinese Chamber of Commerce. The men who ransacked Chor Ee's plantation were charged, the rice trade fell back to the distributors and wholesalers, and life went on as usual. But the flurry culminating from the rice crisis must have been a big blow to a man who prided himself in doing a legitimate trade.

The Hongkong Shanghai Banking Corporation bank note issued on 1 September 1893 in Penang. *National Archives of Malaysia.*

Chapter 9

Drink Tea and
be Married

"Desiring to order well the state, they first regulated their families." –
Confucius

Having made his money Chor Ee needed successors to perpetuate his business. Given the traditional conventions of the time, this meant having sons. Producing male heirs was an obsession for any Chinese family, rich or poor. While it could be argued that this preoccupation applies to many cultures, the Chinese take it a notch higher. A son is referred to as *kia* (child), while a daughter carries a secondary title of *cha-wa* (daughter). Linguistically the distinction between the words for son and daughter meant that if a couple had daughters but no sons, they would literally have no children. The fixation of having male children came from Confucius's teachings of filial piety and ancestral worship. According to the old sage, every man must marry and raise sons to preserve the continuity of the family and to perform the rites of ancestral worship. Over the centuries millions of Chinese had been brought up with these beliefs, and until 1911 these rules dictated how Chinese states and governments were run. There was a saying that China was made up of families and nothing else, and the term *kok-ka* (country and family) was often used to refer to the Celestial Empire.

Sometime around the mid-1890s, and in his mid-twenties, Chor Ee returned to China to get married. He would have exceeded the average man's marriage age but age did not matter for a man, as it did a woman. The village matchmaker found him a girl named Lee Han Nyoh. Not much is known about the bride except that she was younger, came from the neighbouring village and had never met Chor Ee before. Likewise, Chor Ee had never set eyes on her before. He might have received news about her by mail, but everything else was organised on his behalf. Arranged marriages were not uncommon at the time, and romantic love was a minor consideration. More important were the birth dates of both bride and groom, the family backgrounds, the readings of the fortune-teller, and the abilities of the matchmaker. The long-held idea that getting married was the most important ceremony in a person's life meant that in a ritual-obsessed nation like China, weddings became tedious affairs.

Chinese marriage customs have been around since time immemorial, some say for about four thousand years. The earliest rites are believed to have been introduced by the legendary Emperor Fuxi, who was also the creator of the I-Ching. Although no records of these ancient rites exist today, classical writings three thousand years ago, particular those introduced by the Duke of Zhou, remain. Known as the man who set the cultural foundation of China, he established what is popularly known as the "the Three Documents and Six Ceremonies" — a must-do-list of marriage formalities. It starts with the families negotiating through an exchange of written documents facilitated by the appointed matchmaker and fortune-teller. A marriage managed directly by the couple would be a no-no and would constitute a serious breach of decorum. What's more, the services of a prissy matchmaker was needed to attest the virginity of the bride and those of the prophetic fortune-teller to pick out propitious dates and good omens. The contents of the documents would include essentials including gifts and dowries and how much the bride's parents are willing to part as "bride price" — the bride price tends to hold weight in the making of an affable relationship between mother and daughter-in-law. Also included in the negotiations are auspicious dates. Once in order, couples like Chor Ee and Han Nyoh, were processed through a number of improbable rituals — that of the bride and groom bathing in citrus-infused water to cleanse their soul and their hairs combed by hand-picked relatives who possessed certain physical and social traits. The wedding day itself is filled with a list of activities starting with the fetching of the bride procession and ending with the tea-ceremony. Unquestionably every wedding must include a serious amount of feasting and a set of post-wedding rituals. Even the nuptial chamber would need to be kept open for days for inspection by inquisitive guests. By then, Chor Ee and Han Nyoh's wedding would have lasted two to three whole months.

Why did Chor Ee and so many of his contemporaries go to all the trouble of finding a wife in China rather than Penang? For the simple reason that there weren't many women in Penang's male-dominated society, and the few that were might not have passed the matchmaker's chastity test. Another reason for finding a bride in China relates to the idea of ancestral worship. Chor Ee returned to Penang to attend to his business while his new bride stayed in China to carry out the duty of paying respects to her new family's ancestors. As his own parents had passed away, Han Nyoh was now under the supervision of Chor Ee's sisters-in-law.

The newlyweds adopted two sons, Lean Seng and Lean Hong, and on Chor Ee's subsequent visit to China, Han Nyoh gave birth to a son, Kim Hoe. No pictures exist of Han Nyoh, but judging from Kim Hoe's facial features, she may have had immensely high cheekbones and almond-shaped eyes. She might also have been fairly tall for a Chinese woman, as Kim Hoe was among the tallest in the family. Chor Ee was not bad looking himself. He had a square face, round eyes framed by the trademark ancestral brows, fairly full and balanced lips and a high forehead. He spoke with a deepish voice and just stood above five feet five tall.

Sometime at the turn of the 20th century, Chor Ee took another wife in Penang, Gan Geok Siew. She was the sister of Gan Ngoh Bee, a wealthy Chinese merchant who traded in pepper and rice as well as an opium farmer. Geok Siew was his second wife and his marriage to her was more of a business merger than a twining of hearts. While in European history peace between nations was sealed by monarchical marriage, the Chinese would marry to seal a business alliance.

Geok Siew gave birth to two children, a girl called Twa Nya and a boy called Lean Ho. Eventually, she ran off with a Chinese sorcerer, or a *kong-tau sin-seh*. No one really knew why she left. Perhaps she fell under the sorcerer's charm, or it might have been that Chor Ee was not as dutiful a husband as she had hoped for. Without a mother to discipline him, and a father who was always busy at work, Lean Ho grew up defiant and wayward. Chor Ee was not ready to get married again, so he sent his bratty seven year old son to China to be looked after by Han Nyoh. Perhaps being the son of the Penang wife had something to do with it, but the story goes that Lean Ho might not have been cared for properly and eventually died in an accident. Many years later, the family decided to adopt a little boy in memory of Lean Ho.

This arrangement sums up the way Chinese families were organised during that era. If a man emigrated he would still marry a wife in China to fulfill the ancestral rites on his behalf, and regularly remit money to make sure she was looked after. If he could afford it, he would also take a local wife, or wives, to look after him in the foreign country. Having multiple wives was legal and a morally accepted practice, and a man was allowed to marry as many wives as he could support. The emperor himself seldom married less than four 'head wives' and had anywhere from seventy-five to a hundred 'assistant wives' or concubines. From the sons these wives bore, he selected the one best qualified to succeed him. The first wife had precedence over the others. The children however, were all equally legitimate.

A number of years passed after his local wife, Geok Siew, left him. Chor Ee was in his mid-forties. He was extremely wealthy, but without the growing family society expected of someone his stature. He was engrossed in making money, building his name and business, sparing little time on leisure and his private life. But it was time to find another wife. Through a matchmaker, he married his third wife, Ooi Kim Suan. Since she bore him no sons during the initial years of marriage, Chor Ee took another bride as insurance. He sought the services of an illustrious go-between, who was also the town's diamond dealer and the aunt of the potential bride. Through her intricate network of attractive fertile virgins of decent upbringing, she arranged for Chor Ee to marry her own niece, Lee Cheng Kin.

Cheng Kin was born on the 7 February 1897 and was only fifteen years old when she was betrothed to the forty-five year old Chor Ee. She was known for her beauty. Her petite ballerina-like frame stood at just five feet tall. Her facial structure was delicate, accentuating her large velvety eyes. An early photograph shows her legendary jet-black hair pulled neatly into a bun, her face placid but filled with composure. She wore a white cotton blouse with the Nyonya *kerongsang* (brooch), matched with a dark three-quarter length skirt, white stockings and laced-up plimsoles. This was quite unusual attire. Considering it was a big deal to have one's photo taken at the studio, young girls would normally have been decked out in a more traditional outfit, wearing heavy make-up for such an occasion. The go-between aunt was quick to bring the marriage proposal to her family. They were delighted by the prospect of having Chor Ee as their son-in-law. Cheng Kin however was initially against the idea. Chor Ee already had wives — one in China, one in Penang, and on top of that he was much older than her. But in the end, she yielded to her parents' wishes and married him. A fortune-teller later said it was her karma to marry an older man.

Cheng Kin was fifth generation Straits-born. Her family was working-class and sold charcoal, living in the neighbourhood of Weld Quay. Her grandfather had three wives, and she was the only child of an only child from the principal grandmother. As in Chor Ee's case, her parents passed away when she was just a baby and she was brought up by her grandmothers. Her youngest grandmother, a prolific woman who was still bearing children of her own, nursed little Cheng Kin for a short while. This young grandmother allegedly had the peculiar trait of having four nipples and was able to nurse more than one baby at a time. The family adopted a little brother to keep Cheng Kin company, but he was more an irritant than a companion.

Though life was freer and less irksome than for those born and raised in China, Straits-born girls were the embodiment of subservience, their worlds often confined to the four walls of their rooms. Even in their homes, girls were forbidden to look out windows, for fear neighbours might consider them frivolous. The only occasion they were allowed out was the annual event of *Chap Goh Meh*, when all the young maidens, dressed in their best, could be seen throwing mandarin oranges into the sea with the hope of finding good husbands. Another preposterous rule of etiquette imposed on a girl of that era was having to supress her laughter. If one was born female, it was regarded indecent to laugh wholeheartedly, particularly in the company of men, for the advocates of this custom believed that having a sense of humour, however wicked, might be misconstrued as attention seeking. But the most unjust form of female subordination was denying girls any opportunities to develop their minds. Quite apart from not being allowed to be seen in public and subjected to a life of seclusion, the customary practice for raising girls was to deny them of any form of education. Most parents regarded it a waste of money to send their daughters to school, since once they were married, their status and identity would be subsumed in their husbands'. They were only expected to cook, wash, sew, and bear children.

But young Cheng Kin was different. Determined that she wanted an education, she coerced her family into sending her to school. Her aspiration was to enter the medical profession. Initially, the family resisted, leery of undermining the social order, but it might have been because Cheng Kin, being the only child of an only child, was the apple of her grandfather's eye that they finally agreed, on the condition that she had to bring the brother along. The boy was obviously disinterested, habitually disappeared on school days, disrupting Cheng Kin's schedule, and never amounted to very much.

A year into her marriage with Chor Ee, Cheng Kin gave birth to a boy named Hock Hoe. The couple also adopted a baby girl. Hock Hoe was Chor Ee's third natural born son. Shortly after his birth, Kim Suan, Chor Ee's third wife, gave birth to another son, named Hock Hin. When Hock Hin was only a year old, Kim Suan contracted tuberculosis and passed away, so at the age of about seventeen Cheng Kin ended up mothering two young sons.

We know Kim Suan had two children with Chor Ee — Hock Hin and a daughter — but beyond that we know very little of Kim Suan, and nothing about her character, intelligence, religious views, and family background. Towards the end of her life, she spent most of her days confined to her room.

Cheng Kin's relationship with Chor Ee was one of a dutiful wife. Over the course of their marriage, mutual affection developed. Etiquette among Chinese in those days demanded that neither husband nor wife should show affection in public. In the early days of their marriage, the couple often brought Cheng Kin's younger cousin, Nyah Ee, along on outings. It was not because they needed a chaperone to ensure nothing improper occurred, but because the little cousin was what locals called a chatty *lau heoh chien*, a busybody so to speak. She was there to help ease conversations and fill those awkward silent moments. But Cheng Kin's little cousin took every opportunity to surreptitiously listen in on their conversations. Chor Ee was one of those conservative *low yeh* (old husband) who often found it difficult to converse with his young wife. Even in a calamity, old-fashioned Chor Ee would put propriety above safety, such as the unfortunate day when an outing turned into a misadventure.

It was an unusually windy day as they drove out in the hackney carriage. A branch from an angsana tree came crashing down, spooking the horses and causing them to bolt. The yoke attached to the harness gave way, and both Chor Ee and Cheng Kin were thrown from the carriage. The Malay driver, not wanting to lose the horses, held onto the reins and was dragged several feet. Instead of losing the horses, the conscientious driver lost his sarong. Instead of worrying about Cheng Kin's well-being, Chor Ee was more concerned by this half-naked man lying face down with his brown derrière exposed for all eyes to see, especially those of his young innocent wife.

Cheng Kin was accorded the status and functions expected of the number-one wife, and it didn't take her long to boldly take on that role. She kept an exceedingly tight hand on the tiller of the house, playing mother to over a dozen children, even though she gave birth to only one. Several of them were actually older than she was. She had help from her own family, who spent a great deal of time in the house. Marrying into wealth did not alter her values nor spoil her either. Chor Ee was never one to indulge in luxury nor an exuberant lifestyle. His family lived relatively comfortably but not excessively. Instead, he steadily accumulated wealth and led a prudent regime. Cheng Kin and the rest of the family obediently followed. She learnt to cook, sew, and manage the affairs of the household as efficiently as possible, and delegation became one of her key strengths. Like a tactical commander, she orchestrated outings and occasions with ease and lot of big-heartedness. Because she could read and write, Chor Ee also found her useful in his business affairs, often taking her along for meetings. She became his confidant and the pair became inseparable. In due time, she garnered the respect of the business community. The conventional male assessment that women, like children, should only be seen and not heard, did not apply to Cheng Kin. A number of Chor Ee's business associates often approached her first before seeking an appointment with Chor Ee. Cheng Kin basically ran his life for him — she fed him, cared for him, kept track of his appointments, and occasionally advised him on business matters. Perhaps it was the lack of a meddling and overshadowing mother-in-law that allowed her to flourish in housewifery.

The traditional assumption had been that the sons would inherit Chor Ee's mantle when he passed away. Instead, Chor Ee made Cheng Kin the head of his household and chairperson of the bank, making her the first woman in British Malaya to not only serve as a director but to be appointed chair of a bank. Cheng Kin broke ranks again when she was thrust into the limelight as chairperson of Yap Kongsi and the Chinese Clan association — two intensely male-dominated institutions. By then she wore her confidence like her jewels — flawless — the greenest of jade, the reddest of rubies, and the most brilliant of diamonds. Still in her fifties, Cheng Kin took time to travel, returning with experiences as memorable as any young lady has ever enjoyed. She never remarried, not for the lack of suitors. She was attractive, well-respected, and insanely rich, enough to draw any male suitor knocking at her door. Her granddaughters recalled a time when out of the blue a neighbour declared his undying love for her, incessantly calling her on the phone. Annoyed by his persistence, and not wanting to encourage such performance, she told him off, slamming the phone down in disgust. He was a much younger man and although she was unmarried, she was not about to set tongues wagging. Besides, she had a whole new life ahead of her as the matriarch of the family, the business, and community.

Chor Ee's choice of wives was typical of the age — they invariably include one from China and one to seal an alliance — but consistently, they had to be young, fertile and able to produce sons.

Much the same could be said of Tiong Ham's spousal selection. Chor Ee and his business partner had a great deal in common in their private lives even though they differed in their business approach. Both practiced polygamy. Tiong Ham took eight official wives, Chor Ee four. From the wives, they bore Tiong Ham twenty six children, while Chor Ee's women gave him six natural born and four adopted.

Of Tiong Ham's wives, the most venerated was Goei Bing Nio, whose family name partly helped his social standing and gave him his first big break in business. She was also mother to Hui-Lan, who later became the celebrated wife of China's ambassador to America, Mr Wellington Koo. In her memoirs, *No Feast Lasts Forever*, published in 1975, Hui-Lan recounted the time she was barely three years old running around the compound of her home wearing an 80-carat diamond on her neck. The gemstone was so large it created a bruise on the pit of her throat. While not as prominent as Bing Nio's family, Chor Ee's second wife — Geok Siew (the wife the sorcerer made disappear) — also had a family name that was quite well-noted in society. Though her marriage to Chor Ee was an ill-fated one, their union might have given him some standing, both in social and business circles.

The other notable wife of Tiong Ham was Ho Kiem Hoa Nio, also known as Lucy Ho. She was his seventh wife. Born into an elite but financially diminished old Semarang family in 1901, her family lost their fortune just before Lucy was born and was forced to move out from their family mansion. Her marriage to Tiong Ham was arranged. Lucy initially refused his hand in marriage but just like Cheng Kin, she was coerced to marry a much older man than herself. The age difference between Lucy and Tiong Ham was almost the same as Cheng Kin and Chor Ee's — over three decades apart. Unlike Tiong Ham's other wives, Lucy was unusually well-educated and had a liberal outlook in life. Her ability to converse in fluent Dutch allowed her to play a role in Tiong Ham's business affairs, particularly in dealing with Dutch-speaking associates. Like Cheng Kin, Lucy was a woman ahead of her time. Education was held in high regard by both women and they had the mettle to consider pursuing careers at a time when women were not even allowed to be seen in public. Equally, they had an inborn strength of character that allowed them to become trusted confidantes to their powerful husbands. The saying goes that behind every great man stands a great woman. In the case of Cheng Kin and Lucy Ho, this was clearly true.

A young Lee Cheng Kin. Photo taken after her marriage to Chor Ee. Early 1910s. *House of Yeap Chor Ee.*

Oei Family Photo. Standing from left: Tjong Le (Jack), unknown girl, Leonide (Nini). Seated from left Lucy Ho with Tjong Hiong (Horry) on her lap, Oei Tiong Ham and Tjong Bo (Hervey) on his lap, Twan Nio (Lovy). 1923. *Oei family archive.*

Cheng Kin seen here with her adopted grandson. Early 1910s. *House of Yeap Chor Ee.*

Chor Ee and his only son with Cheng Kin, Hock Hoe. Chor Ee would have been in his early 50s. Late 1910s. *House of Yeap Chor Ee.*

Chapter 10

Moving to Uppertendom

Chor Ee was already rich when he married Cheng Kin. By the turn of the twentieth century he was Penang's newest millionaire. At Tiong Ham's suggestion, Chor Ee bought himself a 1904 Daimler to mark the occasion. Owning a car today is not much a novelty, but in those days it was considered the height of extravagance.

The first car that residents of the colony had seen was the Motor Velocipede, built by Benz and Cie in 1894. Shipped to Singapore by Messrs Katz Bros, it was referred to as an auto-car. The vehicle had a neatly built carriage on springs, with bicycle wheels and rubber tyres, and could accommodate two passengers. The one-and-a-half horse-powered benzene engine was at the back and the whole car weighed two hundred and eighty kilos. On a trial run, the car had a top speed of eighteen miles an hour, and only cost one cent a mile to run. It could turn in the width of the road and the "stopping mechanism" (brakes) were in order. The only snags were the rather loud pulsating noise of the engine at a standstill and the steep price tag of $1,600. In the same year, car licences were introduced. A "motor charioteer" — as drivers were called then — could apply for a licence by passing an examination before the chief of police. If, in his estimation, the candidate was capable, the licence was granted for a fee of $1.

At first, there was hardly any infrastructure to support cars in the colony. There were no macadamised roads, no traffic lights, no road maps, or insurance policies. One observer noted that car owners left too much care to "ignorant native attendants" (chauffeurs) who were often reckless when it came to handling petrol. But it was not only the native attendants who were irresponsible. Many of the road accidents reported year after year were caused

A portrait of Chor Ee in western attire. Late 1910s. *House of Yeap Chor Ee.*

by errant car owners themselves crashing into pedestrians and livestock, the damaged vehicle towed away by the pragmatic service of the bullock-cart. Cars were not only considered costly and unreliable but also terrifying. A weekly newspaper at the turn of the century sarcastically quipped "this discovery of the motor-car was, one might say, an accident." Livery stable keepers regarded then as a "calamity".

But not everyone disapproved of this new mode of transport. By the first decade of the 20th century car ownership quickly picked up, particularly in Singapore and the Federated Malay States (FMS). Car clubs organised races to display the speed and prowess of the drivers and their vehicles. Newspapers started publishing regular columns educating the general public about engines, new models, and the latest technological inventions. By 1911, the Motor Car Ordinance came into effect, setting out guidelines for car owners. Insurance companies began offering coverage and protection. Tin miners and planters took to them, preferring them over horse-drawn hackney carriages. Because of the tropical heat, horses could only go short distances, and only at certain times of the day, whereas the motor car didn't seem to suffer much from exhaustion. A popular car was the French-made De Dion-Bouton. Established in 1883, the firm first designed steam-powered vehicles, before moving on to combustion engine models. By the turn of the 20th century, De Dion-Bouton

Chor Ee's old Daimler (second from left) parked in front of Wearnes Brothers Limited, Penang. 1950s. *House of Yeap Chor Ee.*

had become the largest automobile manufacturer in the world, overtaking German manufacturers. From there, new words associated with motoring emerged — "chassis" replaced "undercarriage", "chauffeur" replaced "motor charioteer", and "garage" replaced "stable."

Chor Ee's British-built black Daimler was one of the first — if not the first — cars in Penang and attracted a good deal of interest from the town's residents. It outperformed and outshone every moving vehicle in Malaya. The few other cars then were powered by four-cylinder, ten to twelve horsepower engines, but Chor Ee's model was backed by a sturdy six-cylinder, twenty-eight horsepower engine. Known for their "noiseless" engines, the Daimler cars were advertised as "Silent knights. The wonder of the motor world." It also came with a two-year guarantee from the sole agent, Messrs Guthrie & Co.

A Richshaw puller. Early 20th century. *National Archives of Malaysia.*

A European lady on a hackney carriage. Late 19th century. *Penang Museum.*

Because town houses had no covered car porches, Chor Ee presumably had his precious car parked in a covered shed, and eventually at the garage of Wearnes Brothers when they opened a branch in Penang. Apart from the occasional pleasure rides, Chor Ee continued to move around town in his dependable horse-drawn carriage. In fact, hardly anyone could recall a story of him in his Daimler. The car was so under-utilised that when the family finally sold it to Wearnes Brothers over fifty years later it was still in tip-top condition.

Before the advent of cars, affluent residents of Penang moved about in hackney carriages, while the working classes opted for the light, two-wheeled hand-pulled Japanese jin-rickshaws. Introduced first in Singapore in 1882 and later, Penang, the jin-rickshaws were an exceedingly popular mode of transport and became a formidable rival to the hackney carriages. They scuttled along, carrying passengers, providing them shade from the sun and the rain. The extra thick rubber tyres also offered a smooth ride. Because of their popularity, the numbers rose. By the end of the 19th century there were about five thousand jin-rickshaws in Penang. This gave employment to about ten thousand men, as men invariably took shifts to pull them — one during the day and the other in the evening.

If cars dominated newspaper columns with the number of accidents, bicycles filled the pages with the highest number of thefts. Bicycles were not as common as they are now, and due to their relatively high cost were mostly favoured by Europeans. In 1889, a light, well-made "Facile" bicycle fitted with patent ball bearings was advertised in the *Straits Times* at the cost of $125, or almost two years' wages for a lowly coolie. Bicycles were stolen because of their value, but also because they were easy to steal. To curb the high level of theft, harsh penalties were imposed on offenders, with two to three months imprisonment and sometimes a half-dozen strokes of a rattan cane. For serial thieves, a sentence of two years imprisonment, followed by another two years of police supervision, and twelve strokes of the rattan was quite common. They took bicycle theft rather seriously back then.

With wealth came the luxury of an up-scale home. The newly moneyed, wishing to gain respectability, chose to settle in exclusive neighbourhoods. Chor Ee quickly snapped up No. 4 Penang Street, when it came on the market sometime in the mid-1910s. The property was previously owned by Khaw Joo Keat, a second generation Hokkien from the Khaw na Ranong family that had held the governor's post in Ranong for generations. Joo Keat was governor of Trang in Siam (present-day Thailand), and nephew to Khaw Sim Bee, the high commissioner of Phuket. Khaw's family traced its Penang origins to Khaw Soo Cheang, a migrant from Fukien who arrived in Penang in 1822. Soo Cheang initially went into vegetable farming, but did not make much of the enterprise. He ventured north to Southern Siam, drawn by the promise of opportunities in tin mining and shipping. There he found a niche as a recruiter, supplying workers to the tin and shipping industries within Siam and Penang. He gained a reputation for his honesty and loyalty and was made a royal collector of tin royalties in the Ranong area. For his allegiance to the Siamese royal family, Soo Cheang was made Governor of Ranong, the first foreigner to hold such an esteemed position. Sim Bee was his youngest and most celebrated son, instrumental in reviving the ailing economy of Southern Siam. Joo Keat's family sold the terraced house to Chor Ee after Joo Keat died from complications of gunshot wounds received in an assassination attempt in February 1913.

No. 4 Penang Street was part of a row of houses known as Kau Keng Choo (nine houses), though no one really knows why they were referred to as nine houses, since there are more than nine houses along that row. Built around the early 1890s, they were one of the first experiments with terraced housing

— grand residential blocks designed in the early Straits Eclectic style. They offered respite from the cramped quarters to the south of town, with a lot more width, length, and height than their predecessors, the Southern Chinese Eclectic-styled houses. Apart from size, these homes were more decorative, with European touches added to the structure, including French shuttered windows framed by Corinthian pilasters and topped with fanlights — decorative semi-circular windows — that allowed some daylight indoors while the shutters were closed to keep out the worst of the tropical heat. At the front entrance, geometric-patterned coloured clay tiles replaced the usual terracotta tiles. The main entrance to Chor Ee's new house was on Penang Street, but one could also enter through the parallel King Street. Compared to the decorative façade, the interior remained sombre. As one entered the front hall, one was greeted by traditional Chinese black-wood furniture, inlaid with mother of pearl, and placed against the walls. A wooden screen separated the front hall from the dining area. The opening of the air-well cast the morning light over the sparsely decorated space. An ancestral shrine with lacquered tablets faced the dining table. Aside from a few family portraits, a clock, and a few Chinese scrolls, the lime-washed walls remained bare. There was not much in terms of soft furnishings — no cushions, carpets, or draperies. Next to the dining hall was another hall, with a wooden staircase leading to the top floors. The kitchen was located towards the back of the building. The stove was slightly to the side of another air-well. Bedrooms were located on the first floor. Chor Ee's own sleeping quarters faced King Street. It was quite a sizeable room, with an en-suite bathroom. The second floor above his bedroom, housed his collection of deities, among which was the *Kuan Imm* statue he had brought with him when he first left China to seek his fortune. In the world of geomancy, the uppermost floor was the most strategic position, as it met the *ceh-sua-kua-hai* (views of the sea from the hillside) requirements for a shrine. No. 4 Penang Street was a far cry from the crammed, dingy tenement housing Chor Ee lived in not so long before.

More importantly, No. 4 Penang Street was considered a posh address by Penang's standard — bordering Light Street, to the north of town. That part of town was once the European quarter, occupied by early settlers, including Captain Light and the British Navy officers. Captain Light's trading partner, James Scott, was also a resident of Light Street. Development of the neighbourhood was spurred by the prosperity that came from when rubber and tin dominated global trade. Penang, being a major trading port for these commodities, benefited, and so did its residents. So great were the fortunes accumulated over the decades that by the turn of the century Penang was home to a number of Chinese millionaires. They were mostly engaged in mercantile pursuits, shipping, and opium farming. As the new class of social elite emerged, so did bold public displays of their newly acquired wealth and power through the houses they built. By the third quarter of the 19th

LIM EU TOH. PENANG JAN, 1904

21/7/04
Dear Madam,
    Many thanks for your P. C.
and I am glad to hear that you are
married & living happily in Berlin.
    Herewith my best wishes.
                    yrs. Lim.

Lim Eu Toh. Chor Ee's neighbour. 1904. *Courtesy of Cheah Jin Seng.*

century, a number of European households moved further north west, towards Northam Road, making way for the growing affluent Chinese community to establish grand residences along and around Light Street. Chor Ee's new house was a stone's throw away from the esplanade grounds and the town hall, the power base of the island and home of the municipal commission. To the north was the Supreme Court. Slightly south were more government buildings, and to the east was China Street, the heart of Chinese commerce.

No. 4 Penang Street had many distinguished neighbours. Penang's mercantile elite lived within a radius of three hundred meters. Next door was Lim Eu Toh, English educated, Straits-born, and co-founder of Messrs. Tiang Lee & Co, one of the first Chinese firms to open direct business with merchants in Europe and America. Lim was then a municipal commissioner and a justice of peace. Behind his house, was a bungalow at the corner of Light Street and King Street (current location of Great Eastern Insurance), home of Madam Chung Siew Yin, the daughter of the great Chung Keng Kwee, formidable leader of the Hai San Secret society and founder of modern Taiping in Perak. Chung's own imposing residence was a few blocks away on Church Street. Just in front of Chor Ee's house was No. 1 Light Street, one of the first non-European mansions built in 19th century Penang (current location of Hong Leong Bank). Living there was Lim Boon Haw, a wealthy settler who made his money in tin mining and real estate. Mr Lim had served as the president of the Lim clan, among other Chinese associations. Before Mr Lim, the mansion was owned by another influential community leader, Foo Tye Sin. Mr Foo was one of those early Straits-born Chinese with a British education, which he received from both the Penang Free School and St Xavier's Institution. He was regarded as the only non-partisan Chinese at a ceasefire conference during the Larut Wars, and was one of three Chinese commissioners appointed by the British to sit on the inquiry board into the 1867 Penang Riots.

The list of gentry along Light Street didn't end there. Just in front of the Supreme Court was Sunbeam Hall, a mansion owned by Khoo Cheow Teong, the Kapitan Titular of Asahan in North Sumatra. Khoo came from a privileged background, being grandson of Khoo Wat Seng, a prominent leader in Penang and one of the founders of Penang's powerful Khoo Kongsi on his paternal side, and great-grandson of Koh Lay Huan, Penang's first Chinese Kapitan, on his maternal side. Opposite Sunbeam Hall was Aurora House (current location of Bank Negara Malaysia). Aurora House belonged to Gan Ngoh Bee, an influential member of the Chinese community and an opium and spirit farm merchant. Gan was also Chor Ee's brother-in-law and brother of Geok Siew. Nearby, at the upper end of Bishop Street and Pitt Street, was the house of Quah Beng Kee, a Straits-born English-educated member of the social elite. Quah ran a highly successful steamship company, providing logistic services between Penang and Singapore. He was one of the few Chinese decorated with an Officer of the Order of British Empire award, and served as committee member in various Chinese associations. Another distinguished member of society was Cheah Chen Eok, whose residence was located along Green Hall. A son-in-law of Foo Tye Sin, Cheah was Straits-born and had great interest in English education and everything British. In 1897, when Queen Victoria celebrated her Diamond Jubilee, Cheah funded the construction of Penang's famous Clock Tower at the junction of Beach Street and Light Street.

But the most regal of all residences, and the nucleus of uppertendom, was Edinburgh House, belonging to Koh Seang Tat (current location of Dewan Sri Pinang). Scion of an old family, Mr Koh came from an impressive lineage whose forefathers played key roles in the establishment of two strategic British colonies, Penang and Singapore. Mr Koh's great-grandfather, Koh Lay Huan, was Penang's first Kapitan Cina. A wealthy and educated man, Koh Lay Huan was an anti-Manchu hero who fled China to Siam. He was part of a pioneering party led by Captain Light when Light claimed Penang on behalf of the King of England and renamed it Prince of Wales Island in 1786. His leadership qualities, and the trust Captain Light had for him, earned him the role of leader of Penang's Chinese community. He settled in Penang and contributed to the island's development as a statesman, merchant, planter, and liquor farmer under his popular known name 'Chewan.' Years later, his son, Koh Kok Chye, became part of the contingent that accompanied Sir Stamford Raffles to Singapore when the latter took possession of the island in 1819. The Koh family was regarded as Penang's earliest aristocracy. Koh Seang Tat initially led an enterprising life as a merchant and opium farmer. Together with Foo Tye Sin, they co-founded the general merchant business Tye Sin Tat & Co located on Beach Street. After an extensive tour of Europe and America, he returned with his wife and was made the first Chinese justice of peace and municipal commissioner in Penang. In 1867, he built himself a home befitting of an aristocrat, on a piece of land that was previously a nutmeg plantation belonging to George Scott, who also owned the Ayer Rajah Estate. Christened Edinburgh House, in honour of the Duke of Edinburgh who stayed there during his visit in 1870, Mr Koh's house was certainly the grandest bungalow at that time on the island.

One final famous personality worth mentioning is the Hon. J.M.B. Vermont, manager and proprietor of Batu Kawan Estate in Province Wellesley — who lent his name to the steel and stone Ben Vermont Water Fountain. The structure stood on the edge of the Esplanade, directly facing Penang Street, and was completely destroyed during WW2. Whether a coincidence or premeditated, it was fitting for Chor Ee to choose a house next to a monument built in honour of the man who significantly contributed to improving sugar supplies in the 1880s–1890s, the commodity that propelled Chor Ee to his elevated status.

Almost everyone who lived in uppertendom belonged to a society, an association, or a club, often more than one. For a relatively young community, there was a staggeringly high proportion of associations in Penang to the number of residents — about one to every hundred people. In a new country, without family and social structure, these associations provided pioneers with a sense of cohesion and helped foster a shared identity. Most were voluntary

Edinburgh House. *Penang Museum.*

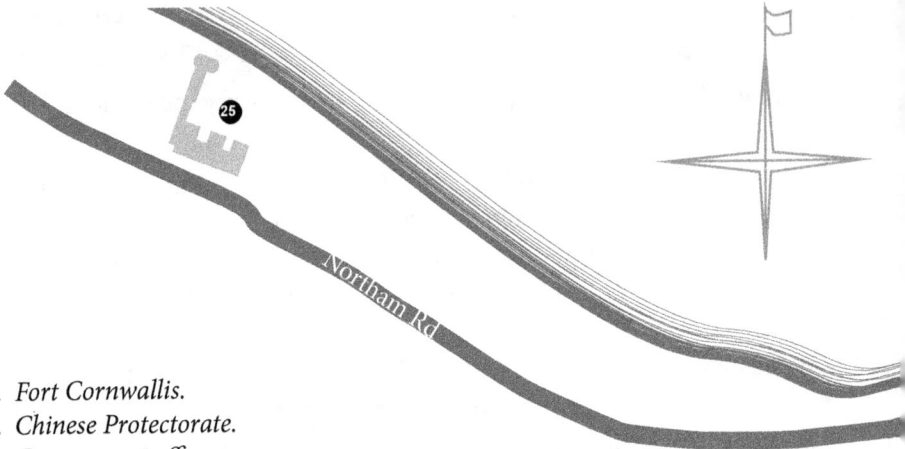

1. Fort Cornwallis.
2. Chinese Protectorate.
3. Government offices.
4. Central police station.
5. Magistrate Court.
6. Town Hall.
7. Municipal Office.
8. High Court.
9. Light St Convent.
10. Ben Vermont Monument.
11. Kuan Imm Teng Temple.
12. 141 Beach Street. Chop Ban Hin Lee premises (late1890s)
13. No 4 Penang St.
14. Lim Eu Toh's residence.
15. Madam Chung Siew Yin's residence.
16. Lim Boon Haw's residence.
17. Sunbeam Hall.
18. Aurora House.
19. Quah Beng Kee's residence.
20. Cheah Cheng Eok's residence*.
21. Edinburgh House.
22. 86 Beach St. Chop Ban Hin Lee premises (early 1910s).
23. Yeap Chor Ee Buildings 1920s-30s.
24. Headquarters of the Ban Hin Lee Bank mid 1930s.
25. Homestead**.

* approximate location
** future location of Homestead.

Figure 3 – Map of George Town circa early 1990s

George Town

LOCATION OF BUILDINGS & SITES
Early 1900s

Leith St

Farquah St

Green Hall

Bishop St

Church St

Penang St

Light St

Pitt St

Queen St

King St

China St

Chulia St

Beach St

Weld Quay

Downing St

Ben Vermont's fountain. The house that Chor Ee bought from the Khaw family is on the right side of the photo. 1910. *Courtesy of Dr Cheah Jin Seng.*

associations, established in the first half of the 1800s by early Chinese settlers. Admission was based on four general criteria — dialect, district, kinship, and craft or trade. The earliest were the cemetery associations — Kwangtung Public Cemetery and Hokkien Public Cemetery — both formed around 1800. Land was either acquired or donated to provide burial grounds for deceased members, who were mostly from the Cantonese and Hokkien communities. Clearly, getting proper burials and preparing for the afterlife, rather than partaking in frivolous social gatherings or athletic amusements, were foremost on the minds of these Chinese pioneers.

Another important organisation in the early days was the Kong Hock Keong, or the Kuan Imm Teng temple on Pitt Street. Funded mostly by the Hokkien and Cantonese merchants in town — all four hundred and forty nine of them — the temple was erected in 1800. Initially devoted to the worship of Kuan Imm, the Goddess of Mercy, it soon evolved into a venue for town-hall style assemblies as well as serving as a prayer hall. The temple's powerful board of trustees, equally represented by Hokkien and Cantonese clansmen, undertook the role of arbitrators for disputes within the communities. They sat and listened, and their words carried weight. This arrangement of indirect-rule had evolved from the early days when the Kapitan system was used to govern Penang's diverse community, thereby allowing each ethnic group to follow its own customs. Through these leaders, the British were able to indirectly control the entire community, in much the same way they used heads of secret societies to oversee their respective groups. That they could settle disputes and punishments based on their own community laws seemed hardly to matter. This was an age when governance and transparency had not entered Penang's vocabulary. Weaknesses within the arbitration system inevitably surfaced when tensions swelled over opium concessions between the Hokkien Kian Teik Tong and the powerful Cantonese Ghee Hin secret societies in 1867. When the riots finally ended, so did the role of the temple trustees as mediators. Because a number of the trustees were involved in the riots, they could no longer resolve conflicts. Realising this predicament, the British donated land to the community in 1881 to build a Chinese town hall, which then took over the role from the Kong Hock Keong.

As it prospered, the Chinese business community took on a newly organised quality. In the two decades since the arrival of Chor Ee and thousands like him, the number of Chinese businesses grew, creating new merchants, traders, commission agents, and general traders. The most important institution uniting mercantile interests at large was the Chinese Chamber of Commerce, established in July 1903. Much like its European counterparts, the chamber of commerce facilitated business dealings within the community and resolved commercial conflicts. But more importantly, it also gave the community a collective voice in local government, particularly in the town's municipal council, where the Straits Chinese of Singapore had tended to dominate. The Penang-based Chinese Chamber of Commerce raised a series of issues affecting the business community, many of which were published in the local English and Chinese newspapers, including concerns about income taxes and estate duties. It made proposals on how best to create employment for the unemployed, and along with the much longer established Chinese Town Hall, it soon became the highest representative body for Chinese society. The trustees of the chambers, some of whom were also on the board of the Chinese Town Hall, accepted a number of the newly-minted rich and professionals as members, Chor Ee among them. By the first decade of the 20th century, the chamber's members included merchants, shipping magnates, wealthy tin miners, heads of clan houses, the managing director of a newspaper, and leading lawyers and physicians. While it appeared as though a cross section of the community was being represented, on the whole the Chinese Chamber of Commerce actually spoke for a small minority elite, rather than the lot.

In addition to this landscape of formal associations came the social clubs. The oldest, the Chinese Merchant Club, had been formed in early 1880. Its cachet was having a long list of who's who of the mercantile community as members, regardless of dialect groups, clans, or trade. This meant most of the residents of uppertendom. Many of them went by the honorific title towkay — a Hokkien word that means "head of family", but can also be used to describe the prosperous merchants in the colony. The title was used as far back as Captain Light's time, but it didn't carry as much weight as the other honorific title, Kapitan. Borrowed from the Dutch, Kapitan referred to the headman of an ethnic group, who could be Chinese, Malay, or Indian. While the term might have been Dutch, the concept was Chinese, dating from as far back as the 9th century. In his early days of governing Penang, Light deployed the Kapitan system as a form of indirect rule to manage the different ethnic communities on the island. Kapitans were given administrative and sometimes judicial powers over their stronghold, often in return for lucrative concessions. When the system began to fade in importance by the 19th century,[23] the British authorities turned to wealthy towkays to maintain order, creating a Chinese Advisory Board (1889) and co-opting heads of associations like the Chinese Chamber of Commerce to govern the Chinese, sometimes appointing them as justices of peace as well.

But beyond motor cars and new homes in fashionable parts of town, perhaps the greatest show of wealth was to own real estate, and plenty of it. With not much available in the form of investment opportunities, the new class of tycoons poured a substantial amount of money into buying properties. Aside from their impressive residences, newly-rich merchants clamoured to join the old established firms along Beach Street, the main commercial thoroughfare on the island. Beach Street was the yardstick of business success. It was distinctly segmented into four parts. The upper end, towards the north,

---

[23]   Ching-Hwang Yen, *The Chinese in Southeast Asia and Beyond*, Singapore: World Scientific, 2008.

was the exclusive segment, George Town's administrative centre, reserved for government offices. Next came the European segment, owned by large-scale merchant houses with networks in the west and regional headquarters in Singapore. They built offices and godowns (warehouses) facing Beach Street and the waterfront. From a commercial point of view, the area was advantageously located, first to the authorities, secondly to the banks, and thirdly to Swettenham Pier, a deep-water wharf capable of servicing large ocean-going vessels. After the European section, was the area dominated by large Chinese merchants. Finally, further down towards Prangin Road was the less salubrious end of Beach Street where Chor Ee had established his first shop, and the smaller merchants were based.

By the first decade of the 20th century, Chor Ee had moved his operations at least three times, always edging further north along Beach Street. By the second decade, flush with profits from commodities trading, Chor Ee's real estate interests became more strategic, more dynamic, and more visible. In 1920, he acquired a large stretch of land along China Street Ghaut, which bordered the European part of Beach Street. The land was believed to have been previously owned by Quah Beng Kee, the shipping magnate. Between 1920 and the mid-1930s, Chor Ee commissioned a well-known architectural firm, Messrs Stark & McNeil, to design a complex of offices and godowns which became his business headquarters. The first building, a three-storey edifice, was completed in 1922. It housed Chor Ee's mercantile operations. Designed along modern lines, the building fronted Weld Quay on one side and the FMS Railway building on the other. The interior was airy as well as modern, and organised around large warehouse spaces with huge loading doors on the ground floor, and a staircase leading to spacious offices on the upper floors. The building also had a lift. Before World War I, two-storey buildings were common, with commercial life carried primarily at ground level. Chor Ee's building was among the first few, if not the first building in town with three storeys, and with improvements in technology his architects installed a lift operated by steel cables over a pulley system to haul the cage up and down the shaft. Though he may have been antiquated about technology, and often reluctant to spend on modern conveniences, Chor Ee had the sense to know that lifts made the upper floors profitable, bringing in rents that offset the costs of construction. Even before the building was completed, a suite of offices on the upper floors had already been let to a European firm. In October 1922, the *Straits Echo* described the building as constituting "a notable improvement on our waterfront and a credit to all concerned in the provision of such a handsome block of offices."

Chor Ee built two additional godowns. But these were not just any normal godowns. They were uncontestably magnificent structures. Designed to store tin slabs which he acquired during the slump years, more importantly, the godowns exuded security and confidence. As Lai Tet Loke, president of the Selangor Chinese Chamber of Commerce, observed, "You do not go to find anyone's bank balance in the solitary bank in town, but look at the amount and quality of carving and state of gilt in front and the quantity of tin slabs inside, to determine the solidity of the chop or sign-board, which again is another indication of opulence apart from the protruding belly and puffed cheeks of our towkay friend."[24] Chor Ee did not have a protruding belly, nor puffed cheeks, but he certainly had a lot of tin slabs and spared no cost to build his godowns, even at a time when the economy was at the brink of collapse. Consistent with the previous building, the façades featured elegance and monumental strength. Using modern construction methods, they were the first buildings in Penang to be built with ferro-concrete or reinforced concrete. Thick walls, floors and columns not only provided fire-proof safety, but also ensured goods were stored at constant temperature and more importantly in Penang's humid tropical climate, kept dry. Large windows and loading doors provided ample light and air circulation. On the upper floors, air vents above the window sills and teak lanterns on the rooftop offered additional light and ventilation. Workers' safety and comfort were also taken into consideration, from the provision of latrines and even bathrooms, to less obvious features such as natural lighting and moderately graded staircases. The fourth and final building was the Ban Hin Lee Bank headquarters. Built soon after its official incorporation in 1935, Chor Ee moved his banking operations into the new building in 1939. Apart from real estate, Chor Ee also amassed thousands of acres of estate land towards the south of Penang Island, which today is the location of the island's airport and the Free Trade Zone, Penang's engine of growth.

Despite the splendour of his real estate and his mercurial rise in the business world, Chor Ee still had a lingering past. Before newspapers and magazines portrayed him a great success and hailed him Penang's merchant

---

[24] 'Memories of Chinese In Singapore and Kuala Lumpur', *The Singapore Free Press and Mercantile Advertiser*, 8 June 1939.

prince, there was a time when he was still referred to by his old trade name, Thi-Thau-Ee. A good deal of it stemmed from habit — from old-timers and clients who used to call him by that name and sometimes, from plain economic rivalry. But when children started to partake in the name-calling, Chor Ee went into an outburst. On a Sunday afternoon in November 1920, on his way back home from an outing, a few of the neighbour's children were playing around the five-foot way of his house. They cheekily sang out a rhyme repeatedly to Chor Ee's supreme annoyance — "A.B.C. Thi-Thau-Ee, chiak curry," (A.B.C. Barber Ee, eat curry). In a fury, he slapped one of the boys on the face. The youngster ran into his house and promptly reported the incident to his uncle, who happened to be Lim Eu Toh, president of the Penang Chinese Chamber of Commerce and a member of the municipal commission. Lim was also in the committee attending to the issues of the rice crisis in 1919 when Chor Ee was accused of profiteering. The municipal commissioner's family summoned Chor Ee to court. The Magistrate found Chor Ee guilty and, ironically, slapped him back with a fine of $50. It was certainly a humiliating ordeal for Chor Ee and probably explains why no one in his household was allowed to utter the words Thi-Thau-Ee ever again.

Back in Semarang, Tiong Ham encountered a similar incident too. A group of young Dutch hooligans led by an obnoxious ringleader had apparently jeered and mocked him when he walked passed a school during recess. But instead of telling the boys off like his friend Chor Ee, Tiong Ham controlled his temper and pulled out a "bright silver coin." He approached the biggest boy in the group and quietly said to him in Malay, "If you want to earn this money, just beat up that boy over there — if you get more boys on your side, I'll pay them too." His scheme apparently worked. Within seconds, the boys were fighting each other like wild tigers. Ever since that day, when Tiong Ham walked past the school, the boys would greet him politely and with respect. Tiong Ham's wily method seems to have done the job — two similar incidents with two different solutions resulting in two different outcomes.

Chapter 11

The King's Chinese

|

As George Town's upper-ten neighbourhood became crowded, a number of wealthy families moved to Northam Road. What had originally been a coconut plantation in the mid-1800s, and an enclave of European planters and professionals in the late 1800s, was dubbed 'Millionaire's row' by the turn of the 20th century. Seduced by the large parcels of land, beach frontage, and proximity to town, the town's elite bought and built palatial homes designed to look as if they belonged in the country estates of Europe. The basic elements — columns, pediments, cornices, and wrought iron gates leading into impressive driveways — created a sense of opulence, and to an extent, a connection with Western traditions. Many of these wealthy merchants and their children had travelled abroad, visiting great European cities. Upon their return, and wishing to emulate old world dwellings, they engaged prominent Western architects to design villas on their own soil, these asymmetrical grandiose mansions with imposing facades asserting social dominance and displaying their new-found wealth.

Among the earliest grand residences on Northam Road were the Cheah Tek Soon Mansion, Aloes, Chakrabongse House, Raja Muda's bungalow, and Hardwicke. These were precursors to the more opulent Western-styled mansions that appeared during the first two decades of the 20th century. Between 1910 and 1930, more than half a dozen examples of such architecture dotted the tree-lined thoroughfare. Mansions such as Northam Lodge, Woodville, and the Leong Yin Kean residence sprouted one after the other. But the most imposing of all was Homestead.

Touted as the finest site on Northam Road, the property was originally owned by a lawyer named Thomas Gawthorne, who lived there with his wife

Northam Road. Late 19th century. *National Archives of Malaysia.*

as far back as 1889 when Gawthorne was admitted to the Bar of the Courts, becoming the first Indian to be admitted to practice in Malaya. In October 1917, a shipping magnate named Lim Mah Chye bought the four-acre property from Gawthorne at Lean Chong Hin's auction for a sum of $49,800. Mah Chye commissioned the architects Messrs Stark & McNeil to design a grand Italianate villa for his family. Two plans were submitted. The first version, in the style of mercantile classicism, provided an annex to an existing bungalow which included servants' quarters facing the sea at the back of the building. The second, submitted three months later, took more of an English country house design, possibly influenced by C.G. Boutcher, a young architect who had recently joined the firm.[25] Gawthorne's house on the property was demolished and the construction of Homestead started in 1919, taking over three years to complete.

Homestead stood out among the other mansions along Northam Road with its distinct Elizabethan "E" shaped plan, impressive portico, and towers on both ends of the main wing. There was an elaborately landscaped Italian garden — added by the Lim family in 1928 at a cost of $10,000 — overlooking

---

[25]   Jon Sun Hock Lim, *The Penang House and the Straits Architect 1887-1941*, Penang: Areca Books, 2015.

Homestead. Late 1930s. *House of Yeap Chor Ee.*

Homestead with its distinct Elizabethan 'E' shaped plan. 2004. *House of Yeap Chor Ee.*

Homestead's pavillion by the sea. The pavillion was added after Chor Ee purchased the mansion. Late 1930s. *House of Yeap Chor Ee.*

Interior of the pavillion with its beautiful stage in the background. 2004. *House of Yeap Chor Ee.*

Homestead. 2004. *House of Yeap Chor Ee.*

the North Beach at the back of the house, with a clay tennis court beside it. By the side of the house were the servants' quarters, stables, and a garage.

The interior of the mansion was as grand as its imposing exterior, measuring in excess of thirty thousand square feet. Messrs Stark & McNeil gave Homestead grand spaces for entertaining, including an airy drawing room, a billiard room, and a library. Upon entering, guests were greeted by an impressive high-ceilinged reception hall with floors and columns lined with black and white Italian Carrara marble. To the left of the reception hall, was a grand imperial staircase that rose to a half-landing before dividing into two symmetrical flights. With wrought iron railings, solid teak banisters, and built of marble, the staircase led to a colonnaded hall and six rather large bedrooms. Standing guard at the bottom of the staircase balustrade were two marble water nymphs. Above the staircase was a magnificent crystal chandelier suspended on a pulley system. To the right of the reception hall was the formal living area, the library, and the billiard room. An impressive dining hall, large enough to cater for eighty guests, occupied part of the west wing.

The interiors were sumptuously and extravagantly furnished. The Italian statuary, draperies, chairs, tables, porcelain, glassware, and

Homestead's imposing grand imperial staircase. 2004. *House of Yeap Chor Ee.*

cutlery were mostly imported from Burma and Europe. Craftsmen transformed Burmese teak into doors and window frames. Furniture made of richly carved Chinese black-wood, and inlaid with mother of pearl, lined the window bays. Glass-fronted teak almirahs stood tall against the walls, displaying racing trophies and the household silver collection. Hung next to them were intricate Venetian mirrors and beautifully framed silk tapestries of Chinese motifs. Interspersed among the oriental pieces were stately grandfather clocks and Queen Anne and Chippendale-styled furniture from Messrs. Pritchard & Co. Combined, these elements formed an elegant contrast and typified the Straits-Eclectic style. The bedrooms, located on the upper floor, were large and had attached bathrooms. Homestead was also rich in automated trappings. Electric ceiling lights operated by bakelite light-switches illuminated the halls, corridors, and rooms, in place of the hot, smoky, and unsanitary oil lamps more commonly used at the time. Electric fans replaced hand-operated *punkahs*. Water closets, bidets, and water taps that gushed into porcelain basins, replaced chamber pots and privies.

Like its contemporaries along Northam Road, Homestead was stylistically in keeping with the great mansions of that period. It was palatial in every respect and reflected an era when glorious structures were symbolic of the achievements and affluence of those who owned them.

In 1927, when Mah Chye passed away at the age of seventy, his son Chin Guan inherited Homestead, along with vast sums of money and real estate. The turning point for the family was when Chin Guan entered into a financial arrangement to manage the funds of an Indian moneylender. It was a common practice then for wealthy Chinese to act as fund managers for Chettiars. For much of the 1920s, people were making fortunes in the stock market with no apparent effort. As long as share prices kept rising, the system worked fine. Chin Guan also informally managed funds for other people, but when markets collapsed, as they did in the wake of the great depression, the value of their stocks and properties tanked. With debts amounting to $500,000, the courts declared Chin Guan bankrupt. Homestead became the first iconic mansion to hit the market. The Lim family approached Chor Ee, who at first was reluctant in making the purchase. The world economy was on the brink of collapse and Chor Ee was already financially committed to completing the construction of his buildings along China Street Ghaut. But through much persuasion by his young wife Cheng Kin, who felt a genuine concern for the Lim family, Chor Ee yielded and bought Homestead for a reported sum of $600,000.

Before Chor Ee moved in, he engaged Boutcher to add an annex by the sea that included three apartments and a bathing pavilion. The bathing pavilion housed a small private theatre with a miniature stage specifically built for puppet shows and Chinese operas. Although a private theatre might have been considered an ostentatious indulgence, Chor Ee's one great passion was Chinese opera. If he was to fork out a handsome sum for a building he felt indifferent to, he might as well indulge in something for himself. Chor Ee spent most of his time in this new annex. The few times he made his way to the main wing were for prayers and just before nine in the evening to make sure all the lights were off. The exterior of the pavilion was in keeping with the rest of the design, but the interior was restrained, without the pomp and opulence of the main house. A simple passageway, half walled and half meshed, connected the main kitchen to the new apartment. Instead of marble, the floors were mosaic tiles, and unlike the ornate wrought iron lamps in the rest of the house, the rooms were lit by a lone bulb housed in a simple shade made of plain white glass. Rather than having views of the gardens, the apartment wing overlooked a small yard with fruit trees and an animal pen.

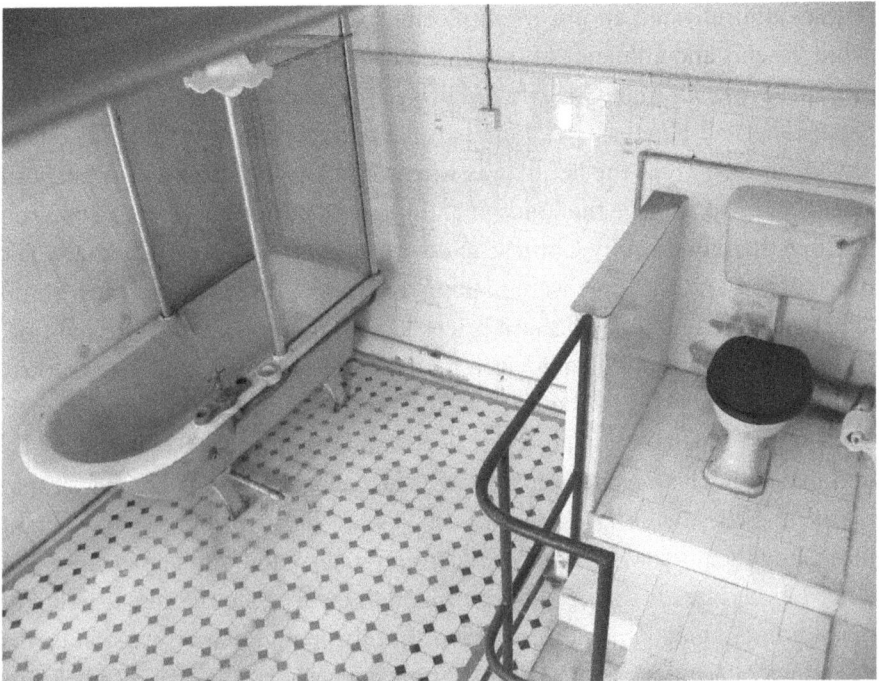

Chor Ee's bathroom with its original fittings. 2004. *House of Yeap Chor Ee.*

The first room was the staff quarters. The second and third were the living and sleeping quarters of Chor Ee and Cheng Kin. The rooms were much smaller than those in the main wing, simple and unadorned. Each room had a lanai, or a roofed patio, which overlooked the beach. Not only did the lanais brighten up the rooms, but they also caught the sea breeze, making conditions extremely pleasant throughout the day despite the incessant tropical heat. An interesting feature of Chor Ee's bedroom was the en-suite bathroom, almost the size of the bedroom itself. The bathroom had a side door that opened to the beach. Another interesting feature of Chor Ee's quarters was a secret side door that led directly to the private theatre. Chor Ee's love for Chinese Teochew opera and puppet shows stemmed from his days as a *sinkhek* when these were popular forms of entertainment. Cheng Kin often recounted tales of how Chor Ee would try to get to the front row before the crowd during the opera season. He probably found an escape of sorts from the gloom of working life in the colours and sounds of the opera.

II

Almost immediately after the family moved into Homestead there was an important announcement. Hock Hoe, Chor Ee's fifth son and Cheng Kin's only son, was to be wed. Hock Hoe was a timid youngster. Chor Ee had already amassed quite a fortune by the time Hock Hoe was born, which gave him a privileged childhood. He was sent to Penang Free School, the oldest English-medium school for boys in the country, but was at best a mediocre student, neither academically inclined nor sporty. Unlike many of his peers, who went to England to further their education, Hock Hoe's parents decided he should be close by, and sent him to Singapore for a college education. When Hock Hoe returned, he joined the family business as an assistant at his father's bank. He chose to remain close to a small circle of friends throughout his adult life, preferring to be selective rather than socially popular. Despite his inhibitions, he was a dashing young man. From his father, he inherited a high forehead, and of course the bushy Yeap eyebrows, from his mother her large penetrating eyes and refined jawline. He always wore his hair slicked back and was often seen in well-cut suits. The fact that he was the couple's only son might have explained his sheltered childhood, but with his good looks and family wealth, Hock Hoe was quite an irresistible catch.

A young Yeap Hock Hoe. Early 1930s. *House of Yeap Chor Ee.*

On the other end of the personality spectrum was his bride, Ida Oei, daughter of Tiong Ham from his fifth wife, Ong Tjiang Tjoe. Tiong Ham's earnings kept his family living in splendour and meant that Ida and her siblings grew up in extravagant and luxurious excess. The Oei children were educated at home by a European governess and tutors, and learned to speak multiple languages, including English, Dutch, Malay, French, and Mandarin. They were also taught the social graces of European aristocrats. They knew which fork to use for which dish, the correct way to hold a cup, and the proper salutations. They had money and spent it on the most fashionable of clothes and jewels, the right addresses, and the latest in modern technology. When aeroplanes first appeared in early 1920s, the family became enthusiasts. The older brother, Tjong Swan, built a runway in Java to receive the first flight from Amsterdam to Java in 1924. Hailed as a tremendous achievement the flight was undertaken by three Dutch aviators, Van Der Hoop, Poelman, and Van der Broeke. It was around this time the family took to flying. Both Ida and her sister Noes learned to manage these flying machines at a young age, with Noes becoming the first female to fly solo in Asia. But what catapulted the family to international fame was not that they could fly planes, or their father's immense wealth, but their oldest sister, Hui-Lan, more famously known as Mrs Wellington Koo.

Hui-Lan was the wife of Dr Wellington Koo, a dashing Chinese diplomat and former acting prime minister and finance minister of China, and China's representative in the founding of the League of Nations. The couple were often seen hobnobbing with global leaders, royalties, and celebrities. As First Lady of China, Hui-Lan captivated the world with her flawless complexion, exquisite taste in fashion, and alluring personality. Hardly anyone could imagine a Chinese person, and a woman for that matter, could be so fluent in all the major languages of the world, or as intelligent and cosmopolitan in outlook. Her sense of style intrigued both sexes — men were drawn to her beauty, and women were in awe of her flair of tastefully adapting traditional Chinese dresses with modern day apparel. She was, what one newspaper described, "Western to the fingertips."[26] Vogue magazine labelled her a "citizen of the world."

Though not as celebrated as her famous half-sister, Ida was attractive, vivacious, and charming, with a taste for travel, fast cars, and horses. She was only nine when her father passed away. As a result of a settlement with the trustees, both she and her sister Noes inherited 400,000 guilders each. Considering that the average adult Javanese male was only earning 160 guilders a year in 1930,[27] the amount was a vast sum for a young woman back then. Sometime in the early 1920s, Ida's mother brought her two daughters to Penang, as Noes was to be wedded to Chor Ee's son, Kim Hoe. The match was an arranged one, intended to fortify the business links between the Oeis and the Yeaps. Wanting to further cement the relationship, the two families formed another union between Ida and Hock Hoe. It would appear that this second union was orchestrated as far back as the early 1920s, when the children had not even reached ten years of age. A photo taken soon after Noes and Kim Hoe's wedding, shows Cheng Kin and Chor Ee seated in the centre as matriarch and patriarch of the family, with Hock Hin, their youngest son, between them. Behind them were Kim Hoe, Noes, and an unidentified gentleman. Ida stood next to Cheng Kin, with Hock Hoe by Chor Ee's side.

---

[26] 'Mr. Wellington Koo', *The Straits Times*, 4 February 1921.

[27] Peter Boomgaard, *Weathering the Storm: The Economies of Southeast Asia in the 1930s Depression*, Singapore: ISEAS, 2001.

Family photo (Late 1910s). Standing from left: Ida Oei, Noes Oei, Hock Hin, Kim Hoe, unknown man, Hock Hoe. Seated from left: Lee Cheng Kin, Yeap Chor Ee. *House of Yeap Chor Ee.*

The girls were exquisitely dressed, while the two younger boys appeared as if they might have outgrown their suits. In any event, the photo symbolised the union between the two families.

Malaya's attention moved to Penang, where on a Wednesday morning on 22nd November 1933, Ida and Hock Hoe joined in matrimony. Newspapers across the country broadcast it as the "Wedding of the Year" and the grandest social event in town. It was a day looked forward to by George Town's high society. Homestead gave itself over to a flurry of preparations. The household laboured night and day for weeks to get the house looking spick and span. The halls and rooms were decked in red silk and transformed into a sumptuous wedding venue.

On the morning of the wedding day, invited guests and well-wishers convened at Homestead and the bride's residence, a few doors away along Northam Road. Chor Ee made a rare appearance in suit and tie with a boutonniere on his lapel. His wife Cheng Kin, wore an elegant *cheongsam* with matching diamond earing and rings. Around midday, Hock Hoe and his best men accompanied by their entourage, set off to Ida's residence to escort her and her bridesmaids back to Homestead. Hock Hoe wore a well-cut tuxedo. He had a fresh hair-cut a few days back and looked extremely dashing. If he was nervous, he gave no hint of it. His manner was calm and composed. Outfitted in true movie-star style, with a juliet cape veil with beaded floral lace and holding a sumptuous ostrich fan with studded crystal handle, Ida dazzled the guests in her stunning bridal gown. Guests oohed and ahhed at the sight of the young couple as they entered the main hall, enchanted by the glitz, glamour and romance of it all. With the town brass band playing in the background, Khoo Boo Cheang, the Master of Ceremonies proceeded with the tea ceremony in the hall which had been redecorated for the occasion. Speeches were delivered. The registry was signed followed by cutting of the cake and free flow of champagne — all of which were not typical features of Chinese weddings but had recently become fashionable. Dinner for three hundred of the family's Chinese friends was served on the lawn at the back of

Wedding photo of Yeap Hock Hoe and Ida Oei. Standing second row from behind: third from left is Kim Hoe, Ida's mother, unknown man, Chor Ee, Cheng Kin, Noes. The two little bridesmaids in between the bride and groom were Kim Hoe & Noes' daughters, Nancy & Gladys. 1933. *House of Yeap Chor Ee.*

恢閒堂

Wedding dinner party held in Homestead for European guests.1933.
House of Yeap Chor Ee.

Yeap Hock Hoe and Ida Oei. 1933.
House of Yeap Chor Ee.

Homestead. The guests took the opportunity to visit the mansion, viewing the various apartments and the new pavilion. Ronggeng dancing, which was also in vogue at that time, started after dinner.

The following evening, another banquet was held in the formal dining hall for the family's European guests. Chor Ee, Cheng Kin, and the newlyweds graciously presided over a beautiful sit-down dinner. The tables were set with a blinding array of silverware. Among those invited were Mr H. S. Russell, managing director of Messrs. Sime Darby and Co. and Mr F. H. Grummitt, owner of the three main English newspapers in town — *Straits Echo*, *Pinang Gazette* and *Sunday Gazette*. They raised their glasses, and wished the young couple a blessed union. Grummitt expressed pleasure and thanked Chor Ee for hosting a magnificent evening that helped them "forget the weariness of the slump, even for a day." Russell also delivered a speech announcing the "union of two well-known families. Mr Yeap Chor Ee's rise to fame as Penang's leading business man they all knew. The bride's father was one of the most illustrious Chinese in Java and Sumatra."

After the marriage, Ida moved into Homestead, where they lived not so happily after. Their period of wedded bliss was a short one. The couple became estranged right from the start of their marriage, which ended in divorce ten years later.

Hock Hoe and Ida's wedding was not entirely in keeping with the traditional Chinese style. Their marriage was what was called the Reformed Wedding, a term coined by the younger generation of Straits-born Chinese who pushed for a less onerous ceremony. The reformed movement started in China where a group of ardent reformers, mostly students, wanted greater freedom and a simpler, speedier, and less costly form of wedding ceremony. The trend soon reached the shores of British Malaya when in 1905, a Chinese Reform Association was set up. One of the prime objectives of the Association was to "discourage as much as possible useless customs involving unnecessary expenditure, especially those relating to marriage ceremonies, Funeral rites, ghost praying."[28] And thus, began a move away from the old to the new, with the earliest recorded Reformed Wedding taking place in 1912 in Singapore, though it didn't become popular until the early 1930s. The idea was mostly adopted by the affluent and educated younger generation of Straits Chinese, who saw it as a symbol of modernity and sophistication.

---

[28] 'Reform Among Chinese', *The Straits Times*, 16 January 1905.

Ong Tjiang Tjoe Nio, fifth wife of Oei Tiong Ham and mother of Noes and Ida. 1960s. *Courtesy of Dr Loh Wei Leng.*

If getting married was cumbersome, getting the marriage recognised was equally troublesome. Of all the Chinese customs practiced in Malaya, the traditional Chinese marriage proved to be the most delicate to govern in the colony. Before laws and ordinances were revised and passed, the courts were constantly called upon to unravel a chaotic tangle of claims and refutations arising from Chinese marriages. Judges commented on the difficulties of continuing to administer the law in cases where there was no final authority or means of being completely informed on whether a Chinese woman was the legal wife. Chief Justice Sir William Murison of the Singapore Supreme Court in 1926 remarked of Chinese marriage litigation, "big sums of money are needlessly spent, the time of our Courts is uselessly expended and a hazardous decision is the most that can be expected, particularly in cases where the evidence is both obscure and conflicting, as it generally is."

The problem boiled down to the lack of ability to define a woman's position, particularly when there was more than one wife involved. Under English laws, when a man dies intestate the widow is entitled to one-third of his estate. In the Settlements, complications arose because a Chinese man may have had more than one wife. There was also the added problem of trying to distinguish between a first wife, a secondary wife, and a concubine. The law treated the children of these various women as having equal rights, but the women themselves were not treated as such.

In late 1910s, a movement sprang up to push for modification of marriage laws for all Straits-born Chinese. When judgement was made on the celebrated "six widows case", where the court of appeal decided that a Chinese man in Malaya could have as many wives as he pleased and the property would be equally divided between them at his death, outspoken locally born women denounced the verdict. Wealthy principal wives in Penang, including the wives of most of the leading local Chinese, objected and took matters in their hands. In 1918, they organised a Ladies Movement, urging the government to recognise the status of Straits women. What Penang needed, argued Nyonya Chuah Guat Beng, were marriage laws for Chinese men and women who were British subjects. She organised a meeting at Holland House on Northam Road and spoke of the need of a one man-one woman policy. If a man died intestate neither his wife nor his children would know how they stood in regards to accession to the estate of the deceased. A petition was then proposed, to be forwarded to the governor, requesting that a modified form of the English Law of Marriage be adopted in the colony for all Straits-born Chinese.

The problem was debated in Penang in 1926 and a commission was appointed to look into the question, but the committee included some men who had three or four wives. The men shook their heads, convinced it was a ludicrous proposal. Nothing came from the commission, but the issue persisted. One man took it upon himself to champion the cause. His name was Lim Cheng Ean. Cheng Ean came from a wealthy and well-known family in Penang. His father was Phuah Hin Leong, founder of the rice and oil industries in Penang. He had two older brothers, Lim Cheng Teik and Lim Cheng Law, who were rice-millers and well-known men in social circles in Penang. A brilliant student, Cheng Ean started his education at St Xavier's Institution before reading law at Clare College in Cambridge, where he met his future wife Rosalind Hoalim who herself was studying to become a medical practitioner. When they returned to Penang, Cheng Ean set up his own legal practice and was appointed a municipal councillor, then later member of the Legislative Council. Articulate and reform-minded, he fought hard and supported worthy causes, one of which was the introduction of a Marriage Ordinance. He proposed that there should be laws providing for the registration of marriages issuance of marriage certificates, as well as legal provisions for the enforcement of conjugal rights and for separation and divorce. Registration he contented, would solve much of the predicament the community currently faced concerning the matter. Naturally, there was much opposition, as some felt compulsory registration would mean government intervention and nobody welcomed interference in this matter. Opponents argued that it was difficult to completely abolish the age-old customs all at once. Most men in Penang were against registration and the vast majority of supporters were the women. Towards the end of 1930s, provisional drafts of two bills were brought to the public, one permitting the monogamous marriage of non-Christians and another for the registration of polygamous marriages. The Marriage Ordinance was introduced in 1952 and registration came into force in 1955, two years before women in Malaya finally gained the right to vote.

III

Lim Cheng Ean, Lim Chin Guan, Yeap Hock Hoe, Ida Oei, the guests who attended Hock Hoe and Ida's wedding, the residents of the palatial mansions along Northam Road, and Nyonya Guat Beng were all regarded as the new breed of the younger generation. Together with their forefathers, like Chor Ee, who chose to settle in the colony, these Straits-born individuals were British subjects. Most were ardently loyal to the king and the empire. At first, their fathers landed on the shores of the colony, leaving the motherland to make a living in their new home. They started as coolies and labourers, and under British rule they found opportunities to progress. They obeyed the laws, in which they had a voice in making, and whatever they earned they kept. Once they saved enough, they formed a chop and hired their relatives to help run their businesses. Many took one wife in China, and another in the colony. Their children, born and bred on British soil, mastered the rudiments of the English language, and after completing their education, became professionals and merchants, while some entered the colonial administration. A number adopted Christian names, such as Nancy and George, in addition to their Chinese names. Typically they favoured Western attire. During the day, they wore suits, straw hats, and ties of the latest style, discarding the *Tng Sah* (Chinese jacket). At night, they attended cinemas, dances, and cabarets, instead of the antiquated Chinese street operas. They developed a taste for Western music and took pleasure in Western sports such as badminton, tennis, football, horse racing, and polo.

A number of inhabitants formed the Chinese Company of the Straits Volunteer Infantry, offering their services in defence of the colony. In time of war, they marshalled their resources, pledged support for Britain, and contributed generously to the relief funds while supporting the War Tax Bill. They gifted Britain the HMS Malaya, the Queen Elizabeth-class battleship built for the Royal Navy. A handful became members of the municipal commission and the Straits legislative assembly. They joined the Chinese British Association and vouched to foster a patriotic and imperial British spirit among the subjects of His Majesty King Edward VII.

The British paid tribute to them. One newspaper said, "The Chinese in the Straits are essential to us, and we are indispensable to them. In the mines, the plantations and the towns white labour would be impossible. Climate and expense are two grounds for the proposition. Chinese therefore provide the labour and produce for us the lion's share of our revenue. We give them in turn, and for the first time in their history, honest rule and justice before the law. And they vastly appreciate us."[29]

---

[29] 'The King's Chinese', *The Singapore Free Press and Mercantile Advertiser*, 10 May 1906.

Another said, "The Chinese is ubiquitous and indefatigable. His working hours, no matter what his trade or profession, seem to be limited only by his physical strength. It is not easy to imagine what British Malaya would be without the Chinese."[30]

C.W. Harrison, author of *The Illustrated Guide to the Federated Malay States*, one of the best guide books to Malaya ever written said, "if ever a monument was raised to the man who was responsible for the country's fortunes, it would be a statue of a Chinese coolie."[31]

But perhaps the greatest compliment came from governor of the Straits Settlements, Sir Shenton Thomas, who said, "I and my Government have no intention of denying the great share that the Chinese have taken in making Malaya one of the greatest, if not the greatest, of the Crown Colonies. Chinese have played an important part in developing the resources of a rich country. They have been the friends and advisers of Sultans since long before the coming of British influence. They were the first tin miners and in every industry they have been leaders, for they possess that essential accompaniment of the pioneering spirit, the ability and readiness to take chances. Many, thanks to their exertions, have built up great fortunes and have given employment to thousands of people."[32]

Yet it was only half a century earlier they were labelled the "lemon-coloured sphinx...a being in whom there are neither morals nor truth." But now they were grandly titled the King's Chinese.

---

[30] 'The Chinese in Malaya', *The Straits Times*, 22 June 1928.
[31] 'Chinese and Malaya', *Malaya Tribune*, 20 December 1934.
[32] 'Chinese and Malaya', *Malaya Tribune*, 20 December 1934.

Chapter 12

Domestic Matters

That throngs of illiterate Chinese peasants, many of whom had never stepped foot out of their villages, could in the late 1800s sail the South China Seas, settle in a foreign land, and be branded as the King's Chinese seems little short of preposterous. But the fact is that they did adapt and they demonstrated it most through their domestic lives.

Like most Chinese parents in George Town, Chor Ee and Cheng Kin brought their brood up on the Confucian principles of filial piety, which demanded that the first loyalty and duty should be to the family. But while the values of Chor Ee's family were distinctly Chinese, a mix of cultures formed part of the fabric of everyday life. Food served in the family home was a blend of Chinese, Malay, Indian, Thai, and sometimes Burmese cuisines. Household servants came from different backgrounds. There were Chinese black and white *amahs*, named for the white tops and black trousers they wore, Malay drivers, Indian gardeners, and Javanese coolies. Hokkien was the predominant lingua franca of the household, but different from the conventional Hokkien spoken in China. Malay words, like *batu* (stone), *balai* (station), and *jamban* (toilet), all entered the local Hokkien vocabulary. The local mix of different cultures also influenced the choice of dress. Cheng Kin wore a *sarong* and *kebaya*, and indulged in the local habit of chewing *sireh*. Her favourite pastime was watching Hindi movies.

|

Unlike the Western nuclear family, comprised of a married couple and their immediate children, the Chinese family is an extended patrilineal one, including everyone from paternal great-grandparents, grandparents, parents, grand uncles, uncles, brothers, and cousins, along with their respective wives and children. The aim of every Chinese family is to have four generations under the same roof. Cheng Kin and Chor Ee were intent on filling Homestead with as many children as possible and made it very clear to the wives of their sons that whoever gave birth to a son would be the *tua boh* (principal wife). And so, the race for sons began. Both Hock Hoe and Kim Hoe were known to be men about town. They were not overly particular about the background or social standing of the women they wooed, so long as the girls were attractive, young and fertile. After his divorce with Ida, Hock Hoe had five more wives and seventeen children — seven boys and ten girls. His older brother, Kim Hoe whose first wife was Ida's older sister, Noes, also had five wives, who gave birth to thirteen children between them. Hock Hin had two wives who bore fifteen children. The other two sons, Lean Seng and Lean Hong, were more restrained, with only one wife apiece at any given time. Lean Seng had seven children. Lean Hong and his Chinese bride remained childless at first, but later adopted Lean Hong's nephew as their son. One thing must be said about Lean Hong's wife. She was the only member of the family with bound feet, a practice her parents had inflicted upon her since she was young. Her original name was Ng Siew, but the family referred to her as Hong Ah Soh, or Aunty Hong. Since foot binding was mostly practiced by the upper class in China, Hong Ah Soh most probably came from a well-to-do family. Perhaps her upbringing made her far more guarded and distant than the other wives. But when Cheng Kin, being a pragmatic matriarch, insisted that her daughter-in-law stop the practice of binding her feet and discard her putrid smelling bandages, she grudgingly obeyed.

Chor Ee's daughters gave birth to eight grandchildren. In total, Cheng Kin and Chor Ee had sixty-one grandchildren — thirty-one boys and thirty girls. Most of the grandchildren were sent to English curriculum schools — St Xavier's for the boys, and Convent Light Street for the girls. When they came of age, most were shipped off to the UK for further schooling.

Even though Homestead was huge, it could not accommodate all the wives and grandchildren. Some made their homes elsewhere, with the husbands visiting each wife in turn during the week. Cousins regularly came to Homestead to play and visit their grandparents.

If a marriage had no male offspring, adoption was accepted. All adopted children were treated equally. Since a family line could only be perpetuated by sons, the adoption of boys was more important for would-be-parents. Adoption took many forms. Children could be adopted from within the family, for example from a brother who already had a few sons of his own,

Three generations of Yeap. Standing from left: Goh Bee Chui, Yeap Kim See, Baby Lim, Lee Cheng Nee, Goh Bee Imm, Yeap Leong Sim, Goh Eng Tuan, Leong Kui, Goh Eng Toon. Seated from left: Geck Geok, Teoh Phaik Kheng, Hooi Kum Chee, Noes Oei, Ng Siew, Guat Imm, Lee Cheng Kin, Yeap Leong Huat (sitting on lap), Yeap Chor Ee, Yeap Lean Seng, Yeap Kim Hoe, Yeap Hock Hoe, Yeap Hock Hin, Goh Hock Siew. Seated front from left: Goh Eng Kee, Goh Eng Kiat, Yeap Leong Hin, Yeap Poh Suat, Yeap Poh Tin, Yeap Poh Tee, Yeap Poh Jin, Yeap Leong Beng. 1950. *House of Yeap Chor Ee.*

who then regarded his natural father as an uncle. This adopted son had all the rights and duties of a real son. If the family had a natural son after the adoption, the adopted child would be treated with more care and love than the natural son. If the brother had no sons, the grandson of an uncle could also be adopted to ensure the continuity of the family line. Sometimes even when a couple had a son, they would adopt another so that the natural son could be shielded from the rigours of life, while the adopted son was trained to take on a more demanding role, such as managing the family's company business. The natural son in such an instance would be called an *Akua-Kia*. This custom of an adopted son often puzzled Westerners, who were unable to grasp the motives behind Chinese adoption.

Another peculiar convention was giving names to children. Chinese names are generally made up of three characters — the surname, being the clan from which the person comes, the generational name, ranking the child according to their relationship within the family, and the individual personal name. The head of the family, usually with the help of a fortune teller, had the honour of naming a newborn child. Since the process took some time, the family often gave the baby a temporary nickname. If he was a boy, he would be named *Ah-Bah* (Sonny) and if she was a girl, she would be called *Ah-Nya* (Girlie), which explains why in those days the record books of the registrar of births where filled with these names. Nicknames also served another purpose — as a disguise to trick malignant spirits from harming the children. People believed that evil spirits might take vengeance on those who had offended them by causing sickness or even taking the life of the child. In order to confound the demons, children were given nicknames such as *Ah-Kow* (dog), *Ah-Too-Kia* (piglet), or *Ah-Loo* (donkey). But not all nicknames were given for superstitious reasons. When names were left to unofficial sources, as with a number of children in Homestead, the results were generally livelier. They were often based on the child's characteristics, such as *Hwey Siong* (priest), *Tua Thau* (big head), or *Huan-Choo* (potato). Chor Ee's children were all given Chinese names, but from the following generation onwards a number of his grandchildren had Western names — Nancy, Gladys, Stephen, Jeffery, Jennifer, Natalie, Janet and so forth, in addition to their Chinese names, so as to ease their way in colonial society.

About a month after Chinese New Year in 1948, Kum Chee, one of Hock Hoe's wives passed away from complications of the anaesthetics she was given when she went in for a simple surgical procedure at the general hospital. Kum Chee had four children with Hock Hoe — Jennifer, Natalie, Janet, and Stephen. Jennifer, who was the eldest, was just six years old when Kum Chee passed away. Overnight, at

Hooi Kum Chee, third wife of Hock Hoe. Late 1940s. *House of Yeap Chor Ee.*

Kum Chee dressed up in typical nyonya attire. Late 1940s. *House of Yeap Chor Ee.*

the age of fifty, Cheng Kin became a mother to these four children, plus to one of Hock Hoe's daughters, Angela, whose mother had separated from Hock Hoe not too long before. The grandchildren recalled their grandmother as a kind-hearted Empress Dowager — commanding yet compassionate, generous, and most of all, highly respected. They grew up relatively pampered, with each child having a nanny to look after them from young until their late-teens. For most of the day, while Cheng Kin was at the bank, the children spent time with their *amahs*, who accompanied them everywhere they went — even to school. The *amahs* controlled the children's movements and disciplined them by telling them old wives tales of how the gods might be offended if they were naughty. Often, the *amahs* restricted the children's diets, avoiding anything that might cause indigestion. When one *amah* didn't get along with another, the child was unable to play with his or her own sibling. Despite being left to the mercy of these nannies and their peculiar whims, the children of Homestead had fond memories of the time they spent together, with their pint-sized grandmother encouraging them to lead an active social life and be exposed to new experiences. In many ways, it was as if Cheng Kin was re-living her own childhood vicariously through these children.

Cheng Kin with her grandchildren in Homestead. Sitting on the far left, Janet, Natalie, Jennifer, Angela, Cheng Kin. Standing: Stephen, Kam Lean (Hock Hoe's forth wife) and her sons sitting on Cheng Kin's lap and standing on her right. Late 1940s. *House of Yeap Chor Ee*.

Chor Ee had a holiday bungalow just below the second station of the Penang Hill Railway and the family often spent weekends there, fleeing from the muggy heat of George Town. Cheng Kin took charge of the outings like an army commander, supervising basket-loads of provisions, food, and linen that had to be carted up for the weekend. Extra care was taken to look after Chor Ee, who was in his early eighties by then. Four men carried him on a sedan chair between the station and the bungalow. Most of the time, the old grandfather sat on the balcony and watched the children play in the garden while their grandmother gave directions to the staff. What seemed a mammoth effort for a weekend's outing, was quite a normal affair for Cheng Kin. Children behaved and fell silent on her command. Food, and plenty of it, was served at her request. Chor Ee often requested all the lights out at 9 p.m. sharp, as he hated wasting electricity.

After Chor Ee passed away, Cheng Kin took to watching matinee shows in the cinemas at least two or three times a week, with the children and their *amahs* tagging along. Cinema was a form of escape for Cheng Kin, and later, a place for afternoon naps. The smaller children sat on their *amahs'* laps, while the bigger ones had their own seats, eyes wide with delight, ready to tuck into their snacks as soon as the movie began. If there were no new movies showing, they sat through the same ones over and over again. Cheng Kin enjoyed watching Chinese, Tamil, and Hindustani movies, anything but Western. The first Western movie the children ever watched was at Homestead. Leong Sim, an older cousin who was a photography and movie enthusiast, set up a projector and a reel, while Cheng Kin gave instructions to turn the dining hall into a makeshift movie theatre. The curtains were drawn, doors shut, lights dimmed, and lo and behold, Laurel & Hardy appeared, projected onto a suspended white bedsheet. There was no sound, but everyone was mesmerised, especially the children. The excitement generated and the sense of marvellous ingenuity are difficult to conceive now. Home movies went from a craze to a compulsion. The library on the eastern wing of Homestead was turned into a home theatre and every week Cheng Kin held movie nights at home screened by Uncle Cheong, the owner of Lido photo shop. He brought his equipment on his motorcycle and the entire household was treated to an hour of entertainment. While the children were happily preoccupied by Charlie Chaplin's slapstick comedy, old Uncle Cheong was in the next room wooing one of their aunts. On days when they were not watching movies, the children played on the grounds of Homestead. They climbed trees, flew kites, accompanied their grandmother to the temples, and went fishing in the evenings, grandma included.

Another pastime was attending race days at the Turf Club. Hock Hoe and Kim Hoe were equestrian enthusiasts as far back as the early 1930s when they took up polo and owned a string of race horses. Hock Hoe whetted his mother's appetite for racing when he encouraged her to take over Froggie, a bay thoroughbred mare, from his string. On race days, Cheng Kin would drive south to the Turf Club with the children and nannies and spend the afternoon at the VIP stand, happily betting and watching the fastest mount race to the cheers of the crowds. Froggie went on to win the Gold Cup, the most prestigious, highest stake, annual meet on the island. Bitten by the racing bug, Cheng Kin bought another thoroughbred bay named Cash Inn. Cash Inn also won a Gold Cup for her proud owner, but the third mare Cheng Kin bought, Froggie II, turned out to be a duck. Such is the fate of horse racing. It was also the end of Cheng Kin's horse-mania days.

Cheng Kin spent many of her evenings sewing clothes for her granddaughters. Initially, they all shared the same style of dressing, but when the older ones began to request for more stylish dresses Cheng Kin

The children's afternoon dance party at Homestead. Sitting: Second from right, Jennifer. Fourth from right Angela. 1950s. *House of Yeap Chor Ee.*

took inspirations from the movies. She memorised the patterns and came up with cuts and pastel combinations that parodied elite fashion to fit their tiny eighteen-inch waists. Cheng Kin preferred the *sarong kebaya*, an outfit most associated with the Nyonya and modified from the Malay *baju panjang*. With its lightweight embroidered blouse secured at the front by a set of *kerongsang* and worn over a camisole and paired with a sarong, the dress was a far cry from the body-hugging *cheongsam*, which she sometimes wore for formal occasions. To complement their dresses, grandma bought them rouge, lipstick, and *eau de cologne*. When Angela, the oldest granddaughter was of age to mingle, Cheng Kin organised social events for her which also benefited her younger siblings. Once a week for several years, their grandmother staged dance parties at Homestead, transforming the dining hall into a dance hall. The friends, especially the boys, who made the cut, were thrilled to be invited. At the appointed hour, the children turned up and danced the evening away with Cheng Kin and Kotek Emm, her friend and partner in crime, acting as chaperons for the evening.

Kotek Emm was an unflattering name, *kotek* being a Malay slang word for the male genitalia, and Emm meaning aunty in Hokkien. She got her

Cheng Kin and her friend Kotek Emm in the family dining room. 1970s. *House of Yeap Chor Ee.*

name because her husband was called Kotek, and through that connection, the whole town referred to her as Kotek Emm. Political correctness was not a concept often observed back in those days.

Having exhausted themselves, grandma and the aunty with the funny name packed all of the children into cars to go for a supper of *Sar Hor Fun* (fried noodles) at Kampung Malabar, or sometimes at the Dato' Keramat junction coffee shop.

One of the crazes to hit George Town at that time was dancing at the Green Parrot, a nightclub located at the end of Gurney Drive and a favourite hangout for returning allied forces army and navy men. Joe Roselle had his band there, belting out the latest songs. Another attraction of the club was the cabaret girls who could be booked to dance with patrons. Cheng Kin sportingly agreed to take the children there and had the van's seats converted so that they could accommodate more than the prescribed six people. The nightclub owner happily welcomed the well-known Mrs Yeap Chor Ee and her coterie of giggly teenagers into his establishment and didn't mind the boys sneaking in their own F&N orange drinks. Their hawkeyed grandmother and Kotek Emm passed the evenings eating rambutans in a corner, or indulging in the local habit of chewing *sireh*. But they still kept a watchful eye over the girls, especially Angela who was the belle of the dance floor. Once in a while the two old ladies found themselves in a battle to keep the undesirables away, while Angela rock-and-rolled the night away. When the children were older and closer to marriageable age, Cheng Kin and Kotek Emm, took them to City Lights cabaret to watch Rose Chan, the striptease queen of Malaya, perform her raunchy acts.

Angela was Cheng Kin's favourite, Jennifer was Hock Hoe's pet, while Stephen, being the oldest grandson was the apple of Chor Ee's eye. But despite the personal favourites, the children were all well-loved, genuinely fond of each other, and a happy bunch. Whatever they needed, their grandmother provided. Every evening after dinner they would line up before Cheng Kin to ask for pocket money to buy knick-knacks from school and the grandmother happily obliged. She was hardly ever cross with them, neither were they disrespectful towards her. When the girls reached an age where they were old enough to travel to the UK for further education, their grandmother made them sign an agreement to pledge that they would not marry a foreigner, for fear they might not return to Penang. Cheng Kin visited them twice in London, one visit coinciding with the coronation of Queen Elizabeth II. It was

Cheng Kin's first trip to Europe. She went again in 1959, when Stephen turned 13. Both times, she brought boxes of food and gifts, most memorably cast-metal star pendants with each child's name embossed on it. For some odd reason, of the many gifts they were given, these stayed longest in their memories.

II

By the time the family moved to Homestead, Cheng Kin had refined the business of feeding the family to an exact science. She was indulgent of Chor Ee's desires, although his requests were far less elaborate than the family's. All he wanted was to dine on his favourite meal of steamed pomfret Teochew style, and braised eels which were bred in a pond at home. The gastronomic requirements for the rest of the family were far more demanding. There was a main kitchen and a secondary kitchen in Homestead. The main kitchen had four brick counters with two open fire stoves on each counter. Copious amounts of vegetables, and meat of all sorts, were chopped up, boiled, stir-fried, braised, and steamed each day. The kitchen prepared four meals a day for a very large family, including children, grandchildren, in-laws, and the household staff. The staff of Ban Hin Lee was also fed from the same kitchen, their meals served in tiffin carriers transported to the office daily. The provisioning for the household was an enormous preoccupation for Cheng Kin and the staff. Groceries were brought in a few times a year and stored in bulk — dozens of five-gallon tins of cooking oil and sacks of rice from Chor Ee's mills. Sugar, tea, and flour purchased by bag loads, carbonated drinks by the crate. Marketing for fresh food was done on a daily basis by the Hainanese cook and his wife. The family sat down to bountiful quantities of food. A typical meal might consist at least three or four proteins — fish, chicken, pork, prawns, or shellfish - with a variety of vegetable dishes and a soup. There was always a curry dish and a *sambal* (spicy paste) — two categorically alien foods by Chinese standards, but by then the average diet of George Town's Chinese had adapted to the varied flavours and tastes that Penang's different cultures offered.

When the early Chinese settlers first arrived in Penang, they brought supplies of preserved ham and fowl, salted vegetables, sausages, dried mushrooms, fungus, and salted ducks eggs. Ignorant of food other than their own, they initially showed reluctance to tuck into local food and looked upon it as wholly peculiar. They stuck to a diet that was for the most part relatively bland. The Cantonese preferred to use plenty of starch, the Teochews liked their soups clear and clean, while the Hokkiens and Hainanese usually took the middle course. The Cantonese excelled in half-fried half-stewed dishes, the Hokkien in roasting suckling pigs, Teochew in steaming, and the Hainanese cooks were fairly competent in fusion food, cooking semi-Chinese and semi-European dishes. The new arrivals learned to plant crops based on local soil and weather conditions and over time as they took on local wives they gradually became acquainted with, and even developed a fondness for a litany of exotic products, including betel leaves, torch ginger bud, lemongrass, sweet chili, galangal, banana flower, palm sugar, candle nut, turmeric, tamarind, *buah keluak* (kepayang nut), cardamom, cumin, star anise, kaffir lime leaves, coriander, and *santan* (coconut milk). Their local wives introduced them not only to new foods but to more interesting ways of preparing them. Some of the techniques were heavily borrowed from the Indians — *tumis*, a way to sauté until the oils separated from the paste, *giling* to grind, and *tumbuk* to pound. The womenfolk also took inspiration from the epicurean methods of the Burmese, Dutch, and Thai. Even the English contributed. Oddly enough, pickled vegetables and Perrin's Worcestershire sauce also seeped into their culinary creations. The women toiled in the kitchens, meticulously amalgamating local and foreign ingredients and techniques with Chinese products, carefully balancing flavours to concoct a style of cooking called Nyonya cuisine. The *mise en place* was painstakingly laborious and elaborate. Ingredients had to be carefully peeled and plucked, finely chopped and uniformly diced. Sauces and accompaniments were prepared days in advance and the sequence of cooking had to be exact. But when it came to the actual cooking however, measurements were wonderfully imprecise, calling for a dash of this and a dash of that — what the locals termed *agak-agak* (thereabouts). It was all about the taste, the visuals, and the aroma, and when all the elements came together in perfect harmony the end result was a delightfully spicy and colourful gastronomy, a true feast for the senses. To compliment this highly vibrant cuisine, crockery was specially designed for curries, salads, pickled fish, stewed meats, fried vegetables, grilled pork, steamed custards, accompaniments, sauces, and so on — blue and white crockery for everyday use, and the exquisite late-Qing ceramics in pastel colours for festive occasions. This innovative cooking became so widespread that almost every Chinese household in Penang began adopting it. It was what the kitchen in Homestead served for family meals. Remarkably, no one became particularly overweight.

Before we momentarily part from the delights of cooking, one other peculiar food item introduced to the once unadventurous Chinese palate needs mentioning — the *belacan* (fermented shrimp paste). *Belacan* has been part of Nyonya cuisine for as long as anyone can remember and is believed to have derived from the Burmese *ngape*. It is a condiment used to add flavour to *sambals*, curries, stews, and stir-fries, and is perhaps the ingredient closest to embodying the savoury Japanese flavour umami. The most distinct characteristic of *belacan* is its strong pungent smell, particularly when heated. Once even a modicum of this unusual condiment hits a hot wok or grill, a putrid smell wafts not only through the kitchen, but the entire neighbourhood, much like the release of a genie out of its bottle. The stench of *belacan* is like no other smell; the closest comparison would be that of a small decaying rodent. It lingers farther and longer than the smell of a durian. But once cooked and infused in the dish, it imparts deliciousness. At the turn of the 20th century Bagan Luar in Province Wellesley, across from Penang Island, was one of the main suppliers of *belacan*. Its products were dispatched across the Malay states and exported to Siam, Sumatra, Celebes, and as far as Australia and Christmas Island.

As cooking techniques changed so did kitchen appliances. Apart from the usual wok and cleaver, novel utensils entered the kitchens of Chinese homes, including the *batu giling* (grinding stone) for example, which had its origins in India. Before electric blenders, spices were manually ground to make *rempah* (spiced paste), the foundation of Nyonya food. The English called it the curry stone, as it was a solid granite slab. Its portable variant was the *cheng-ku* (pestle and mortar), another indispensable household appliance. Like the well-seasoned wok, a well-seasoned *cheng-ku* is one of the most important tools in a Nyonya cook's culinary arsenal. The well-seasoned *cheng-ku* produces far superior *rempah* than a new one. The smoother patina allows for even bruising of the spices, which releases the aromatic compounds in the oils and produces a creamy velvet-like texture to the paste — something the electric blender is unable to replicate. And like a well-worn shoe, the well-seasoned *cheng-ku* is very personal, the shape of the pestle moulded to the motions of the user. Another peculiar appliance is the coconut scraper, an invention from Ceylon which consists of a circular iron burr mounted on the end of a goose neck shaped wooden stool. The kitchen helper sits astride the stool and scrapes the coconut meat on the burr, producing a finely shredded mass which is then soaked in water and pressed by hand to produce coconut milk. Because it was such an unusual looking tool, it initially caused some confusion to those unfamiliar with Asian cooking. A railway guard in the 1920s, fresh from England, who had to list one of these odd looking contraptions in his waybill, racked his brains for a good five minutes before labelling it as "one musical instrument."

Invented in the early 1840s, a contraption that changed diets and improved food storage was an ice maker. Ice was a luxury in the tropics, on very rare occasions imported on cargo ships sailing to Penang as early as the 1850s. By the 1880s, Penang opened its own ice factory — the Penang Ice Company — producing the ice used to keep food safe and fresh for longer periods and to make ice drinks and desserts. The company was so efficient in producing ice that it was able to compete with Singapore by sending ice there and selling it at one cent per pound, or half the price of its Singapore counterpart. Ice was so well received, that by the turn of the century Penang had three ice companies, and factories kept opening throughout the Settlements and Malay Peninsula. After ice came refrigeration, which really came into its own with refrigerated ships, allowing for the shipment of meat and other fresh food from distant markets. Beef, mutton, and lamb could be imported from England and Australia, and even as far away as Argentina. With the opening of the Cold Storage Co Ltd at the turn of the 20th century, Singapore became the epicentre of the frozen food market. The company opened a branch in Penang a decade or so later. When the fortnightly service of Robert Dollar steamers from San Francisco that sailed round the world began in the 1920s, a wide variety of Californian food products were made available to Malaya. Each steamer had over a thousand tons of refrigerator space and was able to keep peaches, cherries, apples, oranges, pears, grapes, asparagus and even dairy products fresh. For the first time in history Malayans didn't have to consume food near where it was produced. By the late 1920s, home refrigerators entered the Malayan market and within a few years, it was considered an essential household appliance. But despite the improvement in extending the shelf life of fruits and vegetables a number of the old-timers in Homestead weren't always quite sure what to make of refrigerators and would still insist on steaming fruits before consumption, no matter how fresh. Children of Homestead were often deprived of the fresh stuff because the *amahs* believed fresh fruits created wind in the stomach or induced coughing. The children were not even allowed to eat fresh home-grown fruit. But whenever they came across a fruit that had dropped from a tree, no matter how decomposed it was, they would pop it in their mouths, thereby validating the old wives' tale that uncooked fruit was bad for you. Undaunted, they often stole a fruit or two from the altar when no one was looking — repeatedly surprising the unwitting *amah* who thought either the rats or the gods had been feasting. Sometimes their mischief backfired when they mistakenly picked an unripe *ciku* (sapodilla), biting into it to find the gummy sap from the skin so sticky that it sealed their lips, again validating the old wives' tales that if children misbehaved, they were punished by the gods.

When Lim Mah Chye built Homestead, he asked for a formal dining hall in which to entertain. Messrs Stark & McNeil gave Homestead an eighty foot long dining hall — big enough to accommodate over eighty guests at any one seating. In the hall were two rectangular art deco dining tables made of teak. Depending on the function, the tables were elegantly laid with bone china plates and monogramed silver cutlery when Western food was served, or Peranakan tableware when Nyonya cuisine was served. Chor Ee and Cheng Kin only formally entertained a handful of times a year — for Chor Ee's birthday, Chinese New Year, and the occasional celebration such as a wedding. For the rest of the year it was quite a lonely hall. Most meals were held in the family dining room where only senior members of the family sat together for meals. Small children ate at the kitchen table, but when there were not enough adults to fill the main table, Cheng Kin would request some of the children to fill the void. It was a privilege to be asked, because it meant the child was considered sufficiently well-behaved to join the adults.

The tone at the main dining table was formal. The table rule was that the youngest member must pay token respect by beckoning their elders to eat, somewhat like the French practice of saying "*bon appétit*". Elders could never be addressed by their given names, only by their designated title based on the nomenclature developed thousands of years before to distinguish relationships within the family. Titles were given to determine the different positions of family members, ranked according to the order of birth and between the paternal and maternal links. Elder sisters were clearly distinguished from younger sisters, direct male ancestors from female, junior cousins from senior, and so forth. If you happened to be the most junior member in the family, your nomenclature would inevitably be longer, and therefore more to memorise. When the relatives around the table were familiar faces, addressing them was not a problem. But if there was a visiting relative, remembering the correct title just to avoid the embarrassment could be quite stressful. Once the token respects were paid, the next rule was to wait for the eldest at the table to take the first crack at a dish before anyone else could eat. The elders engaged in some small talk, but the social vivacity, wit, and humour that characterise modern dining were uncommon.

In his older years, Chor Ee hardly left his room, so meals were often brought to him. Occasionally, little Stephen would end up on his lap, being fed by his grandfather. While they ate, the other grandchildren sat on the timber floor, with Cheng Kin reading them folktales. They listened intently to their grandmother reading the stories of *Sam Pek Eng Tai* (Butterfly Lovers), the tragic story of a pair of lovers, and the *Legend of the White Snake*. The stories were meant to instil values in children. As they sat and listened, they watched with amazement as their grandfather meticulously ate his fish, carefully lifting the white silky meat off the bone from the head to the tail. When the meat was consumed together with a mouthful of rice, he worked his way to the head and the fins, sucking every single bit of flesh attached to the cartilage. Once everything edible was gone, old grandfather Chor Ee picked up a kettle with hot water, poured it over the bones, swirled the plate, then drank the resulting broth so as not to waste anything. Unsuspectingly, the children sat through lessons on benevolence, righteousness, prudence, and wisdom delivered by their astute grandparents.

III

The 1930s was an age of servants in British Malaya. Homes had helpers the way modern people have appliances. As families and homes got bigger, along with furniture and other possessions, they demanded an increasing level of maintenance. Wealthy residents of Penang solved this with teams of servants. By the time they moved to Homestead, Cheng Kin ran the house with over twenty domestic helpers. There was a servant for every function. But unlike Western households of that era, the position of the domestics in Penang was not as formal and as well-defined. There was no particular hierarchy as in Western homes to determine the place of the butlers and the housekeepers. In Homestead, the kitchen was manned by a Hainanese *chompor* (cook) and his wife. The title *chompor* was only reserved for male cooks. Women who cooked were just referred to by their names. Each child had a nanny. Each couple had their own personal helper. There were underservants, a laundress, grooms, a driver, errand boys, and gardeners. There was no chain of command except for Cheng Kin, the matriarch of the house.

Most domestic helpers were sourced from Kwangtung (Guangdong) in China. When the authorities clamped down on migration into Malaya shortly after the great depression in the 1930s, a monthly quota for migrant deck passengers was created. The move forced the cost of passage upwards for male migrants from about $15 to a high of $100. Female migrants on the other hand, could enter without many restrictions and for the fee of $15. Political conditions in China had become unstable again because of the Kuomintang-Communist conflicts. A number of Chinese families encouraged their womenfolk to emigrate, resulting in shiploads of female migrants arriving in Malaya. By the mid-1930s close to two hundred thousand women arrived on the shores of Malaya. The most common way for them to earn money was to work as domestic servants. There were special *kongsi pang* (lodging houses) that took them in when they first arrived in Penang. From there, and through recommendations from friends who were already working, they found jobs as domestics for families. Their standard attire of white *samfoo* and loose black cotton trousers earned them the name black & white *amahs*. Local Chinese referred to them as *amah-chieh*. They were hard-working and completely devoted to the family. Most of them were unmarried and celibate. Their single status enabled them to live apart from their parents and family. According to historian Ooi Keat Gin, a probable reason accounting for such a high proportion of unmarried *amahs* was because they originated from parts of Guangdong where it was traditional for women to resist marriage. He writes, "For approximately one hundred years, from the early nineteenth to the early twentieth century, numbers of women in a rural area of the Canton delta either refused to marry or, having married, refused to live with their husbands. Typically, they organised themselves into sisterhoods."[33]

Cheng Kin kept a number of this *amah-chieh* to look after the children, and as general workers. Among the more notable was Ah Kooi, a gentle soul who was brought in as a nanny to look after Angela. Ah Kooi was the granddaughter of a Chinese physician who was a member of the Po Chi Lam medical centre and martial arts school in China. Her family originated from Foshan, and was steeped in the traditions of Cantonese Kung-fu, Chinese opera, and lion dance. As a child, she accompanied her grandfather to work, and this perhaps explains why she was relatively educated compared to the

---

[33] Ooi Keat Gin, 'Domestic servants par excellence: The black & white amahs of Malaya and Singapore with special reference to Penang', *JMBRAS*, vol. 65, no. 2, 1992, p. 69-84.

rest of the other servants. She was knowledgeable in Chinese medicine, could read and write, and would tell tales of martial arts master Wong Fei Hung long before any Hong Kong and Hollywood versions came to the big screen. After having cared for Angela, and later Angela's children, Ah Kooi was assigned to looking after the altars and preparing ceremonial provisions for festivals. She adopted a daughter who lived in Penang. After serving over forty years with the family, Ah Kooi retired and left to live among her sister *amah-chieh* in a *kongsi pang* on Love Lane. Another fondly remembered *amah chieh* was Ah Chan who also came from Guangdong. Ah Chan started life as a laundress at Homestead before being elevated to the post of household cook after the Hainanese *chompor* passed away. She was a hardworking and vivacious woman with a strong personality. She turned out to be a talented cook with an ability to whip up a delicious meal with just a few ingredients. After her retirement, Ah Chan went back to Hong Kong to live with her nephew. She too served the family for more than forty years.

Another conventional practice of wealthy households at that time was to adopt young girls to live with and work for the family. These girls were commonly known as *char-bor-kan* (servant girls). They came from poor families, or sometimes from the Po Leung Kuk, a girl's home for orphans and abused children. Founded in 1889, a year after Singapore's Po Leung Kuk, the Penang branch, along with the leper asylum on Jerejak Island, was one of perhaps a handful of social welfare programs in the colony. Funded by the local Chinese community, and later by the government, Po Leung Kuk was set up to take care of destitute or sexually abused young girls who had been discarded by their families or brothel keepers. The home took care of them and taught them to cook, sew, wash, and other household chores so that they would be ready for domestic service. Eventually, when the time came for the girls to leave, the home found them respectable homes to work in, while some were married off to applicants in search of wives. Cheng Kin had a soft heart and every now and again would adopt one of them to live in Homestead. She gave them board and food and a small monthly allowance. They didn't have a specific job per se but generally helped out in the kitchen prepping food, setting the table, washing up, and performing general household chores like folding joss paper money with Ah Kooi. Very frequently they accompanied Cheng Kin and the children on their outings. These girls became part of the household, some even took on the Yeap surname, while the prettier ones would normally stay on until a marriageable age and then move out of Homestead.

Young orphans adopted by Cheng Kin. Late 1930s. *House of Yeap Chor Ee.*

Ah Hong was one of these girls. When Cheng Kin brought her back to Homestead, she was only about thirteen years of age. Because she was still quite young, Ah Hong followed Cheng Kin everywhere and became her personal maid, helping her dress and combing her hair in the mornings. Ah Hong was the first person to greet Cheng Kin in the morning and the last to see her at night. She accompanied Cheng Kin to temples, social functions, the cinema, and on other outings. One of her fun outings was to cycle Cheng Kin on a Raleigh bicycle to buy the freshest catch from the fishermen in Batu Ferringhi. It was a fourteen kilometre bike ride on the coastal road. Ah Hong pedalled in front and Cheng Kin sat at the back. They occasionally stopped along the way for a breather. Once, on their way to Batu Ferringhi, the bicycle went over a bump and Cheng Kin was catapulted off the back seat. Ah Hong only realised her light-weight passenger had been thrown off when she heard faint screams from Cheng Kin scolding her from afar. They could have easily taken a car to Batu Ferringhi, but Cheng Kin's adventurous spirit often saw her opting for unconventional means. Ah Hong grew up to be a large woman, with dark skin and jet black hair. When she reached a marriageable age, she was married off to a fisherman in Taiping, Perak. She bore him a son, but increasingly dissatisfied with married life and living in a small fishing town, Ah Hong came back to live with the family in Homestead and only visited her husband and son every now and again. When Cheng Kin's oldest grandson,

Stephen, got married and started his own family, Ah Hong was seconded to become cook and nanny to his children. She gained a reputation for her no nonsense approach to bringing up children, her awesome cooking skills, but most of all, for her world-class profanity. Ah Hong had become a dear and loyal member of the family and took on the name Yeap Guat Imm. She continued living with the family until 1993, when she died of a heart failure. She had been with the family for over sixty years.

Yeap Guat Imm (Ah Hong), Cheng Kin's loyal helper. 1992. *House of Yeap Chor Ee*.

Chapter 13

A Case for Merriment

The seedy pleasures of prostitution and gambling were not the only distractions available to George Town's young immigrant men, though far from their families, and with few women to socialise with, certainly many indulged in these escapes from the dull monotony of manual labour. There were festivals to be celebrated, with special events occurring almost every month of the lunar calendar, with sumptuous feasting and drinking.

In the early days of Penang, festivities were relatively austere by Chinese standards, with celebrations centred on the Kong Hock Keong Temple. Before the fresh influx of immigrants, the island's Chinese settlers mostly originated from neighbouring territories, such as Kedah, Southern Siam, Northern Sumatra, and Malacca. Although they were not from the elite of Chinese

No. 124   CHINESE TEMPLE, PITT STREET, PENANG

Kong Hock Keong Temple or the Kuan Yin Teng Temple. The building next to it was the Chinese Town Hall, established in 1880s to take over the function of the Temple. *Courtesy of Dr Cheah Jin Seng.*

society, they were not devoid of culture and tradition either. They brought with them warm memories of village life and found common ground in practising and perpetuating customs, some of which went back as far as three thousand years. A number of the settlers took local wives, and though they adhered to Taoist and Buddhist beliefs, and ancestral worship, they also embraced much from the Malay socio-cultural traditions, particularly in terms of food, language, and attire. Over the years, as tens of thousands descended on Penang and made their homes and lives there, the celebrations became more regular and elaborate.

There were over a dozen festivals and feast days celebrated every year in China, of which half became perennial mainstays in Penang. The favourite, and most important holiday for the town's Chinese residents, was Chinese New Year. The celebration starts on the thirtieth day of the twelfth day of the old moon and ends on the sixteenth day of the first moon. In 1912, when Dr Sun Yat Sen became president of China, he introduced a number of new proposals for social reforms, among them the abolition of the traditional lunar calendar, to be replaced by the Gregorian (solar) calendar. Given that China had shut herself away from the rest of the world for over five centuries, she was not prepared to obediently hop from an ancient monarchical system to a modern republic just like that. Neither were her people, especially when over ninety per cent of them were illiterate. There were numerous practical issues to be considered. For one, how would they know which day of the Gregorian calendar to make offerings and which day should be chosen to let off firecrackers or pay respects to their departed ancestors? In the absence of the lunar almanac, how would their highly revered fortune tellers be able to advise them on the best day to get married, or open a shop, or build a house? Dr Sun's proposals were met with hostility. His government fell two years later and his orders were forgotten until 1929, when China officially switched to the Gregorian calendar. Despite this, Chinese festivals are still based on the lunar calendar. For this reason, Chinese New Year is often one or two months after the Western New Year. The celebrations usually last for two weeks, during which rituals and special days are observed.

Traditionally no one was allowed to cut their hair or shave their heads during Chinese New Year celebrations. Floors were not to be swept, and brooms were kept out of sight, as they were thought to bring bad luck. Shops, stalls, and businesses all closed for the celebrations. Many shut business for a week, some even extended to the fifteenth day, for the longer the shop was closed during the New Year, the more respectable and reputable it was. The Chinese residents in town smoked, drank, ate, and spent money buying new clothes. This was also the time when debts had to be settled and dues collected so that they could start afresh in the New Year. They gambled, played boisterous games, and of course set off firecrackers and fireworks that erupted in noisy jubilation. Throughout New Year, as well as most other festivals that mattered, this Chinese invention was fired at all hours to ward off evil spirits and bring luck; much to the annoyance of the town's other residents. Fireworks had already been around in the colony for some time before Chor Ee arrived in the 1880s. The earliest available record dates from February 1834, when fifteen chests of fireworks arrived in Singapore from Canton aboard a junk. Presumably, Penang's supply of pyrotechnics came earlier considering that it was the older Settlement.

Towards the end of the 19th century and the beginning of the 20th century Chinese New Year celebrations in Penang became more bourgeois and family oriented. Among the customs that added to the merriment of an increasingly polite society were the reunion dinners. With more migrants settling down to start a family, reunion dinners became widespread. Family members gathered to eat the yearly feast cooked in charcoal-fuelled steam-boats or hot pots. And because there were more women in town, the variety in Chinese New Year cuisine expanded, especially in the department of sweets and cakes. No less than twelve different kinds of cakes were made for the celebrations, including the ever so time-consuming *tee-koay* (sweet rice cakes), *koay-bangkit* (tapioca cookies), and *koay-kapit* (love letters). In the early decades of the 20th century the Nyonyas took over most of the preparations for New Year, sewing, washing, cooking, cleaning, and decorating. Homes were scrubbed, washed, dusted, and brightly lit. Chinese sundry-goods shops and grocers did a roaring trade at this time of the year, often by hiking up the price of goods on the back of increased demand.

More families meant more children, and where children were concerned the one indispensable treat at Chinese New Year was the *ang-pow* (red packet). Inside the *ang-pow* were gifts of money and always in multiples of two. Odd numbers were not viewed favourably because according to old Chinese logic it always took two to make a complete whole. From *amahs* to merchants, from cooks to children to salespeople, nearly everyone was entitled to an *ang-pow*. But it was the children who took the most joy in receiving the red packets. The origins of *ang-pow* date back more than two thousand years, from during the Qin Dynasty, when coins threaded on red strings were given to children to protect them from being harmed by evil spirits. When printing became popular they were presented in little red envelopes and soon the Chinese made a custom of giving *ang-pow* during Chinese New Year. Over time, the money inside the red packets became larger in value. There was a point in the early 1930s when the practice of handing out *ang-pow* encountered some opposition. The attitude felt then was that *ang-pow* was unnecessary, embarrassing, and out-of-date. Presumably because the whole world had just experienced the worst economic depression in history, critics asserted that *ang-pow* encouraged youngsters to gamble away the money they received. But very quickly discussions fizzled out, and life went back to normal, because Chinese New Year without *ang-pows* would be the same as Christmas without gifts. This ancient custom of handing out *ang-pows* became so widespread that even the other races in Penang borrowed the concept for their own special days.

The new level of domestication allowed a number of New Year rituals once performed in temples to be observed at home, such as paying respects to the family gods and ancestors with food offerings on an altar. Having a home also meant having to pay respects to the *Chao Kun*, the Kitchen God. *Chao Kun* is probably the least glamourous deity in the Chinese pantheon. He is only represented by a few characters written on a piece of wood or red paper. The fact that he resides in an obscure corner of the kitchen makes him seem unimportant, but in fact, the Kitchen God is a quintessential part of Chinese culture. Every year, on the twenty-fourth day of the twelfth moon, *Chao Kun* ascends to heaven in a chariot of smoke and fire, accompanied by the explosions of firecrackers and burning of incense paper. Up in heaven, he reports on the conduct of the family to *Thi Kong* (*Yu Hwang Shang Di*, the Jade Emperor). If the report is a good one, the household will be blessed by the Jade Emperor. Burning joss paper and red paper, offering pomelos, boiled fowl, *tee-koay*, joss sticks, and red candles are all part and parcel of the send-off. Those who don't wish to face the perils and anxiety of a bad report sometimes offer *Chao Kun* candies and toffee to seal his jaws and prevent him from speaking ill of the household. On the fourth day of the first moon, *Chao Kun* returns back to earth, to his corner of the kitchen, with a new red paper or gold painted piece of wood on the altar.

George Town's rapid prosperity at the turn of the 20th century likewise enabled homes to be more lavishly decorated. At Chor Ee's residence, all

Hap-su-ee (mother of pearl) furniture was dressed with embroidered crimson silk coverings and cushions. Silk bands were draped over doorways, new red strip of papers with well-meaning messages were posted on the doors, and large cloth lanterns were hung and lit above the front entrance. Even the fruit offerings to the Gods were decorated with cut-out red paper doilies. Indoors, lamps were brilliantly lit from hall to kitchen. Large trays of homemade cakes and biscuits, sweets, dried longan, *kuaci* (melon seeds), and snacks of all sorts, decanters of liquor, wines, and soft drinks were laid out in the living room and quickly replenished when relatives and friends, wearing their best clothes, visited to *pai-ch'ia* (New Year calls). One particular *pai-ch'ia* custom which seems to have died out, but was quite popular in the early 20th century, was the handing of red-coloured rectangular visiting cards with the name of the carrier printed in large characters. These were usually carried by the China-born men when they went around town to call on friends. The local-born Chinese had pink cards printed with *pantuns* (Malay poems) which they left at their friends' houses. A typical New Year *pantun* would read:

> *Bintang timor tergulong*
> *Rumpot tekil di-tengah hutan*
> *Mintak umor setinggi gunong*
> *Mintak rizeki sebesar lautan*

> The east star turns
> Wild grass in the heart of the jungle
> Wish for an age as high as a mountain
> Wish for wealth as big as an ocean

Pai-ch'ia went on for several days during New Year. On the 9th day, sometimes called the "Birthday of God", Chor Ee usually hosted an open house. The day was celebrated in grand fashion and visitors arrived throughout the day. The kitchen worked round the clock to ensure there were generous quantities of food to feed the hundreds of guests who sat at long tables called *tng-tok*. Sugarcane was abundant. Another special delicacy served was *leng-kok* nuts (water caltrops), wing-shaped nuts that look like the heads of buffalos. Children often found these nuts fascinating and enjoyed scraping the fleshy bits inside the shells and then linking the shells in sets of threes with sticks and threads to make them into toy spinners.

A latecomer to Penang's Chinese New Year festivities, but no less popular for that, was the lion dance. The custom dates back a thousand years, but the lion dance only became a familiar sight in British Malaya as late as the 1950s. Together with the equally popular dragon dance, it is traditionally performed to bring good luck and fortune. There is always the clash of cymbals and gongs and the loud crackle of firecrackers during a lion dance performance. Nowadays, lion dancers are engaged to perform not only during New Year celebrations, but also at the opening of new shops and businesses. On the other hand, a New Year convention that had lost its significance is *Chap Goh Meh* (Lantern Festival) which marks the last day of the New Year. Before the 1940s, *Chap Goh Meh* provided the only opportunity for bachelors to have some say in the choice of brides. Unmarried girls in the olden days were not allowed to go out except on *Chap Goh Meh* evenings, when they had their hair done, faces powdered, and dressed in all their finery. The girls rode in gharries and rickshaws and paraded around the Esplanade. It was also customary for homes to be lit up and merchants to put up dazzling lights on the streets. Boys grouped along the route would admire the beauties and cheer them on as they passed by under the full moon — eager eyes in search of prospective wives.

After Chinese New Year, the next most important festival was *Cheng Beng* or tomb sweeping day. Since early settlers were preoccupied with death, burials and ancestor worship were a focal point of the year and an opportunity to engage in traditional funerary rites. The extent of their preoccupation went as far as pre-booking their own coffins and making funeral arrangements before their demise. Some went as far as consulting fortune tellers to pick an auspicious day to dig their own graves. Chor Ee was very meticulous when it came to planning his own funeral. Years before his death, he ordered a coffin made of hard wood from China. He had one made for his wife, Cheng Kin as well. The coffins were stored at the dealer's shop-house on Carnarvon Street until called for. Every year on the sixth lunar month, the shop proprietor made sure the coffins were polished. An unfortunate mishap took place with Cheng Kin's coffin when the premises caught fire. The flames set the entire shop ablaze, including the caskets in it. The shopkeeper and the neighbours watched helplessly as the fire burnt through the roof. In the aftermath, a new coffin had to be reordered for Cheng Kin. Such was the peril of planning too much ahead of time. Chor Ee also put a lot of effort into selecting a final resting ground for himself and his family, including setting aside money in his will to provide for his wife's funeral expenses. Every year in April, Chinese families including Chor Ee's, made a pilgrimage to the cemeteries to pay homage to their departed ancestors. They swept the graves, cleared the weeds, wiped down the altars, repainted the inscriptions on the tombstones, made food offerings, burnt incense paper, and carefully cover the mound on the grave with ghost money, just as was done in China.

After *Cheng Beng*, the next great feast-day is the Dragon Boat festival, held on the fifth day of the fifth moon. It is held in honour of a statesman who committed suicide by throwing himself into the river because he was accused of treason. The local people in admiration of the minister commemorated the day of his death by an annual festival. The way it is celebrated by the Chinese varies according to the different dialect groups, but the *bachang* (rice cakes wrapped in bamboo leaves) is always featured in the festival, like plum-pudding with an English Christmas, except more so. To be without the savoury sticky rice cakes during the fifth moon season is worse than having no festival at all. Traditionally, *bachang* were cast into the river as a sacrifice to the spirit of the great hero. Today, they are offered on altars together with *koay chang* (another form of rice cake) to the gods and patron saints. They were also exchanged among friends and relatives, along with preserved ducks and sausages. For many others, dragon boat races during the fifth moon festival are as equally essential as the *bachang*. The story behind the races is that the people continued their search for the hero's body. Whatever the early form of the dragon boat ritual was, it is now nothing more than a race, with long narrow boats with dragon heads at the prow and crews of twenty-two people racing against each other to drum beats and cheering crowds.

Rather more romantic is the Seven Maidens' Festival which falls on the seventh day of the seventh moon. The festival is based on a folklore story of a weaving fairy who fell in love with a mortal cowherd. Their union was objected to by the Gods because both had neglected their duties. As punishment, the two lovebirds were transformed into stars each separated by the Milky Way and doomed to live apart. But once a year they were allowed to meet. Since there was no bridge to unite them, magpies hovered wing to wing to allow the weaving maiden to walk across to her husband. Like *Chap Goh Meh*, the Seven Maidens' Festival only became popular in Penang after the turn of the 20th century as it was mostly celebrated by unmarried women, particularly the Cantonese. They prepared elaborate offerings for the star fairy and prayed that they would find a good husband and happy marriage. Over the years, attitudes toward this festival and how to celebrate it have become somewhat ambivalent. Increasingly, the festival is becoming known as the Chinese Valentine's Day, where young couples exchange gifts with one another. During Cheng Kin and Chor Ee's time, on the eve of the festival the entire household participated in washing the floors, from the kitchen, down the corridors and all the way to the pavilion by the sea. Why that was so, no one knows, except that it was a particularly fun day for the children, who got to play with water. They created their own make-believe play, going outdoors in search of droplets of white powder to apply on their faces — their little imaginations believing that the weaving fairy, while beautifying herself for the cowherd, accidentally dropped bits of face powder on earth. But little did they realise, or for that matter cared, that what they applied on their faces was in fact bird droppings.

Perhaps the only Chinese festival with political connotations is the Moon festival, otherwise known as the Mid-Autumn festival. Originally intended to celebrate the harvest, the festival falls on the fifteenth day of the eighth moon, when the moon is at its brightest. This is also the season of moon cakes and children parading their colourful candle-lit lanterns in the evenings. According to folk tradition the festival took a political twist sometime in the fourteenth century, when Chinese civilians plotted a revolt against the oppressive Mongol rulers. For fear of Mongol spies, who were scattered across the land, and with limited means of communication, the leaders of the revolt inserted messages into mooncakes to inform families that a rebellion was taking shape. The message supposedly read "Kill the Mongols on the fifteenth of the eight lunar month," the day of the festival. And thus, the legend was born that the innocuous mooncake was instrumental in the overthrow of the Mongol dynasty.

There are a few other festivals that were prominent in Penang but not in China, and vice versa. For instance, the Kew Ong Eah, or the Festival of the Pilgrimage dedicated to the Nine Emperor Gods from the first to the ninth day of the ninth moon was popular in Penang, but not in China. Another was Chingay, a festival originally held when one patron saint was moved from one temple to another, but over time it was organised to celebrate the birthdays of Chinese deities, or in honour of Kuan Imm, the Goddess of Mercy. The procession originated from China, but it was the Chinese communities, namely the Macanese, Teochews, Hakka, Hainanese, and Cantonese communities in Penang that fully embraced it. The first reported Chingay in the Settlements was held in Penang in 1883 and was referred to by the English community as The Great Chingay, or Thanksgiving Procession. The entire procession was organised at a cost of $25,000. It was so well received, that guests came not only from the Straits Settlements but also from Sumatra and Burma, to witness the event. They all celebrated with the usual feasting and rejoicing. A huge procession, usually a few miles long, of towering multi-coloured banners, decorated lanterns, musical parties playing on drums, cymbals and gongs, and beautifully decorated chariots pulled by bullock carts, paraded through town. Much like a football match, Chingay cemented friendships and united clans, particularly those with differing views. In this regard, the clan houses often organised the event, collecting vast sums of money and planning the itinerary. But due to its prohibitive cost, it has not become a regular event on the festival calendar.

Chingay Procession, Penang. 1928. *Courtesy of Dr Cheah Jin Seng.*

Such was the way the Chinese residents of Penang celebrated festivals and socialised, particularly in the first half of the 20th century. But there was a point in time when these merriments and religious observances were on the verge of being banned, if not for a Scotsman named James Richardson Logan. Logan studied law in Edinburgh and came to Penang in 1839 with his younger brother, Abraham. A year later, Logan made a name for himself when he defended an Indian betel leaf planter against the powerful East India Company, quickly earning him a reputation as defender of native rights.

Subsequently, the two Logan brothers went to Singapore, where Abraham became the editor of the *Singapore Free Press*, while Logan founded the *Journal of the Indian Archipelago and Eastern Asia*, a periodical that promoted and brought awareness of the region, particularly the British colonies. In 1853, Logan returned to Penang to practice law, often acting as legal counsel for the Chinese community. He also took over the *Pinang Gazette*, a weekly English newspaper. Together with his brother, they used the press to influence public opinion and campaigned against Indian rule[34] in the Straits Settlements, which resulted in a transfer of the Straits Settlements to the Colonial Office in London in 1867.

But of all his accomplishments, he was most valued by local residents for defending their rights to pursue their way of life, in particular for religious tolerance. Back in the 1850s, a powerful current had been running between the Kong Hock Temple on Pitt Street and the St George's Anglican Church just down the road. When the Chinese celebrated at the temple, the Anglicans complained about the disturbances caused by the firecrackers and fireworks. To pacify the church-goers, the Chinese rescheduled their festivals so they didn't fall on a Sunday, but that failed to solve the problem, as the Anglicans also worshipped on other days. When a new law, which gave the police comprehensive powers to control processions and issue licences for public performances, was introduced, the colonial governor, Edmund Blundell, quickly took advantage of it. He got Bruce Robertson, the new deputy police commissioner, who also happened to be his son-in-law, to enforce it by refusing to approve a licence for performances at the Kong Hock Temple in celebration of Kuan Imm's birthday on 14 March 1857. This festival was at that time one of the most important celebrations on the island for the local Chinese. The new police commissioner went to the temple with a few policemen, demanding that the stage erected for the event to be dismantled. When their demands were not met, the police took it down themselves. The action sparked outrage and a riot broke out in the town and into the police station where two police muskets went missing. A number of people were injured and one was killed. The following day, Chinese businesses retaliated by closing their shops, but that did little to resolve the tensions. If anything, it further escalated the friction between the Chinese community and the police force. Less than two weeks later, the temple's leaders applied to the

---

[34] Penang became a Presidency of India on 1 March 1806.

police commissioner and resident councillor for a permit to hold another performance at a festival to celebrate the birthday of the Emperor of the Dark Heaven. The resident councillor gave his consent, but when governor Blundell heard of it, he gave instructions to the police to withhold licences for all performances until the muskets were returned. Infuriated by the decision, and with the support of their lawyer James Logan, the Chinese community petitioned the Governor General of India directly. The governor reviewed the situation and quickly rebuked Blundell for the offensive tone of his reply to the Chinese petition and asserted that licences for the celebration of religious festivals should not be arbitrarily refused. As anthropologist and historian Jean De Bernardi concluded, the conduct of governor Blundell and the deputy commissioner of police was an attack on the temple precincts. They stigmatised the entire community for the theft of the two muskets and treated its leaders with contempt and rudeness.[35]

Subsequently a commission of inquiry was appointed to look into the riots. Logan submitted a report to the commission and published it in the government records supplement of the *Singapore Free Press*. Logan's report and his fiery editorials won official recognition for Penang's Chinese communities and its diverse associations. He made a case for religious tolerance and repeatedly sought to convince his European readers "that they should show greater respect for China's ancient (albeit decayed) traditions." He argued that the "Chinese of Penang had enjoyed these rights (to preserve their civil and religious peculiarities) for over seventy years, but, moreover in Penang it was the European who was the sojourner, and the Chinese community that was more permanent, concluding that the European resident has no social privilege denied to the Asiatic." He concluded that "no group had the right to taboo public places against religious celebrations unless these were an 'offence' to the community."[36] As a consequence of the 1857 riots, the Penang Chinese gained greater recognition and tolerance for the religious practices, and a large part of it was thanks to James Logan.

Logan died in Penang of malaria during one of his exploratory journeys. As a tribute and in gratitude to him, the town's residents erected a monument which still stands today in front of the supreme court in Penang. The inscriptions on his monument reads:

---

[35] Jean De Bernardi, *Penang: Rites of Belonging in Malaysian Chinese Community*, Singapore: NUS Press, 2009, p. 53.

[36] *Ibid.*

James Richardson Logan, Advocate, F.R.C.S. F.E.S.

Whose death in the prime of his manhood they regard as a public calamity. He was always first, and sometimes stood alone, in every movement having the welfare of these Settlements for its object and the whole Colony, but most especially Penang, owes much of its present welfare and success to his personal efforts and to his unflagging zeal and great ability. He was an erudite and skilful lawyer an eminent scientific ethnologist and he has founded a literature for these Settlements as the projector and editor of the *Journal of the Indian Archipelago*. Above all he was an upright, true and honourable man, held in the highest respect and esteem by his fellow countrymen and loved and implicitly trusted by all the native races around him. He was born at Hutton Hall in Berwickshire Scotland, 10 April 1819, arrived in the Straits Settlements in 1839. He died at Penang on 20 October 1869.

Logan's memorial, in the supreme court ground, Farquhar Street, Penang. *Penang Museum.*

Chapter 14
Money Men

In the early days, the Straits Settlements' colonial enterprise opened lucrative new markets for farmers, merchants, planters, shopkeepers, and ship-chandlers, as well as creating jobs for hundreds of labourers. But it did not attract a great amount of capital into the local economy. Those who came were mostly sojourners, who at the end of their stay sent the money they earned back to their homelands. Since banks were considered essential for commercial expansion, proposals of one kind or another started circulating around the colony as far back as the 1830s. The first attempt to organise a bank in the colony was in 1833 by Sir Benjamin Malkin who arrived in Penang as the new recorder of the court in February of that year. Malkin was a fellow of Trinity College, Cambridge and had previously been a manager of the Marylebone Savings Bank in London. One of the first things he initiated in Penang was forming a savings bank for which he drew up the rules and called a public meeting to set it going.[37] We don't know if the bank went ahead or if the idea was dissolved, but a similar proposal in Singapore the same year fell through for reasons unknown to us today. Two years later, another attempt was made to establish a bank in Singapore, to be named the Singapore and Ceylon Bank, with a board of directors located in London. That proposal was not well received either. It was only in 1840 that someone made a success of it, when the Union Bank of Calcutta opened its office in Singapore, followed by the Oriental Bank in 1846. Subsequently, a number of banks came along: Mercantile Bank of India in 1855, Nederlandsche Handel-Maatschappij in 1857, Chartered Bank in 1859, and the Hongkong and Shanghai Banking Corporation in 1866. Towards the end of the 19th century, four others appeared — the Banque de l'Indo-Chine, the International Banking

---

[37] Gilbert Edward Brooke, Roland St. John Braddell, and Walter Makepeace, *One Hundred Years of Singapore*, 1921, p. 171.

Corporation, the Deutsch-Asiatische Bank, and the Nederlandsch-Indische Handel Bank. But all these banks were "exchange banks" rather than loan and deposit institutions. They matched foreign receipts with foreign payments, and in so doing reduced the need for international movements of physical money or bullion. The banks were also in a cosy position of being able to issue their own bank notes, that is, print money. Many types of notes proliferated, with the Oriental Bank being the first to issue $5 and $100 notes in the colony, adding to the already diverse variety of money floating about. But by 1897, the colonial government ended the banks' printing privileges, prompting them to put more attention on attracting deposits.

Some wealthy Chinese merchants in Singapore entered the banking world themselves at the turn of the 20th century, marking the beginning of a proliferation of locally-incorporated banks. Hitherto the banks in the colony were branches of British and foreign owned institutions, set up mainly to serve the European community. There were none that catered to the local community. Instead, the locals resorted to alternative forms of financing, including borrowing from moneylenders, often managed by members of the Indian Chetty caste, an influential class of merchants in the colony, or simply borrowing from family members and kinfolk. In 1903, a group of Cantonese businessmen headed by a Chinese migrant named Wong Ah Fook, established the first locally incorporated bank in the Straits Settlements. It was called the Kwong Yik Banking Co. Ltd and had its headquarters in Singapore, and a capital base of $850,000. The name of the bank meant "Cantonese interest" which clearly suggested the bank had a Cantonese-centric market. Ah Fook, like many of his contemporaries who amassed fortunes in the business, came from China to Singapore, aged sixteen. He made a success of his early trade as a young carpenter, then quickly developed into a leading building contractor and gambier planter in Johor and Singapore. Through his business dealings, he became a close confidant of the Sultan of Johor. Since not many Chinese businessmen in those days spoke English, a Chinese bank filled a much-needed service in the economy.

Growing numbers of merchants like Ah Fook transitioned into finance. In 1907, following their Cantonese brethren, a group of Teochew businessmen announced the formation of the Sze Hai Tong Banking & Insurance Co. As Kwong Yik catered to a Cantonese market, Sze Hai Tong similarly catered to the Teochew business community. But management was overly cautious and the bank did not grow much, remaining a rather small entity. Within the next few years competing dialect groups entered the fray with two more banks, both focusing on the Hokkien community — the Chinese Commercial Bank (1912), and the Ho Hong Bank (1917), having a combined capitalisation of four and a half million dollars. Singapore became the de facto capital of the colony, drawing hundreds of merchants and firms who wanted direct access to the banks and their connections to pools of domestic and foreign capital.

Back in Penang, the financial scene, like everything else it seemed, evolved at a much slower pace. After Malkin's attempt in 1833, it took almost thirty years before the next bank served the town's residents when the Chartered Mercantile Bank of India opened a branch along Beach Street in 1860. Twenty-four years later, in 1884, and just a year before young Chor Ee first arrived, Hongkong and Shanghai Banking Corporation and Nederlandsche Handel-Maatschappij ambled in, setting up their branches on Beach Street as well. The bulk of their business was focused on financing external trade and trading of commercial bills. Like their peers in Singapore, their clients were mainly European merchants.

With the amount of trade Chor Ee was doing, and a growing customer base, it was just a matter of time before he acted as the town's local community banker. In 1918, Chor Ee set up the first local bank in Penang, initially offering loans to his clients. In many ways, the transition was a natural one. Cash-poor farmers and the labouring classes often bought goods from small shopkeepers on credit, who in turn purchased their stocks on credit from wholesale merchants like Chor Ee. With a growing circle of customers, Chor Ee was effectively financing this chain of credit. In fact, many principal banking houses in Europe before him had a trading past; Barings and Rothschild's had their early beginnings in the cloth and silk trade. Schröder learned his skills in his brother's merchant house, dealing with sugar and acting as acceptor of bills of exchange. Coutts & Co was originally a goldsmith-banker shop. Jardine Matheson was a commercial agent of the East India Company, trading in Chinese tea and opium, among other things. And of course, the great Medici family, which ruled Europe's finances during the 15th century, derived their wealth and influence from the textile trade.

Ban Hin Lee Bank emblem designed by Chor Ee, with a circle around the Pinang tree and two merchant junks in the background. *House of Yeap Chor Ee.*

Ban Hin Lee Bank Headquarters under construction. Mid-1930s. *House of Yeap Chor Ee.*

There is no question that without the capital Chor Ee was able to accumulate from his trading activities as a merchant, he would never have had the resources to move into banking. But what helped spur this transition was his prescience in trading in Straits tin. In 1914, at the beginning of World War I, tin prices contracted. With nerves of steel Chor Ee took a particular interest in the commodity whose price was fluctuating wildly. Malaya was the world's largest producer of tin, contributing to over half of global consumption. Straits tin was trading at over £230 per ton in 1913. But the tin market collapsed just before war broke out and prices dropped to £140 per ton. When smelted tin became unsaleable in the early years of war prices dropped even further.[38] During this period, shipment of tin became dangerous and expensive, further depressing prices to historic lows. Chor Ee surveyed the weakness of the market from his shop-house godown at 141 Beach Street and decided it was time to invest in a bit of metal. From as early as January 1914,

---

[38]   K G Tregonning, 'Straits Tin – A Brief Account of the First Seventy-Five Years of The Straits Trading Company Ltd', *The Straits Times Press*, Singapore.

he bought supplies from the smelters in Selangor and had them transported from Port Swettenham to his godown on Beach Street. Entries from the Daily Imports & Exports Records published by the chamber of commerce indicate the frequency of his tin shipments in 1914 — averaging twice a week, each cargo weighing around three hundred to seven hundred piculs, or roughly twenty to forty-five tons. It seemed no one else in Penang participated in this single-minded acquisition. By April 1915, the British Government imposed a ban on the export of tin to control the commodity from ending in enemy hands. When the ban was removed at the end of the war, demand from around the world sent prices spiralling upwards to a high of £420 per ton. It was a lucrative investment for Chor Ee, one which single-handedly helped finance his banking operation. He was the only man to own 100 per cent of a bank in British Malaya, whereas the other banks were established by a syndicate of investors.

Over the following twenty years, with the expansion of international and domestic trade, seven other local banks popped up around the country. Like their predecessors in Singapore, small groups of venturesome merchants supplied capital to lead promoters based on proposals to start a bank. By then, British Malaya presented financiers two advantages — a global market hungry for its commodities, and rapid population growth from a stream of work-eager immigrants. Despite the robust business environment, a few banks got off to a shaky start. For instance, in 1914, Kwong Yik went into liquidation just ten years after its formation, primarily from the lack of experience, and partly due to reckless credit practices which saw the bank lending to its own directors. Adding to the instability was the lack of supervising bodies to regulate banking operations. To start a bank, all that was required was to form a company under the Companies Ordinance of 1889 and obtain a licence from the treasury, which was a fairly easy affair. There were no laws to regulate them and unsound practices, including extending loans to directors, were quite common. The central bank, the regulatory body of banking institutions we know today, did not exist until 1959. Disorderly financial practices and bank runs became a recurring feature of the country's economic life.

In 1929, after more than a decade of feverish lending in a get-rich-quick-climate, coupled with the global slump, British Malaya was struck by a disaster of worrying proportions. The collapse of the New York Stock Exchange sent commodity prices spiralling downwards to unprecedented levels. Unemployment reached acute levels, with no prospect of work for many people. Demand for the country's rubber and tin collapsed. The streets were crowded with unemployed rubber estate labourers, tin miners, seamen, and lumber yard workers, all looking to find work in the city as mines and estates closed. Without any unemployment benefits they turned to the Chinese Protectorate for help, but the protector responsible for the well-being of the ethnic Chinese couldn't do much except to put a freeze on the once open-door migration policy, and deported them back to China. The economy reached a point where it could no longer absorb immigrant labourers into the workforce. Business languished and ships lay at the piers with no one to buy their freight. *Malaya Sudah Habis* — Malaya is gone — declared one local newspaper.[39] The country's exports fell from $1,290,000,000 in 1925 to $931,000,000 in 1929, before collapsing to $366,000,000 in 1932.

Dr Lim Boon Kheng. *Courtesy of Family of Dr Lim Boon Keng.*

---

[39] 'Singapore a City of Despair?' *Malayan Saturday Post*, 7 February 1931, p. 20.

Almost everyone, from the richest merchant to the poorest shopkeeper, was affected by the economic crisis, banks included. The sharp contraction sent over-exposed, illiquid or badly managed banks over the edge. Among them were three locally incorporated banks that served a large sector of the Chinese population — the Ho Hong Bank, the Chinese Commercial Bank, and the Oversea-Chinese Bank. Combined, their total paid-up capital and reserves amounted to over $12.9 million, with fourteen branches in Malaya, China, Java, and Rangoon. To allow these institutions to collapse would be devastating to Chinese enterprises and the community at large, particularly depositors, some of whom had kept their life savings with them. A proposal, led by a few promoters including Dr Lim Boon Kheng — who himself was a shareholder of two of the banks — was put forth. The idea was to merge the three ailing banks to form a stronger and more resilient institution. Born in 1869 and brought up in Singapore, Dr Lim was an extremely influential figure in the Straits Chinese community. After earning his medical degree in Edinburgh University, he became active in business and politics. He was, among others, a founding member of the Straits Chinese Chamber of Commerce and a member of the Straits Settlements Legislative Council. The amalgamation, Dr Lim and the promoters stressed would create economies of scale and consolidate costs, and their combined resources would put the merged bank in a much stronger position to serve its clients' interests. But the new entity could not function without a fresh injection of capital to haul it back from illiquidity. Dr Lim went about enlisting new investors from the financial community. Almost as fast as panicked depositors withdrew their savings, a cool and calm Chor Ee stepped in to take a large stake in the new bank, consequently helping to restore confidence. A new board was appointed and a long list of guidelines was put in place to create a bank that could rein in irresponsible lenders and stabilise the community's financial system. On 1 January 1933, the newly merged entity was launched as the Oversea-Chinese Banking Corporation Ltd (OCBC). Chor Ee became the third largest shareholder and a director of OCBC, as it is known today.

When the depression passed Chor Ee had emerged as the merchant-banker of Malaya. Thrifty and clever with his money, newspapers sang praises of this sixty-something year-old man, once a poor itinerant barber who worked the streets of George Town. *The Sunday Tribune* in 1934 said: "A man of humble birth, Mr Yap Chor Ee, one of the wealthiest and most influential Chinese in Malaya, came to this country in the olden days and by dint of hard work and persistence built up a fortune." In the same year, the *Pinang Gazette*, while paying tribute to Chinese enterprises, wrote a piece about his property development project along China Street Ghaut: "The erection of these modern offices and godowns, adjoining the Yeap Chor Ee Building facing the Railway Station were started when the depression was at its zenith but it showed Mr. Yeap Chor Ee's complete confidence in the future of this country and in Penang in particular. Mr. Yeap Chor Ee is now easily the largest land-owner in Penang." Having experienced the fragile and risky nature of the banking industry, Chor Ee came out of the depression eager to restructure his own enterprise. From OCBC's amalgamation he witnessed how banks could be strengthened to weather crises. There was another reason prompting him to restructure. Even though Ban Hin Lee's banking operations were relatively unscathed throughout the slump years, Chor Ee was concerned about personal liability and issues of operating a sole proprietorship, which was essentially what Ban Hin Lee was. Chor Ee ran and owned his entire business empire by himself and was also personally responsible for all its debts. There was no legal distinction between him as the owner, and the business entity.

In 1934, when Tan Kah Kee, a highly respected merchant and community leader in Singapore, struggled to keep his business empire afloat and was forced to liquidate, the country's Chinese community was in shock. Kah Kee was a public benefactor, not only because he created an industry which gave employment to over four thousand people, but also because of his generosity to various charities. Students, educationists, industrialists, housewives, and the proverbial man on the street were worried about the financial positions of the university and schools he established. To assure them, Kah Kee avowed that since "Tan Kah Kee & Co was a limited corporation, its collapse did not alter very greatly his personal situation, and that he had made ample provisions for the maintenance of the university and the schools in the form of immovable property."[40]

Kah Kee's bankruptcy prodded Chor Ee into action. He hired a young man by the name of Walter Lim Kho Leng to help with the reorganisation. Walter was the third son of Dr Lim and had been working in the Penang branch of OCBC where Chor Ee spotted his strong work ethic and clear knowledge of finance. Upon joining as manager in 1935, Walter assisted with the conversion of Ban Hin Lee into an incorporated company, which limited Chor Ee's

---

[40] 'Chinese Topics in Malaya', *The Straits Times*, 18 September 1934, p. 18.

liabilities in the event of a lawsuit. It was renamed Ban Hin Lee Bank, Ltd. (BHLB). Chor Ee also made his three sons, Lean Seng, Kim Hoe, and Hock Hoe and his nephew Swee Ark, directors of the bank, with Chor Ee acting as chairman of the board. He allocated 1,500 shares to his two older sons, Lean Seng and Kim Hoe; 1,000 shares to his two younger sons, Hock Hoe and Hock Hin; 500 shares to both his son-in-law and nephew, Hock Siew and Swee Ark; and 8,000 shares to himself. He also allocated 6,000 shares to a collective group comprising of himself, Cheng Kin, and their four sons. The bank then acquired 86 Beach Street from Chor Ee as its headquarters, and the Singapore branch properties on Boat Quay. Over the following year, Walter was sent to Singapore to set up the branch there. BHLB quickly expanded its scale of services, including establishing connections with Japan, Java, and New York to operate a foreign exchange business. Chor Ee kept his credit under tight control, following conservative precepts of lending against the best collateral and lending on shorter-term credits (overdrafts) of not more than 12 months. The bank also adopted prudent internal measures of making allowances for general and bad and doubtful debts provisions. When it came to investing the bank's own money, Chor Ee favoured cautious capital-preserving vehicles like real-estate or straight up fixed deposits. Much to the chagrin of his shareholder sons, most of the bank's profits were ploughed back into real estate rather than distributed as annual dividends. Chor Ee also managed his liquidity and made the best use of cash by depositing with OCBC, where he, as one of the largest shareholders, received an extra half a per cent more on fixed-deposits.

By the end of 1938, when the last brick was laid, BHLB shifted its operations into its spanking new headquarters designed by Messrs. Stark & McNeil. The bank building finally completed Chor Ee's row of buildings fronting China Street Ghaut running west from Beach Street all the way to Weld Quay. A staff reporter from *Sunday Gazette* wrote: "To Mr Yeap Chor Ee, the owner of the new Ban Hin Lee Bank Buildings at the junction of China Street Ghaut and Beach Street, its completion must have been a dream come true." The reporter went on to add: "Chor Ee's financial rise has made him the wealthiest man in Penang and probably one of the richest in Malaya." The over-enthusiastic reporter also took a shot at estimating his net worth and claimed that he once recalled "Chor Ee signing a bail bond in the police court where he put his worth down at $8,000,000. The magistrate and clerks rubbed their eyes when they saw the document. Since then, his fortune must have trebled."[41] The reporter was probably right in pointing out that opening his bank headquarters was a dream come true for Chor Ee, but he might have erred in his estimation of Chor Ee's net worth. No one really knew how much Chor Ee was worth, except the man himself, and surely, he would not disclose the true amount, not least to a policeman.

What was certain was that BHLB's new headquarters transformed the banking experience for the town's Chinese residents. Instead of the long, dark, narrow shop-house environment, the new building offered levels of convenience and a sense of excitement previously unknown. Standing guard at the main entrance was Seraj Din, the bank's Bengali security guard, who also doubled as doorman. Compared to the shophouse-styled bank, the interior of the hall, with its high ceilings and marble floorings, exuded a whiff of grandeur. It boasted long wooden teller counters and extra staff to facilitate speedier banking transactions during peak periods. The building also possessed a vault the size of a room, to protect valuables against theft, fire, and disaster. For the first time, the local merchant community could safely stash away their valuables. But what truly distinguished the bank's headquarters was that it stood back to back with Chor Ee's two fortress-like godowns packed full of tin slabs on China Street Ghaut. The traditional Chinese view of wealth was based on ownership of physical assets, and to many savers the notion of having their money backed by assets of such magnitude certainly gave them a deep sense of security. Who would have thought an illiterate Chinaman like Chor Ee could have applied the concept of branding in building trust back in those days.

The bank's official hours were from 10 a.m. to 3 p.m., but being family owned, Chor Ee was quite flexible with the opening hours, which could sometimes be at 7 a.m., or on a Sunday if a customer needed to deposit or withdraw funds. Board meetings were held three to four times a year, always at the headquarters and often at 2.30 p.m. in the afternoon. A common practice among banks of that period was to close their accounts every day by settling up with one another directly. When the claim cheques came in, they worked out how much was owed to the other banks and drew a cheque, or sometimes packed a stack of notes to settle the accounts. The clearing came in around 3 p.m. and settlement was usually done by 4 p.m. — runners and messenger boys scuttling hurriedly about the town with stacks of money or piles of

---

[41] 'Penang's Millionaire's Dream Come True', *Sunday Gazette*, 15 October 1939.

Completed headquarters of Ban Hin Lee Bank on Beach Street. 1938. *House of Yeap Chor Ee.*

The spacious banking hall of the new headquarters. 1938. *House of Yeap Chor Ee.*

cheques to settle the accounts. The central clearing system of the modern day only appeared in the country's banking scene in the early 1960s, which then enabled clerks to do in minutes what had previously taken hours.

There were about fifty staff working in both the Penang and Singapore branches. Most started as messenger boys who worked their way up to becoming clerks. Many of them were also kinsmen from the same village, relatives of sorts, or Hokkiens from the same province. Yap Siong Eu, a distant relative of Chor Ee who apprenticed as a clerk in the mid-1930s, recounted his days at the bank. On his first day, Chor Ee gave him a cup of *kopi-o* (black coffee) which was considered quite a big deal for a young apprentice, particularly so when Sir Malcolm MacDonald, the governor-general, also received an almost on par gesture of a cigar and *kopi-o*. Chor Ee was not known to be lavish with gifts. He was quite unlike the charming Tiong Ham who kept bales of expensive batik sarongs which cost around twenty five dollars each in his office. When important foreign visitors called on him, he would generously distribute them — much to the delight of the visitors' wives.[42]

Young Siong Eu was given an allowance of $10 a month. By Western standards, his salary seemed paltry, but the Chinese practiced a commercial custom which European businesses were not familiar with or had not yet adopted at that time — the bonus system. No one knows when the bonus system was invented but it was common for Chinese enterprises to reward their staff members with a bonus of one or two-months' salary at year-end, depending on how well the firm and employee had performed. For many employers, the system kept employees free from dealings with moneylenders and allowed them to pay off their debts before the New Year. Of course, in today's corporate world, bonus compensation has outlived its original intention. In addition to bonuses, other perks which Chor Ee offered employees who were relatives, were room and board, monthly hair-cuts, and at year-end, a suit and a pair of shoes. Cheng Kin saw to these. She would also organise a special *guik-buih* (month-end) dish to be sent to all the staff to enjoy, including the ones in Singapore. Lunch and dinner for staff were provided by the bank and were comprised of four dishes, usually a meat dish, a fish dish, two vegetables, and a soup dish. It was substantial, simple,

---

[42] Hui-Lan Koo (Madame Wellington Koo), *An Autobiography, As Told To Mary Van Rensselaer Thayer*, New York: Dial Press, 1943.

Staff of Ban Hin Lee Bank, Penang. 1939. *House of Yeap Chor Ee.*

wholesome food. Chor Ee ate with the staff at lunchtime. The meals were prepared by Homestead's Hainanese *chomphor* and brought to the bank in tiffin carriers on a daily basis. Tea was available throughout the day, kept warm in woollen cushion baskets. If the employee was prudent and saved his earnings with the bank, he received a special interest rate of between 6 per cent and 12 per cent. There was also an understanding that in times of need, the bank would extend an advance to an employee.

In Penang, customers of the bank came from a cross section of the community, mainly because there were no other local banks. In the Singapore branch, however, most of the business came from "commission agents". These were traders who acted as agents for other parties for a 2 per cent commission, thus, in Chinese they were referred to as "98 per cent" (since they only paid 98 per cent for the goods). There were not many other industries in Malaya at that time. The clans had their own specialties — Cantonese mostly in hardware and engineering, Hokkiens mainly in trade, Teochews specialised in rice, vegetables, farm produce, and textile, and the Hakkas engaged in the supply of household goods. Since local banks tended to serve their own dialect groups, BHLB Singapore, being Hokkien-owned, focused on the merchant community.

Computation of interest rates was fairly straightforward. It wasn't set by a central bank but by the Chinese bankers in town when they came together for their monthly meetings. Loans were charged at 0.90 per cent per month, or 10.8 per cent per year — merchants in those days preferred to calculate on a per month basis. Preferential customers enjoyed a rebate of 10 per cent to 20 per cent, family members up to 50 per cent and always backed by collateral. Higher risk-profile customers paid a slight premium of 1 per cent per month. Assessing risk was Chor Ee's domain. Although Walter did a fine job of implementing measures to bring the bank's internal operations up-to-date, it was still Chor Ee's antiquated method that ruled. As Siong Eu, his clerk, reminisced about Chor Ee's credit analysis techniques: "The boss studies the character of those borrowers. It was pretty simple to him. One glance at the face and having recalled the background of that potential borrower, he just nodded his head and that was that. No loan reports to be written out. At the most, he asked me to scribble the limit on the ledger for the particular customer."[43] The "scribbling" as Siong Eu put it, was all in English. Company minutes, ledgers and accounts were all kept in the English. Official letters were in English too.

After the formation of OCBC, Chinese banks like Chor Ee's quickly evolved from being ancillary arms, created and managed by merchants to facilitate their mercantile business, into stand-alone business enterprises. More banks and more capital enabled the local economy to expand and thrive, and soon even the European banks thawed their frosty attitude towards serving the Chinese business sector. European bankers had long considered the community too difficult to deal with because they had a language and business culture very different from their own. But even they clamoured for their business by employing the services of compradors to act as go-betweens. The Indians too, who had previously depended on the Chetty system, saw the need for a more formal form of financing. In 1937, with the blessings of the Penang Nattukkottai Chettiars Chamber of Commerce, the first Indian bank, Indian

---

43   Yap Siong Eu, Economic Development of Singapore, Accession Number 000316, Oral History Interviews, National Archives of Singapore.

Overseas Bank Ltd, opened its office in Penang to develop trade between India, Burma, Malaya, and Ceylon.

If capitalism was here to stay, thought a few bankers, then banks should be better prepared for the long-haul. They had the idea of establishing a bankers' association to create a collective voice and promote cooperation with each other. The Malayan Exchange Banks' Association was established sometime in the mid-1930s (the year seems unclear), but it was in March 1935, when the association first issued a circular announcing that member banks would introduce a service charge on current accounts, that the country first took notice of them. The action met with some protest from the chambers of commerce, but the association remained steadfast and firm on their decision. The association was a precursor to the establishment of other governing institutions, such as a central bank, vital for national stability and prosperity. Finally, a stable financial structure for the future was coming into being in Malaya.

The Spoils of War

I – INVASION

At half past midnight on 8 December 1941, just hours before the attack on the Hawaiian Pearl Harbour, Japanese troops invaded Malaya. They came from rough seas, landing on the beaches of Kota Bharu, the waves capsizing some of the smaller vessels, drowning Japanese soldiers before they could even engage in battle. But any advantage that gave the 8th Indian Infantry Brigade waiting on the shore was soon lost. From there the Japanese advanced south, travelling on bicycles, with rifles slung on their backs. General Tomoyuki Yamashita led his troops in a well-organised and aggressive attack, punching through the weak lines of resistance as they moved towards Singapore. The Allied troops deployed to protect British interests of rubber and tin retreated. Some deserted. The war went badly for the British, quickly ending in a humiliating defeat. On 16 February 1942 Lieutenant-General Arthur Percival, marching under a flag of truce, called for a ceasefire. The whole of Malaya had fallen into Japanese hands. More than 130,000 Allied troops became prisoners of war. Winston Churchill described the fall of Singapore as "the worst disaster and largest capitulation in British history." It was the beginning of the end of the British Empire.

Lim Kean Siew, a prominent lawyer, and son of Lim Cheng Ean, surmised in his personal account of the war, that the invasion "opened the eyes of the West to the power of the East and the eyes of the countries she invaded... When Japan bombed the island (Penang), they did more than rip open buildings, plaster walls with bits of human flesh and turn the streets red with blood. They shocked the innocence out of our eyes. They also shook the myth of British superiority and invincibility of the Empire to their roots, destroying the myth of Western racial superiority."[44]

Penang had little military significance. Besides a small garrison the island was defenceless. The British reassured the populace that despite the Japanese landing in Kota Bharu, the British forces were well prepared, and in any case Japan was incapable of posing a serious threat since it had exhausted its resources battling China in the Sino-Japanese War. Duped by the false sense of confidence portrayed by the British, when fifty Japanese fighter planes flew in formation over Penang three days later many assumed they were the British Royal Air Force Fighters. No one expected the attack, not even the British, and everyone was shocked when the bombs dropped on the aerodromes in Bayan Lepas and Butterworth. Whether Malay, Indian, Straits-Born, or anyone else, it was the first time Malayans experienced the ravages of war.

At Homestead, the groundsmen and servants were the first to notice the aircraft. They dashed to the seawall to get a better view. As the planes flew past the bombs dropped. Thinking they would be hit, they screamed and ran for cover. But instead, the shells glided across the channel, striking the vicinity of the aerodrome in Butterworth. Later, when they recounted the story of the attack, they swore Kuan Imm, the Goddess of Mercy, had shielded Homestead, protecting its residents. Chor Ee's family frantically packed a few belongings and hurriedly made their way along the rail tracks to the hills, where they had a holiday house just above the middle station of the funicular railway. Chor Ee's son-in-law, Goh Hock Siew, his son, Kim Hoe and their families took shelter in the Edinburgh Estate in the south of the island. Homestead was empty for the first time.

The following day, the planes returned, this time targeting George Town. Pockets of the town were destroyed. Burning buildings were wreathed with dark plumes of smoke. Hundreds of undefended civilians were maimed or killed. For a split second, the dazed town folk stood still in eerie silence. Then horrific reality reasserted itself. Soon, the streets were bustling with panic-stricken evacuees streaming away from the town. The British garrison prepared to evacuate, as did most of the European community, which meant that the town's municipal authorities, police force, fire brigade, and other essential services stopped operating. Penang continued to burn through the night, with over five hundred buildings destroyed, at least a hundred and fifty dead, and several hundred more injured.

---

[44] Lim Kean Siew, *Blood on The Golden Sands, The Memoirs of a Penang Family*, Pelanduk Publications, 1999.

By morning of the following day, bloodshot-eyed looters with rubber sandals appeared, swooping in like vultures, vandalising warehouses, homes, and shops, plundering anything they could lay their hands on, furniture, clothing and blankets and food, jewellery, wrist-watches, kitchen utensils. The planes returned, dropping more bombs. More carnage, more casualties, more buildings destroyed. Propaganda leaflets fluttered down from the sky. Shopkeepers sealed their doors, equally as afraid of looters as Japanese soldiers. News came that the Japanese had sunk HMS Prince of Wales and HMS Repulse, two British warships engaged to intercept the Japanese fleet north of Malaya. The town folk were completely demoralised, but still found the strength to join the rush to hoard food — rice and sugar and flour, and especially anything that came in cans. By afternoon, the decaying corpses started to smell. Medical services were not prepared for the devastation the air raids inflicted. Doctors and nurses worked round the clock, attending to the wounded, who kept pouring in. More families fled to Air Itam, to the hills, to Batu Ferringhi, Teluk Bahang, and Balik Pulau, anywhere but George Town. Meanwhile, the British broadcasts acted as if things were under control, and people huddled around radios eager to believe any reassurances. "Three attempts were made to raid Penang yesterday. In the morning our fighters twice drove the enemy off and no bombs were dropped. There was a third attempt late in the afternoon to bomb the island but fighters again drove the raiders off before they could drop any bombs."[45] The soldiers manning the British garrison had all abandoned their posts. Almost all the European community had been evacuated due to reports of Japanese brutality towards European civilians. Only the Eurasian, Malay, and Chinese companies of the Penang and Province Wellesley Volunteers stayed behind, rejecting the offers to leave, electing to remain with their families.

Salvation arrived in the person of Manicasothy Saravanamuttu. He was a British subject from Ceylon (later Sri Lanka), editor of the *Straits Echo*, and a good friend of the Yeap family. When war broke out, he volunteered as an air raid warden. Though not a Malayan native, he stayed behind to be of use to the people in Penang. Stepping up as the town's commander-in chief, Saravanamuttu called for a meeting. Five hundred town folk turned up. They formed a committee, with Saravanamuttu as chairman, named it the Penang Services Committee, and charged it with the task of maintaining

---

[45] 'Penang Drives off Raiders', *The Straits Times*, 15 December 1941.

order. Even though the garrison had withdrawn, the British continued to claim that Penang was still holding out. Hearing this, the Japanese war eagles continued to bombard the island. To the acute embarrassment of the British administration, Saravanamuttu and his sub-editor, RS Gopal, courageously made their way to Fort Cornwallis where they lowered the British Union Jack and replaced it with the white flag of surrender, signalling to the Japanese that Penang was defenceless, to stop further attacks, and most importantly, call for an immediate ceasefire. Meanwhile the committee organised the Penang Volunteers to bury the dead, transport casualties for medical attention, and police the town to prevent further looting. They instated a makeshift rationing of petrol and rice to thwart excessive hoarding and help maintain calm in the terrified town. Saravanamuttu and his team kept the townspeople informed through daily hand-printed news bulletins. At the same time, he worked on overdrive from his office, receiving cables and phone calls, sending news of Penang's situation to the world, and somehow also finding time to cook for a large number of air raid wardens who might have gone without food for days. His boss, F. H. Grummitt of the *Straits Echo*, dubbed Saravanmuttu a "hero" and the work he did as "a job for a giant."[46] The situation in Penang would have been even more catastrophic if not for him.

In his memoirs Saravanamuttu notes that "the individual Europeans were not to blame for this craven exit. They were merely obeying the orders given to them by their leaders…But the manner in which it was done was reprehensible in the extreme. No attempt was made to inform the local residents so that they could carry on the essential services of the town. They evacuated Penang secretly by night and it led me to write in an article, headed "Penang's nightmare" published on the first Sunday after the reoccupation, "that they ran away like thieves in the night."[47]

But Saravanamuttu's story didn't end there. Just over a month after he lowered the Union Jack, there were news reports that the Japanese had appointed him as high commissioner for Penang. What propagated the misinformation was probably due to the fact that the Japanese instructed Saravanamuttu to carry on with his duties to temporarily administer the town after they occupied Penang. Unfortunately, that might have triggered

[46] 'Epic of Journalism Enacted in Penang', *The Singapore Free Press and Mercantile Advertiser*, 27 December 1941.

[47] Manicasothy Saravanamuttu, *The Sara Saga*, Penang: Areca Reprints, 2010, p. 109.

the impression he was working with the enemy. Outraged by the misleading reports, the House of Commons in London resolved to make an example of Saravanamuttu, its members proposing "to make a declaration that any British subject willingly co-operating with the Japanese in any territories overrun by them will be charged with treason when the war is over."[48] The news soon made its way worldwide. But the truth was that far from assisting the Japanese, Saravanamuttu continuously refused to cooperate, prompting them to lock him up in solitary confinement for nine torturous months in an eight by eight cell. It was only after the war, in July 1946, that the *Straits Times* sheepishly published a public apology to Saravanamuttu for falsely claiming his appointment by the Japanese, saying "we wish to state that we have since learnt that there was no justification for the allegation...Under the circumstances our headline, "M.P.s Question About Puppet in Penang" is wholly incorrect. We withdraw any implication that Mr Saravanamuttu acted as a Japanese "Puppet" or assisted them in the smallest degree and tender to him and to his family our apologies for the damage and pain in mind caused by our headline."[49] Perhaps more disappointing was that after the war, despite L.D. Gammans, the Conservative member who first raised the matter in the House of Commons, verbally promising to officially correct the mistake in Parliament, it never happened.

Penang was defeated solely from the sky, but within days of the air raids Japanese soldiers appeared. Most Malayans had never seen or met a Japanese person before, only familiar with the caricatures that politician, lawyer, and author Lim Kean Siew described. "He was a political creature of the cartoon, a short, yellow, buck toothed, bowlegged caricature of comic opera, and a figure made inhuman by propaganda which the Rape of Nanking made fearful." According to Kean Siew, when some farmers and their families first encountered a group of Japanese soldiers walking up Penang hill in their cloth peaked caps and rubber-soled boots, they exclaimed, "*Alamak!* They look like us...people were genuinely surprised to find that the British were not so superior after all if they could be defeated by such simple-looking people."[50] Farmers weren't the only ones stunned. Those in business circles were astounded by "the devastation the Japanese wrecked in the few bombs they

---

[48] 'MPs Questions About Puppet in Penang', *The Straits Times*, 22 January 1942.
[49] 'Not A Puppet Of The Japanese', *The Straits Times*, 16 July 1946.
[50] Lim Kean Siew, *Blood on Golden Sands*, Pelanduk Publications, 1999, p. 81.

dropped. They lost confidence in British propaganda about their strength."[51]

The Japanese were ruthless, particularly towards the Chinese. Their hatred stemmed from the ongoing second Sino-Japanese war, which started in 1937 and continued until 1945 when the Japanese were finally defeated by the Allied forces. China had appealed to the overseas Chinese for aid and a large group of Chinese in Malaya — mainly those born in China or educated in Chinese language — responded by setting up a Straits Chinese China Relief Fund to procure first aid and medicine, equipment and supplies for Chinese troops. Tan Kah Kee established the fund in Singapore, and his son approached Dr Lim Boon Kheng and Mrs Lee Choon Guan, two well-known and influential personalities in the Peranakan community, to assist in creating a committee,[52] with Dr Lim agreeing to act as chairman. Unlike Dr Lim, who was English educated and locally born, the majority of Straits-born Peranakan babas and nyonyas remained indifferent to the cause. They were not generally interested in the politics of China and would only contribute to alleviate living conditions in the event of a famine or flood.

The 25th Army was responsible for the administration of Malaya, but it was the Kempeitai (Military Police Corps) that people feared most.

"It was difficult to imagine what could be worse than the Kempeitai. We had never seen anything so deliberately brutal and crude. It was as if terror had been turned into a system and an art,"[53] wrote Kean Siew, recalling the dreaded police force. The Kempeitai had their offices in the Wesley Methodist Church on Burma Road in Penang, and the Fullerton building in Singapore. Answerable to the War Minister, the Kempeitai in Malaya was headed by Lieutenant-Colonel Mazayuki Oishi. They were the equivalent of the infamous Nazi Gestapo, working both as spies and counterintelligence agents. It was not a good thing to be in their bad books. They had a vast range of powers — they could restrict travel, seize food and supplies, or indiscriminately detain people without trial. At the same time, they established and cultivated a large native spy network, co-opting, but more often threatening, private citizens into becoming their informants. They brutally preyed on civilians based on the slightest suspicion, violently torturing them until they confessed or strangely

---

[51] Yap Siong Eu, *Economic Development of Singapore*, Accession Number 000316, Oral History Interviews, National Archives of Singapore.

[52] Tan Kok Kheng, *Pioneers of Singapore*, Accession Number 000232, Oral History Interviews, National Archives of Singapore.

[53] Lim Kean Siew, *Blood On Golden Sands*, Pelanduk Publications, 1999, p.103.

disappeared. Worst of all they established prisoner-of-war camps, administered in the most callous manner, often violating international agreements. One of the most powerful measures used to intimidate civilians was execution by beheading. Their notoriety first immediately spread when the severed heads of civilians, impaled on spikes, were placed at strategic points in several cities. In Singapore, they displayed them on busy thoroughfares, like bridges crossing the Singapore River, and in Penang they were paraded through the centre of the market. These were heads of looters caught by the Kempeitai, meant to teach a lesson to all. They were beheaded by one clean swoosh of the sword. It was an effective way of broadcasting their authority and immediately put a stop to looting. Their fearsome reputation enabled them to effectively carry out imperial orders from Japan and keep Malayan society in line.

If the meaning of the message conveyed by the public display of these decapitated heads eluded some, the Kempetai's next mission — operation Sook Ching — rattled even the most cold-blooded criminals. Operation Sook Ching was a systematic purging of perceived anti-Japanese elements in Singapore and Malaya. Thousands of males between the ages of eighteen and fifty were rounded up at various screening centres. They had to bring a week's ration of food to feed themselves during interrogation. Those targeted included people involved with the China Relief Fund, followers of Tan Kah Kee's Nanyang National Salvation Movement, the Chinese Volunteer Force, teachers, lawyers, and other anti-Japanese fronts. With the help of masked informers, suspects were singled out, interrogated, detained, and if found guilty, transported to killing sites for execution. In Penang, a mass screening was carried out on 5 April 1942 in George Town, and other areas of the island the following day. Identified suspects fell into four categories: those who had worked against Japan, communists, educated people, and criminals. Some detainees were eventually released, but a substantial number were executed, while others died when cholera swept through the overcrowded cells. Japan officially claimed that fewer than five thousand deaths occurred during the screenings, but Lee Kuan Yew, Singapore's first prime minister stated that "verifiable numbers would be about seventy thousand."

Not all of the Japanese were merciless and ruthless. There were those who showed compassion and were sympathetic towards the Chinese. One such man was Mamoru Shinozaki, a press attaché at the Japanese consulate before the war. Shinozaki had previously served a sentence for espionage in the Changi Prison. After his release, he was appointed a senior official of the Syonan Tokubetsu Shi (Singapore City Government), serving initially as director of education, and later as head of welfare department. When Dr Lim Boon Kheng was arrested by the Kempeitai, it was Shinozaki who told him of the military's intention to execute all those involved in the China Relief Fund. Shinozaki then broached the idea with Dr Lim of forming the Overseas Chinese Association (OCA) with the aim of getting the Chinese community to cooperate with the Japanese. But the real underlying purpose was to protect prominent Chinese leaders from further persecution by securing their release. Dr Lim, who had a nose for resolution, agreed and put together a committee comprised of prominent members of society, including Wong Siew Qui, Ching Kee Sun, Robert Tan Hoon Siang, Chen Kee Sun, Dr Hu Tsai Kuen, and Heah Joo Seang from Penang. Chor Ee was appointed treasurer of the committee, and Dr Lim was made president.

Not everyone from the Nippon Gunsei (military administration) embraced the establishment of the OCA. When a new military administrator by the name of Colonel Watanabe took over from Major-General Manaki, he got rid of Shinozaki, criticising the latter's "policy of reasonableness" towards the Chinese community.[54] His new team then demanded that the Chinese atone for their past opposition to Japan by contributing $50 million Singapore dollars towards a "Voluntary Contribution Campaign." The amount doesn't seem much by today's standards, but back then it was a staggering sum. According to historian Paul Kratoska, it was "equivalent to half of the entire note issue of British Malaya in 1938 and nearly a quarter of the gross circulation at the end of 1941."[55] The OCA pleaded with the Chinese community to contribute according to assessments of their property and other forms of wealth as determined by pre-war tax records. Many families and housewives were frightened into parting with their life savings. No one dared to object. Money, jewellery, British currency, and title deeds were handed over to Chor Ee's bank for safekeeping. Against this backdrop, dissenters emerged accusing the OCA of being "running dogs" for the Japanese. Even though he had been relieved of his duties, Shinozaki tried to help the victims as much as he could. In his memoirs, he concluded: "there is no doubt that the $50 million 'donation' scheme caused a great deal of misery. Unfortunately some of the Chinese community blamed the leaders of OCA for starting it. This

---

[54] Mamoru Shinozaki, *Syonan – My Story. The Japanese Occupation of Singapore*, Singapore: Marshall Cavendish Editions, 1975.

[55] Paul H Kratoska, *The Japanese Occupation of Malaya, 1941-1945*, University of Hawaii Press, 1997, p. 211.

was not true, but once the Japanese had started the collection, the community leaders were forced to help. They had no alternative if they wanted to live."[56] The OCA only managed to raise $28 million, the balance was borrowed from the Yokohama Specie Bank, which had to be written-off after the war. When the Japanese surrendered, Shinozaki was imprisoned, but later discharged after the Chinese and Catholic communities petitioned for his release. He was later known as the Japanese Schindler.

As for Chor Ee and his family, they were kept relatively safe during the occupation and were not regarded as enemies by the Japanese. Chor Ee had no social or political involvement, nor did he subscribe to the China Relief Fund. Being a man of enterprise, his sole focus was making money. Everyone in town knew that, even the Japanese. As tensions began to escalate between local and Japanese banks just before the outbreak of war, the financial system, like diplomatic relations, approached gridlock. Japanese banks avoided dealing with Chinese-owned banks and vice versa, resulting in a lot of discord within the financial system. A more practical approach was needed to resolve the predicament.

Most other foreign and local banks had directors who supported the China Relief Fund. As such it was unacceptable for the Japanese to deal with them. But Chor Ee was viewed as an apolitical neutral party. Much to the relief of the bankers in town BHLB volunteered to act as a clearing house to settle accounts.

Chor Ee and his family were spared a great degree of hardship during occupation thanks to Dr Lim's son Walter Lim, who was Chor Ee's bright and hardworking bank manager. We cannot be certain of the extent Walter's role played in protecting his old boss, suffice to say that when Shinozaki was made head of the welfare department, Walter was seconded to work for him. We can only assume that this connection might have given Chor Ee and his family a bit of latitude in war-time Penang.

Chor Ee's grandson Leong Sim, by then eighteen, remembered the civility of the Japanese, particularly the naval officers, when they came to meet his grandfather shortly after occupation. They issued Homestead a scroll with Japanese characters and a seal stamped on it notifying other military personnel to stay clear of the property. Homestead, the grandest private house in Malaya, was never ransacked, nor taken over by the Japanese, as happened to Kedah

---

[56] Mamoru Shinozaki, *Syonan – My Story. The Japanese Occupation of Singapore*, p. 57.

House on the neighbouring lot. Leong Sim also recalled the time when the Kempeitai officers came to personally warn Chor Ee and his family to stay indoors during Operation Sook Ching. Chor Ee's bank was never searched and was allowed to operate without any restrictions, but this might also have been to do with the fact that banking was an essential service. Similarly, the bank staff were issued with seal-stamped cloth passes with their names inscribed, enabling them to roam freely without risk of detention.

II – AFTERMATH

After the British surrendered, there was peace for the people of Malaya for a brief moment. Gone were the bombings, explosions, and the sounds of machine guns that had kept the whole country on edge. Initially the streets were strewn with debris and rubble from fragmented buildings. Pavements were littered with broken concrete and rubbish. Public services came to a halt. Portions of the town turned pestiferous. Unperturbed by explosions and bombings, flies and mosquitoes bred profusely. Shortly after occupation the Japanese appointed administrators. City officials, policemen, firemen, engineers, and contractors met to map the course of recovery. Some of the first tasks were to clean the town and restore the water supply and other basic utilities. Since fuel was in short supply, bullock carts once again reigned in the streets. Families returned to their homes in town. But they noticed a different Penang. As Kean Siew wrote, "The city no longer had its familiar noises. The cries of the hawkers could no longer be heard, nor did the ringing of bicycle bells disturb the morning calm. The city had changed. Everything had changed. Instead, it was filled with strangeness and an absence of gaiety."[57]

Through their official mouthpiece, *Syonan Shimbun* — previously the *Straits Times* of Singapore — the Nippon Gunsei sent orders for shops and businesses to resume operations.

But within less than a year living conditions began to deteriorate, dropping below subsistence level. *Syonan Shimbun* published articles about food shortages everywhere in the world, except Malaya and the rest of Japan's occupied territories, but the reality was that food and fuel were hard to come by. Before the war, Malaya imported rice from Burma, Thailand, and Vietnam, but because of a shortage of transport and fuel, it was impossible to ship

---

[57]   Lim Kean Siew, *Blood On Golden Sands*, Pelanduk Publications, 1999, p. 97.

large quantities of rice around the region. Food shortages meant prices went through the roof, and inevitably a black market surfaced. By end of 1942, as food prices continued to soar, Nippon Gunsei formed quasi-monopolies called Kumiai to purchase and sell certain goods such as rice, fish, vegetables, and cloth. The idea was to reduce wastage and control prices, but because of abuse and corruption, the Kumiai made conditions worse for everyone. Families with ration cards had to queue for hours, and if lucky might have been able to buy a few basic essentials. There was never enough to go around. Banker, Yap Siong Eu observed that the Kumiai "did not sell to everybody in the queue. [It was] just a token sale only. The rest, the main portion, went to the black market."[58] The Kumiai diverted a large portion of the rations into this thriving underground economy, because profits were greater. Daring entrepreneurs too, took to smuggling from Indonesia and sold goods on the black market. It was the illegal black market that historians believe provided the population with sustenance, rather than the nutritionally inadequate diet of starchy roots like tapioca and yams which many people had to survive on.[59] Meanwhile to counter food shortages, the administration started a Grow More Food Campaign, distributing free seeds to encourage people to be more self-sufficient. The campaign, however, failed to produce the desired results, which led the Japanese to resort to other tactics, such as cutting the already meagre rations.

Chor Ee moved his family back to Homestead almost immediately after the Japanese regime took over. One of the first things Cheng Kin did was to disguise her young servant girls as boys. Their chests were tightly bandaged, their hair cut short, and they dressed in shorts and short sleeve shirts. This was because of rumours of young women and girls being dragged from their homes and raped by the Japanese troops. Even though the house was protected, she didn't want to take chances, especially since the property next door was occupied by Japanese officers. Food was not really a problem. There were hardly any family accounts of not having enough to eat in occupied Penang. Homestead was relatively self-sufficient. There was enough space for the family and staff to grow crops and rear chickens for eggs. A pond had eels, and there were ducks for meat, a cow for milk. The sea next to the house was

---

58 Yap Siong Eu, Economic Development of Singapore, Accession Number 000316, Oral History Interviews, National Archives of Singapore.
59 Paul H Kratoska, The Japanese Occupation of Malaya, 1941-1945, Hawaii: University of Hawaii Press, 1997. p. 249.

another food source. Chor Ee's plantations also supplied the family with locally grown fruits and vegetables. If anything, the family probably had a healthier diet, with more fruit and vegetables and less sugar and red meat than before. What was absent however were spices, condiments, preserves, sauces, and anything that added zest and flavour to Nyonya cooking.

Medicine and access to good professional medical care were hard to come by. When all else failed, the family resorted to traditional Chinese medicine of two kinds: the medicinal kind, as practiced by Chinese doctors, and the superstitious kind, consulting divine spirits for help. To do that, the help of a medium was required. The spirit medium for the family during wartime was Ah Hong, Cheng Kin's devoted servant girl. When she entered into a trance, her personality took on that of the spirit. She wailed and cried, her nose running, and she repeatedly hit her thighs with her bare hands until they were bruised. While this was going on, the rest of the household remained anxious, praying that her wailing would not attract the attention of the Japanese officers next door. It was risky either way. To quieten the medium might offend the spirit, while to do nothing and allow the crying to continue might have drawn the unwanted attention of the Japanese officers. Questions were quickly asked about treatment, medication, recovery period, and so on. The whole event lasted less than thirty minutes. When Ah Hong came out of her trance she had no recollection of what happened or why she had bruised thighs. The second type of treatment was more "scientific" and based on the concept of Yin and Yang. The family used a great deal of home remedies taught to Ah Kooi, the black & white amah, by her father, who was a trained Chinese physician. The cure for flatulence was eating a spider. Dried toads were pounded into a paste to make an ointment to heal sores and ulcers. The horns of an antelope, burnt and pounded into powder, helped with rheumatism and inflammation of the lungs. But all of these paled in comparison with the ultimate home remedy of pigeon droppings infused with an assortment of herbs and boiled until the concoction turned thick black. Meant for pregnant women, the bitter vile potion was believed to contain properties similar to penicillin.

The bombing and fighting was more severe in Singapore, making living conditions tougher than in Penang. Singapore also had a larger urban population and not much land for food production. The scarcity of food meant diets of the average person became remarkably unvaried. Even though Chor Ee had a rice and sugar dealership in Singapore, he too found it difficult to get access to the commodities. The Kempeitai requisitioned the company's warehouses along Boat Quay and only retained him as storage agent for sugar and rice. The stores were guarded by Japanese soldiers who were under strict instructions to only release to authorised sellers, but when they felt sympathetic enough the soldiers poked their bayonets into the gunny sacks so that the staff could sweep the spilled grains for their own consumption. BHLB was the only bank that continued serving free meals to its staff, but their three meals soon became measly-portioned. The menu for breakfast, lunch, and dinner was the same — a string of boiled *kangkung* (water spinach) with a bit of white rice, and the water used for boiling the *kangkung* served as soup. As the diet grew duller, it inevitably prompted the staff to look for other sources of nutrition, so they followed Chor Ee's example of rearing chickens for their eggs and growing tapioca and sweet potatoes as staples. In the past, tapioca and other root vegetables like sweet potato were considered unsavoury because their edible parts grew below ground, but at times like this no one could afford to be fussy. Compared to *kangkung* the starchy vegetables were godsend for the staff. Periodically, the bank's staff were treated to food from the Japanese military kitchen, brought by one of Chor Ee's customers who was also a food supplier to the military. Whenever Chor Ee visited Singapore, the customer secretly delivered bean curd, pork cuttings, beans and vegetables, which Chor Ee shared with his staff. That probably saved them from debilitating diseases such as beriberi. Being grateful for little gestures, such as pilfered food, only underscored the appalling circumstances to which many residents of the city had been reduced.

As the war dragged on, city people had their own miseries to contend with. The problem confounding them was not that there were sporadic shortages of food and supplies, or of rampant corruption, or even of having to live off root vegetables — all of which might have been relatively bearable — but rather, the constant anxiety of what was going to happen with money. The war created shocking reversals of fortune in every band of society. In the three and a half years after war broke out the prices of goods swang wildly and the value of money fluctuated from being legal tender to illegal tender, to becoming massively inflated, then valueless overnight. The first such blow happened just a few days before occupation, on 12 February 1942. When the British sensed a loss was imminent, they hurriedly issued directives to the public requesting them to surrender things of value to prevent them from falling into the Japanese hands — cash, gold, jewellery, stock certificates, and so forth. Notes, including unissued ones, were burnt and destroyed. Coins were dumped into the sea; their weight would have been too much of a burden to transport back to London. Treasury officials closed in on all the banks to seal British notes. In normal circumstances, it would have been unfathomable for someone like Chor Ee to just hand over his wealth in return for a slip of paper, but the banks had no choice. It was a government directive. Chor Ee did as he was told and handed over a substantial hoard of gold bars, as well as cash from his bank and trading businesses. Just a few days before surrender armed escorts from the treasury collected the gold and cash and issued an acknowledgment of the amount. The angst of not knowing whether the treasury would honour their commitment to return the monies after the war, or whether their wealth would be destroyed and sunk in the middle of the ocean by enemy planes, was on everyone's mind, especially the man who had the most of it.

Panic quickly spread. In the days that followed, hundreds of traders rushed to liquidate stocks. Prices fell. Edgy traders offloaded their supplies to profiteers. Meanwhile depositors lined up to withdraw money that still remained in the banks. Siong Eu recalled that some were in such a hurry that they dropped stacks of cash on the floor as they frantically scurried out the door. The banks remained open as long as they could, until the day of surrender. When the Japanese took over bankers were issued directives to reopen, but working hours had to follow Tokyo time. In just a week, a new currency — the military scrip more commonly known as "banana money" — became legal tender in Malaya. The notes were unnumbered, unbacked, and valued on a par with the Malayan dollar. For a while, the Malayan dollar was still in circulation and used as one and the same currency. Two Japanese banks — the Yokohama Specie and the Bank of Taiwan reopened branches, and by October 1942 a number of local banks, namely OCBC, Sze Hai Tong Banking & Insurance, BHLB, United Chinese Bank, and Lee Wah Bank were extended a ten million loan from the military administration to help inject currency and resurrect the internal economy. Within a year and a half a central bank named the Nampo Kaihatsu Kinko was set up to issue notes.

Despite the rosy picture *Syonan Shimbun* constantly painted, the financial system began to buckle. In order to meet military expenses, Japan authorised Nampo Kaihatsu Kinko to print a bewildering sum of money. An estimated seven thousand million to eight thousand million dollars were printed and issued during occupation, compared to just under two hundred and twenty million dollars issued by the Malayan Currency Commissioner in 1941 preoccupation.[60] The volume of money in circulation was between thirty to thirty-six times more than the normal levels before occupation. The flood of banana money, coupled with a sluggish economy, gave rise to rampant inflation which quickly stifled banking transactions. For the first time in its history, BHLB recorded an operating loss, with loans of close to $500,000 written-off as irrecoverable. By 1943, the Malayan dollars rapidly vanished from the open market and anyone found holding the currency could have been arrested, or worse, had their head chopped off. Cheque deals soon came to a stop, with customers preferring to transact in cash. Siong Eu recalled that the value of currency depreciated so fast that there was not enough time to count. Gunny sack-loads of currency with the depositor's name written on it exchanged hands. It reached a point that the services of the BHLB became nothing but a market place of exchange. When cash became almost valueless, people dispensed with money and relied instead on barter, trading goods, with the bank's staff acting as brokers and earning commissions to supplement their salaries. The banking hall of BHLB turned into an auction room. Initially, the goods used in barter were mostly commodities, but when that became scarce, jewellery, gold-bars, the old Malayan currency, and title deeds went under the hammer.

For Chor Ee, one of his bleakest moments arrived less than three months before Hiroshima and Nagasaki were bombed. In June 1945, fearing that they were about to lose the war, the Japanese authorities haphazardly issued a policy to confiscate all pre-occupation Malayan dollars. Word got around that four banks were in possession of Malayan dollars — OCBC, BHLB, Indian Overseas Bank, and The Indian Bank Ltd. The total sum confiscated from the banks amounted to $962,627 of which, BHLB's portion was over sixty per cent, or $586,000. An order was sent to each bank demanding they hand over the currency. At first, Chor Ee refused to comply, but following threats by the Japanese, he reluctantly succumbed and handed over the money in instalments, in bags labelled and sealed with rubber stamps bearing BHLB's name. In exchange BHLB was forced to accept the military scrips which were almost worthless. After the war about $669,992 of the confiscated money remained in the strong room of the Chartered Bank on Beach Street, where the Japanese had deposited it. It fell into British hands when a Major Dickens, the financial officer of the Civil Affairs Services (Malaya), personally took

---

[60] '300 Tons of "Banana" Notes in Kuala Lumpur', *The Straits Times*, 10 October 1945.

possession of the bags on behalf of the British Military Administration (BMA). The remainder had been withdrawn by the Japanese Navy just before they surrendered.

With the help of their lawyers, Hogan Adams & Allan, Advocates & Solicitors of Penang, BHLB made numerous desperate attempts to reclaim their monies, but to no avail. In 1950, almost five years after reoccupation, Chor Ee's son, Hock Hoe made another attempt, but this time, a petition was made to Sir Henry Gurney, the High Commissioner for Malaya. The matter was passed to Mr A.N. Goode, the financial secretary who sought the advice of his lawyer Mr Shearn, and the attorney general Mr T. A. Brown. By then, the monies had been credited into the accounts of the Custodian of Enemy Property. As to be expected after such a long period, some confusion arose among the officers who took physical possession of the bags. Major Dickens acknowledged receipt of the monies in bundles bearing the bank seals, but another officer later recollected that there were no seals and that the bundles were simply marked with the chop of the Japanese Treasury. In his correspondence with the attorney general — as if finding a justification to not return the money — Mr Goode commented: "The question arises however of Government liability towards the petitioners. Let us assume that the assets remained physically identifiable up to the moment the BMA took possession. This point may take a little time to determine; but if we can show that they were not so identifiable; presumably the petitioners' case falls to the ground."[61] The attorney general concurred, and replied: "The evidence on our side is undeniably conflicting but it does not appear to me that the petitioners have a case that would hold water in court. Even if we conceded in principle the point that some bundles bearing the seals of the original banks survived through the Japanese period to the BMA Treasury, there is no precision in the claim, i.e. no evidence that the precise sum of $962,627 claimed was thus identifiable especially as the assets only amounted to $669,991.88." He further went on to explain that, "In these circumstances I agree with you that, as a matter of law, we cannot admit the claims of any of the petitioners. That is the legal position. Whether there is a moral obligation on us to refund money taken from the claimants as a body under the conditions indicated is another matter."[62]

---

[61] 'The Petition of Ban Hin Lee Bank Limited, Copy of Minutes in F.S. 3561/50', 5 July 1950, Arkib Negara.

[62] 'The Petition of Ban Hin Lee Bank Limited, Copy of Minutes in F.S. 3561/50', 11 September 1950, Arkib Negara.

The Attorney General then replied to the claimants: "Intensive investigations have been made into the question of what currency was found to be in the possession of the NPKSK Bank when it was taken over by the BMA and the circumstances in which that bank acquired any such currency. These investigations have failed to produce evidence that there was in the hands of the bank at that time any currency bearing the seals of your bank far less that any precise amount was so marked....In such circumstances it is regretted that, even without referring to the question as to whether the circumstances in which you parted with the money would give a right to demand the return of that money from the BMA or the Federal Government, it is not possible on the ascertained facts to admit your claim. You may however wish to consider whether you should make a claim as a general creditor of the NPKSK."

A few days later, Hock Hoe's lawyers informed the financial secretary that his clients would be submitting a Petitions of Right under the Crown Suits Ordinance to take legal action against the British Government. We don't know what transpired after that. Presumably Hock Hoe's lawyers lost the case, and the matter was not brought up after that.

For the people on the street, the harshest blow came less than a month after Japanese surrender. The jubilations and spirits of an elated populace were quickly dampened when the British Military Administrators hastily announced that the Japanese banana money had been invalidated and made defunct with immediate effect. It was only worth the paper it was printed on and would not be exchanged for the new Malayan currency. The news sent millions of people up in arms, asking what they would use for money. The great majority of the population suddenly found themselves incapable of buying food and basic necessities. Only a small minority who had been hoarding the former British Malayan currency had something to live off. Everyone else in Malaya however, particularly the labouring class, was left in the lurch. Even those who had kept a nest egg of the former money found it difficult to survive, as prices of goods shot through the roof after the arrival of British forces. Pork, which could be purchased at $0.35 went up to $30 within a week. The Chinese community was aflame with anger. Leaders anxiously spoke up and pleaded with the authorities to act quickly to get the new Malayan currency in circulation. As one Chinese businessman commented: "It is not the scrapping of the Japanese money that has upset people. Nobody expected that anything else would be done with it — although there were some who thought that a nominal exchange rate might be fixed for it so as to get the new currency into circulation quickly. But what has upset people is the suddenness with which this has been sprung on us, without telling us first the measures that would be taken to get the new dollars into circulation and how quickly we might expect that to happen."[63]

---

[63] 'Singapore's Currency Upheaval', *The Straits Times*, 10 September 1945.

Chapter 16

Death and Taxes

Throughout his life, Chor Ee was known to be a very thrifty man. Despite his immense wealth he hardly ever indulged in anything extravagant. His dressing was modest. He often wore a white Chinese coat with mandarin collar and black cotton shoes, not even leather. He was a staunch believer in Kuan Imm, the Goddess of Mercy, and a keen observer of a number of religious activities. He kept his diet fairly simple, slept early, and woke early. His personal frugality was legendary. His grandchildren, remembering his sparing lifestyle, noted that he would never allow anyone to waste food. He disdained activities that were considered to be an encouragement of idleness or sinfulness. Games involving dice or cards were entirely out of the question. Gambling was forbidden. Smoking and drinking could land you into trouble. Snacking outside of mealtimes was equally abhorrent to him. When the children heard the bell of the *kuih* man who came to Homestead at 3.30 p.m. daily with his cart full of treats, "they would happily flock towards the hawkers," said his grandson, Goh Eng Toon, "but when they saw Chor Ee approaching, they all scrambled! Chor Ee didn't approve of the extra meal after lunch."[64] The gates of Homestead were locked and chained by 6 p.m. and it was lights out by 9 p.m.

It wasn't only at home that Chor Ee was famed for his sparing ways. He struck many who encountered him as tight-fisted and thrifty. His employee, Siong Eu, recalled watching him pick a paper clip from the floor to set an example to his employees to not be wasteful. It was when he worked with Chor Ee that Siong Eu started using both sides of the ink blotter to save paper. Chor Ee's oldest grandson, Leong Sim, noted that his grandfather was honest, thrifty and hardworking — and he liked people to be such, regardless of whether the person was of his own blood or not. Saravanamuttu described him as the

---

[64] Interview with Dato Seri Goh Eng Toon, 19 August 2009, Penang.

"most outstanding Chinese in Penang" who had acquired his wealth "by hard work, thrift and a fair share of good luck."[65]

Lim Chong Eu summed Chor Ee up as "a self-confident man who achieved all the things he did without wanting 'money'. He was not a big spender unlike his sons and was a straight laced man who did not fool around with flower girls. He understood life well and did not need money although he was good at making it. Chor Ee did not use his wealth to become a social leader, unlike Cheah Chen Eok who donated funds for the clock tower in order to become a Justice of Peace. Nor did he use his money to engage in shady businesses. Most people who lent money used to surround themselves with gangsters, but not Chor Ee. He believed in honest hard work and as his reputation for sobriety and reliability spread, more people deposited money in his bank. He lends you money and you give back. If a man [customer] approached him with a problem, he may extend the [credit] terms. His contribution was social stability in Penang. He knew what it was like without food but made provisions to fill the gap in an honest way."[66]

We also know that apart from subscribing to a number of small charities to help restore temples, aid the sick and aged, provide relief from famine and floods, and for education, Chor Ee was not known to be a man who devoted much of his resources to social causes. However, things took a change after the war. From an extremely self-restrained and frugal individual, both in his private and business lives, he blossomed into a generous advocate of social reform. What seemed to have changed his course from ostensibly being an Ebenezer Scrooge to a philanthropist extraordinaire was a comparatively new piece of legislation — estate duty.

Estate duty in the Straits Settlement dates back to 1908, fourteen years after it was introduced in England, replacing the stamp duty which had been around since the 1880s. It was a graduated tax, levied on the amount left by the deceased. Estate duty was relatively unknown because it was intended to affect only the very wealthy, but the rise in the number of millionaires and value of real estate, had brought more families into the net in the following decades. Also by the early 1930s, the imperial government set a new get-tough attitude towards the colonies. Opium revenues were dwindling, poverty and unemployment was at its highest, and the world was faced with a severe

---

[65]   Manicasothy Saravanamuttu, *The Sara Saga*, Areca Reprints, 2010, p. 79.
[66]   Interview with Tun Dr Lim Chong Eu, 27 October 2009, Penang.

economic depression. To help plug its revenue shortfall, estate duties were raised to twelve per cent in 1929 and again to twenty per cent in 1931. When Britain went to war with Germany in 1939, another quandary surfaced: How was the government to pay for the defence of the colonies and finance its way into war? It was tempting to raise the colony's income taxes but that might have proven sticky: the income tax paying residents had already objected heavily when the government continued the war tax after World War I and it would be chancy to raise taxes again, particularly when the colony did not enjoy the same level of social services as Britain. Since the wealthy residents of the colonies arrived with nothing, and seeing how much Britain had done for them, surely it was time for them to assume some of the responsibilities to help pay imperial expenses. With that line of thought and without holding any debate in the Legislative Council or consulting the public, the wealthy residents of Malaya were slapped with a whopping sixty per cent estate duty in 1940. The new law was met with much criticism and uproar by the public across the country, calling the measure "oppressive, unjust and unfair." It was obvious that the estate tax was designed to raise money and not remake society by redistributing wealth. Distressed by what they considered a great injustice, the country's property owners spent much time petitioning the government. The basic argument against the excessively high rate was the same: Don't drive away capital. Don't cripple the country. Don't tax the residents without their consent. Don't be unfair by taxing Malayans higher than other colonies. Don't tax the same rate as in England, considering the low level of social services, the comparatively light expenditure on defence, and the comparative absence of public debt in the colony. They argued vehemently that it had taken hundreds of years to reach similar high levels of duties in England and that it was ruthless and unfair to impose such high rates within a few years in a colony which had not reached the same level of social and political development. In response to this pandemonium, the legislation was amended in April 1941 and estate duty was lowered from sixty to forty per cent. It was still relatively high but before anyone could protest, the war reached the shores of Malaya. Estate duty was side-lined — for a while.

Chor Ee's first response when the amended rate was announced at forty per cent was that it was perhaps time to distribute his wealth. How else would a man of such a colossal fortune avoid giving almost half his assets to the government? Forced sale or break-up of the estate was not a practical option simply because he owned so many properties. His estate alone could have easily driven down real estate prices. Chor Ee promptly called for a meeting with his directors the following month in May 1941. For the first time in the bank's history, a dividend of five per cent was paid out to all its shareholders. After the war ended, estate duties came back to haunt and trouble the minds of the propertied and the rich. A month after reoccupation on the 5th of September 1945, the Estate Duty Ordinance was promptly brought into effect. Chor Ee was approaching eighty. He continued his benevolent spirit towards his family by paying fees, again for the first time in the bank's history, to all his directors. He added an extra month's bonus for all his staff, and splashed out on a lavish three-day birthday celebration for himself the following year. But that didn't solve the estate duty predicament. Divesting himself of his properties was out of the question. The world was still licking its wounds from the war, the money situation in Malaya had not been resolved, people were mostly illiquid. The political situation in Malaya had turned hazy, resulting in civil unrest that deteriorated into a full-scale anti-colonial insurgency. To this litany of trouble was the money the Japanese confiscated from his bank – over half a million dollars — by which the British would not return. When Chor Ee died, the British would take another massive chunk from his holdings, hence his focus on benevolence and philanthropy.

Two years later, after the reinstatement of estate duties, the authorities gleefully announced that since their decision to raise rates, estate duties had contributed significantly to government coffers, this without overstretching the purses of the masses, but at the expense of a small wealthy minority. For context — death duties in America and Britain today only contribute about one per cent of government revenues. But back in the late 1940s, estate duties raised over half of total government revenues for British Malaya, essentially replacing opium revenue as the administration's main source of income. Trailing in second place were proceeds from gambling, which often accounted for thirty to forty per cent or revenue, while corporate taxes were the smallest source, at less than three per cent of total revenue. The Chinese topped the charts in terms of contributing communities, providing about half of duties, followed by the British Europeans with about a third, the Indians contributed about an eighth, and the Malays one twentieth.[67] When two Chinese brothers died in 1942 and 1949, their duties alone accounted for about half of estate duties collected that year, which clearly points to one fact — a handful of

---

[67] 'Most Death Duty Chinese', *The Straits Times*, 12 April 1949, p. 4.

individuals could have a huge effect on the country's financial position. The estates of the two brothers were assessed at three and a half million, of which duty paid was close to one and a half million. Chor Ee's estate was worth substantially more. Aside from banking and other businesses, his assets included over a hundred properties, as well as huge tracts of land, company stocks, liquid assets in cash, and other immovable properties. His fortune would have easily outstripped his nearest rivals. After Chor Ee died in 1952, at least one journalist estimated the net worth of the towkay with the "touch of Midas" at over $100 million.[68] The year before that, another suggested he was "easily the wealthiest man in the country."[69] Needless to say, it would have been of great public interest, and a tax bonanza for the government, if this remarkable man and his enormous estate was assessed and taxed on his demise. Taxing the estates of the rich would generate enormous revenues which could be used to improve council services, infrastructure and education in Malaya, but what if part of the revenues were repatriated back to the Colonial Office in London?

Chor Ee's friend Tan Cheng Lock suggested that what was needed was proper estate planning. Born to a Straits Chinese family of wealth, Cheng Lock was a rubber planter who entered public life in the early 1910s as council commissioner and a justice of peace in his hometown, Malacca. Ten years later, at the age of forty, Cheng Lock was appointed a member of the Legislative Council of the Straits Settlement. It was around this time he delivered his historic speech on a politically and territorially united Malaya. His candidness and eloquence earned him the nickname the "silvery-tongued" councillor, while his ardent support for reforms, such as legislation for monogamous marriages, vernacular education, citizenship, and immigration, made him a hero among the grassroots. Chor Ee got to know Cheng Lock when both men served on the board of the newly merged OCBC bank in 1932. Ever since, they had confided in each other on banking, legal, and political matters. When the war began, Cheng Lock moved his family, and lived in exile in India. There, he would be deeply influenced by the struggles of Gandhi and Nehru, and their fight to gain independence. In fact, throughout the colonies, the reaction to Gandhi and Nehru's success was an outburst of discontentment against the colonial system. One by one, the colonies sought

---

[68] 'Towkay Chor Ee's secret yielded him $100 million', *The Straits Times*, 1 June 1952.
[69] 'Mr Yeap Chor Ee's Birthday', *Singapore Standard*, 2 October 1951.

Tan Cheng Lock. Late 1940s. *National Archives of Malaysia.*

their independence.

After the war, Cheng Lock returned to Malaya and found his patriotic energies rekindled by Chor Ee's humanitarian drive. Chor Ee was aware of Cheng Lock's ideas of an Independent Malaya and Cheng Lock was mindful of Chor Ee's concerns with resolving his vast estate. They corresponded by mail and often through phone calls. Goh Hock Siew, Chor Ee's son-in-law, drafted the letters in English on his behalf and read out Cheng Lock's letters to him in Chinese and sometimes Malay. They cordially sent gifts to each other — sometimes baskets of rambutans, bags of *pulut* rice, and once in a while, vitamin pills. On special occasions, they requested the pleasure of each other's company by sending dinner invitations. Cheng Lock became Chor Ee's legal angel, and it was he who recommended Rodyk & Davidson, a legal firm based in Singapore, to help Chor Ee plan his estate and draft his will.

Established in 1861, the firm was one of the oldest in Malaya, specialising in handling trusts and estates. Coincidentally, it was founded by the same Bernard Rodyk who once had his law firm along Beach Street in the 1850s. Over the next year or so, Chor Ee travelled back and forth between Penang and Singapore, meeting with his lawyers to discuss his thoughts, concerns, and wishes. With characteristic precision, they drew up a well-thought-out will that involved the setting up of two main trusts — an endowment trust, which was charitable in nature, and a residuary trust, which provided comfortably for his beneficiaries for generations. He also made provisions for his loyal employees, funeral expenses for both he and his wife, repairs and maintenance of his house in China, ancestral worship and *sinchoo-pai* (ancestral tablets) rites, among others. He put in place structures to safeguard the interests of the people he loved. Meant for charitable purposes, so that part of the estate could be exempt from duties, Chor Ee bequeathed a number of prime assets to the endowment trust, which included Homestead and his real estate along China Street Ghaut. More importantly, the endowment trust allowed Chor Ee to have the final say on how his wealth should be used, rather than allowing the government a free hand on his entire estate. Chor Ee also made provisions to pay the remaining duties on his estate. Throughout the drafting process, Cheng Lock was by his side, reading over and carefully explaining to Chor Ee, line by line the content of the will and how it functioned.

In the meantime, patriotic morale got a boost when the Carr-Saunders Commission issued a report which recommended the immediate establishment of a University in Malaya to prepare the country for self-government. Before World War II, there were only four universities in the colonial empire: Malta, Jerusalem, Ceylon, and Hong Kong. Malaya had the King Edward VII Medical College (1905) and Raffles College (1929) but neither had university status. According to Anthony Stockwell, a leading historian on British imperialism and decolonisation in Southeast Asia, the "British reluctance to develop higher education was influenced by current principals of colonial government, previous experience in India, contemporary attitudes to race and constant financial constraints ... They regarded university expansion in India since the mid-nineteenth century as a mistake .... Indian universities were blamed for the production of numerous overqualified, unemployable, politically ambitious and intractable young men."[70]

But things took a turn when rising political consciousness in the colonies after the war spurred the Colonial Office to reappraise their policies. The commission was chaired by Sir Alexander Carr-Saunders, the architect of colonial universities, who toured Singapore and the Malayan Union in April 1947 with the commissioners, visiting several educational and research establishments. And after much deliberation, they agreed on a plan for a university by merging the King Edward VII College of Medicine and Raffles College in Singapore. The recommendations were supported by the Legislative Councils in Singapore and at the Federal level. Through Cheng Lock's suggestion, Chor Ee immediately agreed to donate $100,000 to the establishment of the country's first university, The University of Malaya.

In August 1949, a month before the inauguration of the university, Malcolm MacDonald, the commissioner general, held a tea party in honour of Chor Ee and Lim Lean Teng, the initial donors to the university. Lim Lean Teng was a land proprietor and Kedah rubber planter who donated $50,000 to the fund. In handing the cheque over, Malcolm MacDonald noted that Chor Ee had "become the pioneer leader of all the great benefactors of the University." To which Chor Ee replied in Hokkien, that he was happy to donate to the cause as it "means that the boys and girls here will not have to go to England or elsewhere for higher studies but will do so in Malaya."[71] He might not have had the eloquence of a seasoned orator, nor the grace and articulateness of a statesman, but he regarded higher learning as a beacon of

---

[70] AJ Stockwell, 'The Crucible of The Malayan Nation: The University and the Making of a New Malaya. 1938-62', *Modern Asian Studies*, 2008.

[71] 'Mr Yeap Chor Ee's "Princely Gift" To University', *Straits Echo*, 20 August 1949.

enlightenment for a young country, and believed that a respectable university would do much to improve Malaya's reputation post-Independence. The amount was the first biggest individual gift to the university endowment fund. When the university was short of funding the following year, Chor Ee donated $50,000 to the university's Chinese library. Three months later, he topped the figure with another $100,000, bringing his total contribution to a quarter of a million dollars. Together with Homestead and his China Street Ghaut real estate in the endowment trust, he would be by far the largest private donor to education in Malaya at that time.

The Right Honorable Mr Malcolm MacDonald, Commissioner-General of the British Colonial Administration thanking Yeap Chor Ee at a tea party hosted by the Resident Commissioner, A.V. Aston. Also honoured at this function was Lim Lean Teng. Also present was Chor Ee's wife, Lee Cheng Kin. 1949. *House of Yeap Chor Ee.*

Yeap Chor Ee handing a gift of $100,000 to the Right Honorable Mr Malcolm MacDonald, Commissioner-General of the British Colonial Administration, for the University Malaya Endowment Fund. 1949. *House of Yeap Chor Ee.*

In recognition of his magnanimous contributions, Chor Ee was granted approval for a private burial ground on his Bukit Gambier estate. A road next to the estate was also named in his honour. But perhaps the sweetest gesture of appreciation was from Cheng Lock. When hearing the news that Chor Ee was not feeling well, he wrote a confidential letter to Cheng Kin. In a letter dated the 6 October 1951, he wrote:

"Dear Madam Cheng Kin,

What I am writing now to you must be kept absolutely secret, and I would like you to tear out this letter after you have conveyed my message to Mr Chor Ee for his information. My motive in writing to you is to make Mr Chor Ee feel a little happier now that he is not in such very good health. I have been a little anxious about his health and hope that he is quite well now. Please ask him to take good care of himself. The news I want to convey to him is that I have spoken to the Government about giving him some token of appreciation by Government of his services to the country during an active business career covering a period of more than half a century. Government have intimated to me that they will do something about it, though it may not be possible to do it this year. It may have to wait till next year. However I have requested Government to try and do it this year if possible. Please keep this matter absolutely secret.

With my very best wishes to you both and the whole family,

Yours sincerely, TCL."

Cheng Kin replied immediately, thanking Cheng Lock for the news to cheer up the old man. A few days later, on 13 October, Cheng Lock responded with another letter informing the family of the assassination of Sir Henry Gurney, the high commissioner to Malaya, by communist insurgents while on his way to Fraser's Hill. Cheng Lock wrote — "The subject matter to which I referred in my letter to you dated 6th October, 1951, was discussed between me and Sir Henry Gurney who was really a great man, unfortunately, met with a tragic death on the 6th October, 1951. I hope Mr Yeap Chor Ee and I will be able to meet soon. In Singapore or Penang, as we have not seen each other for a long time."

Chor Ee passed away from pneumonia early on a Monday morning on 26 May 1952, eight months after Sir Henry's assassination. Chor Ee was 83 years

Yeap Chor Ee and Aw Boon Haw, the "Tiger Balm King", at the opening of Phor Tay insitituition, Penang in 1950.
House of Yeap Chor Ee.

old. He had been in failing health the previous weeks, but continued to go to work until the Friday before his demise. Cheng Kin kept her promise, and her correspondence with Cheng Lock was never brought up again — that is until recently, when it was discovered in the archives of Singapore's Institute of Southeast Asian Studies library, seventy years after Chor Ee's demise.

The day after Chor Ee's death, newspapers across the country announced that "The G.O.M. (Grand Old Man) of Penang is dead." Messages of condolence poured in from all over. Old business associates in England, India, Burma, and Indonesia wrote and paid tribute. His funeral was one of the grandest Penang had seen for a while. His body was placed in a huge coffin adorned with all the trappings of traditional Chinese customs and carried in the *leng cheng* (funeral hearse). Accompanied by several bands, over a thousand representatives from the Yeap Kongsi, Phor Tay Nunnery, Penang Rubber Trade Association, Chinese Club, Chinese Club Football Team, and a host of schools and other associations, formed a procession over a mile long. Scrolls, banners, and wreaths were carried by hundreds of men, women, and children. A mounted rider dressed in white, rode a grey polo pony alongside the *leng cheng*, followed by Chor Ee's old Daimler, which was heavily decorated with flowers and had a large framed photo of him placed on the front. Leading the procession were his sons, followed by the family in mourning clothes. Prominent politicians, including Cheng Lock and leaders from the ranks of business and the professional classes, were also well represented. Starting from Homestead and pacing along the streets of George Town, the procession passed his bank on Beach Street, before proceeding to the burial grounds in Bukit Gambier. The St John's Ambulance was on duty. The Malayan Film Unit filmed the event from start to finish, and several other cine-cameramen filmed sections of it. Lines of people formed on the streets to pay their last respects. Chor Ee was laid to rest on a hill overlooking his bank, the town, and the sea. Surrounding his large tomb were trees, with the hills of Penang as the backdrop, his final resting place meeting all the requirements of Chinese geomancy.

Chor Ee's death marked the end of a remarkable chapter in history. Five years later, Malaya gained independence. Large-scale Chinese migration into Malaya bottomed out by the mid-1950s. By then, as many as seventy per cent of the Chinese diaspora lived in Southeast Asia. If Singapore had not separated from Malaysia in 1965 to become a sovereign state, Malaya would have had the largest overseas Chinese community in the world. The British Empire was on the decline, and not for another generation, by which time the world had changed, would we see China opening its doors to the rest of the world again.

Cheng Lock became one of the founding fathers of modern-day Malaysia. University Malaya continued to expand, and in 1959 divided into two autonomous campuses, one in Singapore, the other in Kuala Lumpur. It counted among its alumni four Prime Ministers of Singapore and two Prime Ministers of Malaysia and countless leaders in politics and business.

A new generation of socialists and activists came together to provide a political platform and improve working conditions for the working class. Penang's free port status was stripped by the Federal Government in 1969, leading to Penang's economy sliding into a deep recession. Beaten by a sluggish economy, its populace would leave the island in search of better job prospects elsewhere. This triggered the state government to transform its economy from trade and agriculture to industry. Through the creation of the country's first Free Trade Zone, the revitalisation soon created employment. All these developments took place on the large strip of land on the south-eastern corner of the island that once formed part of Chor Ee's estate.

By 1991 estate duty was abolished.

Cheng Kin took over the helm of BHLB as chairperson. After her death in 1977, at eighty years of age, the family continued to manage the bank until the year 2000, when a government initiated consolidation plan forced the merger of BHLB with Southern Bank, before being acquired by CIMB Bank in 2006. In the same year, Chor Ee's grandson, Stephen, vested Homestead and the properties in his endowment trust to help establish the Wawasan Open University and provide a campus for Disted College, the first private tertiary institution in Penang. By doing so, Stephen would have fulfilled his

Yeap Chor Ee. Late 1940s. *House of Yeap Chor Ee.*

grandfather's final wishes.

When I reflect on my great-grandfather's life, and the historic legacy he left behind, it is remarkable to consider that an illiterate seventeen-year-old could have amassed one of the greatest individual fortunes in Malaya. But despite his own personal lack of education he would have agreed with educational reformer Horace Mann that "education is the great equaliser of the conditions of men."

He was undoubtedly an unlikely hero, willingly giving away so much of his fortune to support institutions that would help others help themselves. He was a pragmatic visionary, at odds with a materially-obsessed age. In the many years it took to write this book I have tried to understand his thinking. I have come to realise that for Chor Ee money was only ever a means, never an end.

Glossary of Non-English Terms

Agak-agak	Thereabouts
Akua-kia	Precious son
Almirah	Anglo-Indian free-standing cupboard
Amah-chieh	Black & white amah
Ang-mooi	Heaven and Earth Society (*Tiandihui*)
Ang-pow	Red packet given out during Chinese New Year (*Hongbao*)
Ark-tau	Duck broth
Baba	Male descendants of Chinese migrants who came to the Malay archipelago
Bachang	Chinese sticky rice dumpling
Baju Panjang	Malay woman's attire comprising a knee-length tunic worn over a batik sarong.
Balai	Station
Batu	Stone
Belacan	Fermented shrimp paste
Bua-kar-na	Chinese olives
Buah Keluak	Kepayang nut
Cabang atas	Literally 'highest branch' in Malay — was the traditional Chinese upper class of colonial Indonesia
Catty	Chinese unit of measurement
Ceh-sua-kua-hai	Views of the sea from the hillside
Cha-wa	Daughter
Chap Goh Meh	Fifteenth day of Chinese New Year celebration (Lantern Festival)
Char-bor-kan	Chinese servant girl/bonded maid
Chao Kun	Chinese deity. Kitchen God (*Zao Jun*)
Chee	Chinese unit of measurement
Cheng Beng	Chinese festival. Tomb sweeping day (Qingming)

Cheng-ku	Mortar & pestle
Cheongsam	Fitting dress for Chinese women
Chetty/Chettiar	Indian money lender
Chingay	Parade held in conjunction with the celebration of Chinese deities
Chompor	Chinese cook
Chupak	Malay unit of measurement equivalent to a quart
Ciku	A tropical fruit — sapodilla
Corvee	Forced labour exacted in lieu of taxes
Gantang	Malay unit of measurement usually for unhusked rice
Giling	Grind (spices)
Hap-su-ee	Chinese mother of pearl furniture
Hoon	Chinese unit of measurement
Huaqiao	Overseas Chinese
Jamban	Toilet
Kangkung	Water spinach
Kapitan	Title referring to the headman of a community
Karayuki-san	Japanese prostitute
Kee-tong	Spirit medium
Kempeitai	Military police of the Japanese Imperial Army
Kerongsang	Ornamental brooch fastened with a clasp
Kew Ong Eah	Taoist celebration. Nine Emperor Gods Festival
Khek-pang	Boarding house
Kia	Child
Kok-ka	Country and family
Koay-bangkit	Tapioca cookies
Koaychang	Sticky rice dumpling
Koay-kapit	Love letter wafer biscuits
Kongsi	Company or association
Koyan	Malay unit of measurement
Kuaci	Melon seeds
Kuan Kong	Chinese deity. God of War (Guandi)
Kuan Imm	Chinese deity. Goddess of Mercy (Guanyin)

Kumiai	Quasi-government distribution outlets of basic goods during Japanese occupation
Kwei	Evil spirit
Lau heoh chien	Busybody
Leng cheng	Funeral hearse
Leng-Kok nuts	Water caltrops
Low yeh	Old husband
Mui tsai	Prostitute
Nippon Gunsei	Japanese military administration during occupation
Nyonya	Female descendants of Chinese migrants who came to the Malay archipelago
Pai-ch'ia	New Year calls
Pantun	Poem (Rhyme)
Passenstelsel	Laws related to travel movements of the Chinese in the Dutch East Indies
Pikul/ picul	Asian unit of measurement
Phenta	A distinctive headwear of a Parsee man
Por-tiah, ting-wur	Ceramic bowl mender
Pulut	Sticky rice
Punkah	A large cloth fan on a frame suspended on the ceiling, moved backwards and forwards by pulling a cord.
Rempah	Spiced paste (for cooking)
Rottan	Rattan
Regie	Government monopoly used chiefly as a means of taxation
Samfoo	Every day attire for Chinese in south china comprising an upper garment (*sam*) and a pair of trousers (*foo*)
Sam Pek Eng Tai	Chinese folklore — Butterfly Lovers
Sambal	Spicy paste
Santan	Coconut milk
Sar Hor Fun	Chinese fried noodles

Sarong Kebaya	Outfit associated with the women of the Peranakan community made up of a lightweight embroidered blouse worn over a camisole and paired with a sarong skirt.
Seh-Ee	secondary wife
Shen	Good spirit
Sinchoo-pai	Ancestral tablet
Sinkhek	Newcomer
Syonan Shimbun	Japanese newspaper during occupation (previously Straits Times of Singapore)
Syonan Tokubetsu Shi	Singapore City Government during Japanese occupation
Tahil	Chinese unit of measurement, often known as tael.
Tee-koay	Sweet rice cakes
Thi Kong	Chinese deity. Yu Hwang Shang Di (Jade Emperor)
Tng Sah	Traditional Chinese dress worn by men
Tong soo	Chinese almanac
Tok-tok mee	Local name for wontan noodles
Towchang	Hair style of Chinese men during Qing dynasty, otherwise known as a queue
Tumbuk	To pound
Tumis	Sautee until oil separates
Twakows	A single-masted boat with a junk rig, formerly used in the Straits Settlements
Wijkenstelsel	Segregation laws related to Chinese settlements in the Dutch East Indies

Bibliography

Government Publications from Arkib Negara

Annual Reports
Annual Reports of the Straits Settlements, 1855-1941, vol. 1: 1855-1867
Annual Reports of the Straits Settlements, 1855-1941, vol. 2: 1868-1883
Annual Reports of the Straits Settlements, 1855-1941, vol. 3: 1884-1891
Annual Reports of the Straits Settlements, 1855-1941, vol. 4: 1892-1900
Annual Reports of the Straits Settlements, 1855-1941, vol. 5: 1901-1907
Annual Reports of the Straits Settlements, 1855-1941, vol. 6: 1908-1914
Annual Reports of the Straits Settlements, 1855-1941, vol. 8: 1922-1926
Annual Reports of the Straits Settlements, 1855-1941, vol. 10: 1932-1935
Annual Reports of the Straits Settlements, 1855-1941, vol. 22: 1936-1941

Government Gazette
Straits Settlements (S.S.) Gazette – July-December 1884
Straits Settlements (S.S.) Gazette – November-December 1888
Straits Settlements (S.S.) Gazette – April-June 1893
Straits Settlements (S.S.) Gazette – 1903
Straits Settlements (S.S.) Gazette – December 1907
Straits Settlements (S.S.) Gazette – April-June 1912
Straits Settlements (S.S.) Gazette Part II vol. LIX – October-December 1924
Straits Settlements (S.S.) Gazette Part IV vol. LXIV – 1929

Ordinance
Straits Settlements Ordinance 1867 – 1941, Ordinance: 1889
Straits Settlements Ordinance 1867 – 1941, Ordinance: 1898-1902
Straits Settlements Ordinance 1867 – 1941, Ordinance: 1923-1934
Straits Settlements Ordinance 1867 – 1941, Ordinance: 1913-1941
Straits Settlements Ordinance 1867 – 1941, Ordinance: 1867-1889
The Acts And Ordinances Of The Legislative Council Of The Straits Settlements (S.S.), Part II (1 April 1867-7 March 1898)
Act And Ordinance Of The Legislative Council Of The Straits Settlements (S.S.), Part V of 1884-Part VIII of 1887
Straits Settlements Establishment 1884-1941. List of Establishment: 1884, 1905, 1910, 1925-1929. (Singapore, Penang, Malacca)

Straits Settlements Blue Book

S.S. Blue Book For The Year 1881, Government Printing Office, Singapore.
S.S. Blue Book For The Year 1882, Government Printing Office, Singapore.
S.S. Blue Book For The Year 1894, Government Printing Office, Singapore.
S.S. Blue Book For The Year 1911, Government Printing Office, Singapore.
S.S. Blue Book For The Year 1919, Government Printing Office, Singapore.
S.S. Blue Book For The Year 1930, Government Printing Office, Singapore.

Census

Straits Settlements Census Report 1901
Census - 1911 - Population of the Federated Malay States
Census Report for British Malaya, 1921
British Malaya - A Report on the 1931 Census and on certain problems of vital statistics.

Others

Annual Report 1920. Chinese Protectorate
Annual Report on the Chinese Protectorate, Straits Settlements for 1924
Chinese Protectorate - Establishment List 1925
Directory for 1883 - Singapore & Penang
Estimates 1904. Chinese Protectorate
The Petition of Ban Hin Lee Bank Limited, Copy of Minutes in F.S. 3561/50, 5 July 1950

Newspapers and Periodicals

Daily Advertiser (Singapore)
Malayan Saturday Post (Singapore)
Malaya Tribune (Singapore, Kuala Lumpur, Penang, Ipoh)
Singapore Standard (Singapore)
Straits Echo (Penang)
Sunday Gazette (Singapore)
The Eastern Daily Mail and Straits Morning Advertiser (Singapore)
The Pinang Gazette and Straits Chronicle (Penang)
The Singapore Free Press and Mercantile Advertiser (Singapore)
The Straits Times (Singapore)

Oral History Interviews

Chan Kum Chee, Oral History Interviews with Chan Kum Chee by Lim How Seng, Accession Number 000341, National Archives of Singapore, 25 September 1983.
De Cruz, Gerald, Oral History Interviews with De Cruz, Gerald by Foo Kim Leng, Accession Number 000105, National Archives of Singapore, 23 September 1981.
Foo Kee Seng, Oral History Interviews with Foo Kee Seng by Chiang Wai Fong, Accession Number 002017, National Archives of Singapore, 20 May 1998.

Gwee Peng Kwee, Oral History Interviews with Gwee Peng Kwee by Tan Beng Luan, Accession Number 000128, National Archives of Singapore, 18 November 1981.

Hwang Chung Yun, Oral History Interviews with Hwang Chung Yun by Liana Tan, Accession Number 000237, National Archives of Singapore, 18 January 1983.

Lee Kim Tah, Oral History Interviews with Lee Kim Tah by Tan Beng Luan, Accession Number 000211, National Archives of Singapore, 15 December 1982.

Lee Kip Lin, Oral History Interviews with Lee Kip Lin by Cindy Chou, Accession Number 001491, National Archives of Singapore, 6 June 1994.

Lim Kee Lam, Oral History Interviews with Lim Kee Lam by Jesley Chua Chee Huan, Accession Number 000617, National Archives of Singapore, 3 January 1986.

Low Cheng Gin, Oral History Interviews with Low Cheng Gin by Yeo Geok Lee, Accession Number 000517, National Archives of Singapore, 3 June 1983.

Lu Yaw, Oral History Interviews with Lu Yaw by Lu Chisen, Accession Number 001599, National Archives of Singapore, 28 April 1994.

Seow, Betty Guat Beng, Oral History Interviews with Seow, Betty Guat Beng by Ooi Yu-Lin, Accession Number 001048, National Archives of Singapore, 8 July 1989.

Silcock Thomas, Oral History Interviews with Silcock Thomas by Liana Tan, Accession Number 000180, National Archives of Singapore, 13 June 1982.

Sng Boey Kim, Oral History Interviews with Sng Boey Kim by Khoo Ting Poh, Accession Number 000064, National Archives of Singapore, 8 February 1985.

Sng Choon Yee, Oral History Interviews with Sng Choon Yee by Lim How Seng, Accession Number 000064, National Archives of Singapore, 14 May 1981.

Tan Cheng Hwee, Oral History Interviews with Sng Choon Yee by Low Lay Leng, Accession Number 000416, National Archives of Singapore, 26 April 1984.

Tan Chye Yee, Oral History Interviews with Tan Chye Yee bycJesley Chua Chee Huan, Accession Number 000616, National Archives of Singapore, 3 January 1986.

Tan Hoon Siang, Oral History Interviews with Tan Hoon Siang by Lim How Seng, Accession Number 000077, National Archives of Singapore, 24 January 1983 Tan Hoon Siang.

Tan Kok Kheng, Oral History Interviews with TAN Kok Kheng by Lim How Seng, Accession Number 000232, National Archives of Singapore, 25 January 1984.

Tan Sock Kern, Oral History Interviews with Tan Sock Kern by Yeo Geok Lee, Accession Number 000287, National Archives of Singapore, 20 September 1993.

Toh Man Keong, Oral History Interviews with Toh Man Keong by Lim How Seng, Accession Number 000001, National Archives of Singapore, 27 December 1979.

Toh Thiam Seng, Oral History Interviews with Toh Thiam Seng by Jesley Chua Chee Huan, Accession Number 000759, National Archives of Singapore, 25 March 1987.

Yap Siong Eu, Oral History Interviews with Yap Siong Eu by Liana Tan, Accession Number 000316 - 000, National Archives of Singapore, 16 August 1983.

Interviews

Chim Poh & Lay Geok, 4 December 2009

Foo, Thye Chye, Penang, 8 September 2008

Goh, Bee Imm 7th, Penang, December 2007.

Goh, Eng Toon (Dato Seri), Penang, 8 November 2007 & 1 November 2017

Fitzgerald, Aiden (sister), Penang, 21 January 2011

Hooi, Siew Foong, Penang, 19 January 2010

Kwoh, Shoo Chen, Penang, 17 August 2010

Levin, Charles (Brother), Penang, 3 March 2011

Lim, Chong Eu (Tun Dr.), Penang, July 2007 & 27 October 2009

Lim Kean Chye, Penang, 23 January 2011, March 2014.

Limpanonda, Khim, Phuket, 9 December 2007

Ong, Chin Hong, Penang, 4 December 2009

Png, Gek Ling, Penang, June 2007–November 2018.

Png, Seok Pheng, Penang, 16 September 2008 & 4 December 2009

Tanner, Lovy, Bangkok, 3 October 2017

Woo, Sak Khau, Penang, 2 March 2011

Yeap, Boon Huat, Yangon, 22 December 2009

Yeap, Eng Gim, Penang, 7 December 2007

Yeap, Leong Huat (Dato Seri), Penang, June 2007–November 2018.

Yeap, Poh Jin, New York, June 2007–November 2010.

Yeap, Poh Tee, Brisbane, June 2007–November 2018.

Yeap, Poh Tin, Kuala Lumpur, June 2007–November 2018.

Yeap, Leong Sim, Penang, 7 December 2007.

Books & Articles

Allan, C Wilfrid, *Makers of Cathay*, Shanghai: Presbyterian Mission Press, 1909.

Anderson, John, *Political and Commercial Considerations Relative to The Malayan Peninsula British Settlements in the Straits of Malaya*, Printed under Authority of Government, 1824.

Bailey, Warren and Lan Truong, 'Opium and Empire: Some Evidence from Colonial-Era Asian Stock and Commodity Markets', *Journal of Southeast Asian Studies*, June 2001, 173-193.

Bank Negara Malaysia, *Money and Banking in Malaysia 1959-1979*, Kuala Lumpur: Bank Negara Malaysia, 1979.

Bard, Emile, *The Chinese At Home*, London: George Newnes, 1906.

Bernardi, Jean De, *Rites of Belonging: Memory Modernity and Identity in a Malaysian Chinese Community*, Singapore: NUS Press, 2009.

Blakeslee, George H., *China and the Far East*, New York: Thomas Y Crowell & Co, 1910.

Blythe, Wilfred, *Historical Sketch of Chinese Labour in Malaya*, 1947.

Blythe, Wilfred, *The Impact of Chinese secret societies in Malaya: A Historical Study*, Oxford, UK: Oxford University Press, 1969.

Bosma, Ulbe & Jonathan Curry-Machado, *Two Islands, One Commodity: Cuba, Java, and The Global Sugar Trade (1790-1930)*, New West Indian Guide, vol. 84, no. 3-4, 2012.

Boomgaard, Peter, *Weathering the Storm: The Economies of Southeast Asia in the 1930s Depression*, Singapore: ISEAS, 2001.

Brooke, Gilbert Edward, Roland St. John Braddell, and Walter Makepeace, *One Hundred Years of Singapore*, John Murray, Albemarle Street, W, 1921.

Bryson, Mary Isabella, *Child Life in Chinese Homes*, London: London Missionary Society, 1890.

Butcher John and Howard Dick, *The Rise and Fall of Revenue Farming: Business Elites and the Emergence of the Modern State in Southeast Asia*, London: The Macmillian Press, 1993.

Campbell, Persia Crawford, *Chinese Coolie Emigration to Countries Within The British Empire*, London: P. S. King & Son, 1923.

Carroll, John M., 'A National Custom: Debating Female Servitude in Late Nineteenth-Century Hong Kong', *Modern Asian Studies*, vol. 43, no. 6, 2009.

Cheah, Jin Seng, *Penang 500 Early Postcards*, Kuala Lumpur: Editions Didier Millet, 2012.

Cheng, Tien-His, *China Moulded By Confucius: The Chinese Way in Western Light*, London: The London Institute of World Affairs, 1947.

Chin, Edmund, *Gilding the Phoenix: The Straits Chinese and their Jewelry*, Singapore: The National Museum of Singapore, 1991.

Choi, Dong Sull, 'Myth and reality of the Chinese Diaspora', *Comparative Civilizations Review*, vol. 46, no. 46, 2002.

Claver, Alexander, *Dutch Commerce and Chinese Merchants in Java: Colonial Relationship in Trade and Finance, 1800-1942*, Leiden/Boston: Brill, 2014.

Comber, Leon, *An Introduction to Chinese Secret Societies in Malaya*, Singapore: Donald Moore, 1957.

Comber, Leon, *Chinese Ancestor Worship in Malaya*, Singapore: Donald Moore, 1956.

Comber, Leon, *Chinese Magic and Superstitions in Malaya*, Singapore: Eastern Universities Press, 1969.

Conwell, R. H., *Why The Chinese Emigrate and The Means They Adopt For The Purpose Of Reaching America*, New York: Lee and Shepard Publishers, 1871.

Coppel, Charles A., 'Liem Thian Joe's Unpublished History of Kian Gwan' *Southeast Asian Studies*, vol. 27, no. 2, 1989.

Cunnyngham, W.G.E., *History of the Chinese*, Chicago: Fleming H. Revell Company, 1896.

Dobbs, Stephen, *The Singapore River – A Social History 1819-2002*, Singapore: Singapore University Press, 2003.

Douglas, Robert K., *Society in China*, London: Ward, Lock & Co, 1901.

Drake, Peter Joseph, *Financial Development in Malaya and Singapore*, Australian National University Press, Canberra, 1969.

Edgerton-Tarpley, Kathryn, 'Famine in Imperial and Modern China', Oxford *Research Encyclopaedia of Asian History*, Online Publication, 2017.

Edkins, J., *Banking and Prices in China*, The Presbyterian Mission Press, Shanghai, 1905.

Frankema, Ewout, 'Raising revenue in the British Empire, 1870-1940: How Extractive were Colonial Taxes?', *Journal of Global History*, 2010.

Frost, Mark Ravinder, 'Transcultural Diaspora: The Straits Chinese in Singapore, 1819-1918', Asia Research Institute, National University of Singapore, August 2003.

Gambe, Annabelle R., *Overseas Chinese Entrepreneurship and Capitalist Development in Southeast Asia*, Hamburg/London: Lit Verlag Munster, 1999.

Gascoigne, Bamber, *The Dynasties of China: A Brief History of*, Robinson, London, 2003.

Gascoyne-Cecil, William, *Changing China*, London: James Nisbet & Co, 1911.

German, RL, *Handbook of British Malaya*, The Malayan Information Agency, 1930.

Giles, Herbert Allen, *China and The Chinese*, New York: Columbia University Press, 1902.

Giles, Herbert Allen, *China and The Manchus*, Cambridge: Cambridge University Press, 1912.

Giles, Herbert A., *The Civilization of China*, London: Thornton Butterworth, 1911.

Grainger, Adam, *Studies in Chinese Life*, Chengtu: Canadian Methodist Mission Press, 1921.

Gullick, J.M., 'Governors' Houses', *Journal of the Malayan Branch of the Royal Asiatic Society*, vol. LXXI, no. 1, 1998.

Hicks, George, *Chinese Organisations in Southeast Asia in the 1930s*, Singapore: Select Books, 1996.

Historical Personalities of Penang Committee, *Historical Personalities of Penang*, Penang: The Historical Personalities of Penang Committee, 1986.

Ho, Wing Meng, *Straits Chinese Furniture: A Collector's Guide*, Singapore: Marshall Cavendish Editions, 2008.

Holcombe, Chester, *The Real Chinaman*, New York: Dodd, Mead & Company, 1909.

Hoyt, Sarnia Hayes, *Old Penang*, Singapore: Oxford University Press, 1991.

Huff, W.G., 'Currency Boards and Chinese Banks in Malaya and the Philippines Before World War II', *Australian Economic History Review*, vol. 43, no. 2, University of Glasgow, July 2003.

Jones, Russell, *Chinese Names: Notes on the Use of Surnames & Personal Names by the Chinese in Malaya*, Singapore, MBRAS, 1959.

Keaughran, T.J., *The Singapore Directory for the Straits Settlements 1879*, Singapore: T.J. Keaughran, 1879.

Kemp E. G., *Chinese Mettle*, London: Hodder and Stoughton, 1921.

Khadijah Moore Wendy, *Malaysia: A Pictorial History 1400-2004*, Singapore: Archipelago Press, 2004.

Khoo Salma Nasution and Malcolm Wade, *Penang Postcard Collection 1899-1930s*, Penang: Janus Print & Resources, 2003.

Khoo Salma Nasution, *The Chulia in Penang: Patronage and Place-Making around the Kapitan Keling Mosque 1786-1957*, Penang: Areca Books, 2014.

Khoo Su Nin, *Streets of George Town Penang*, Penang: Areca Books, 2012.

Kohl, David G., *Chinese Architecture in the Straits Settlements and Western Malaya: Temples, Kongsis and Houses*, Kuala Lumpur: Heinemann Asia, 1984.

Koo, Hui-Lan with Mary Van Rensselaer Thayer, *An Autobiography*, New York: Dial Press, 1943.

Kratoska, Paul H., 'The British Empire and the Southeast Asian Rice Crisis of 1919-1921', *Modern Asian Studies*, vol. 24, no. 1, 1990.

Kratoska, Paul H., *The Japanese Occupation of Malaya, 1941-1945*, Hawaii, US: University of Hawaii Press, 1997.

Kratoska, Paul H., 'The Post 1945 Food Shortage in British Malaya, 1941-1945', *Journal of Southeast Asian Studies*, vol. XIX, no. 1, 1988.

Kunio, Yoshihara, 'Interview: Oei Tiong Ie', *Southeast Asian Studies*, vol. 27, no. 2, 1989.

Kunio, Yoshihara, 'Interview: Oei Tiong Tjay', *Southeast Asian Studies*, vol. 27, no. 2, 1989.

Kunio, Yoshihara, 'Oei Tiong Ham Concern: The First Business Empire of Southeast Asia', *Southeast Asian Studies*, vol. 27, no. 2, 1989.

Lee, Hock Lock, 'Commercial Banking in the Federation of Malaya and the Borneo States Before the Advent of Bank Negara Malaysia', *Journal of the Malaysian Economic Association*.

Lee, S.Y., 'The Development of Commercial Banking in Singapore and the States of Malaya', *The Malayan Economic Review*, vol. XI, no. 1, 1966.

Leong, Yee Fong, 'Secret Societies and Politics in Colonial Malaya with Special Reference to the Ang Bin Hoey in Penang (1945-1952)', *The Penang Story - International Conference*, 2002.

Leong, Y.K. and L.K. Tao, *Village and Town Life in China*, London: George, Allen & Unwin, 1915.

Lewis, Su Lin, 'Cosmopolitan and the Modern Girl: A Cross-Cultural Discourse in 1930s Penang', *Modern Asian Studies*, vol. 43, no. 6, 2009.

Lim, Jon Sun Hock, *The Penang House and The Straits Architect 1887-1941*, Areca Books, 2015

Lim, Jon Sun Hock, 'The Shophouse Rafflesia: An Outline of its Malaysian Pedigree and its Subsequent Diffusion in Asia', *Journal of the Malayan Branch of the Royal Asiatic Society*, vol. 66, 1993.

Lim, Jon Sun Hock,' Typologies of Historical Exploration: Constructing History from Research Methodology, Documents, Narratives and Memories', *The Penang Story - International Conference*, 2002.

Lim, Kean Siew, *Blood on The Golden Sands, The Memoirs of a Penang Family*, Pelanduk Publications, 1999.

Lim, Kean Siew, *The Eye Over The Golden Sands*, Pelanduk Publications, 1997.

Lim-Loh, Lin Lee, *Traditional Street Names of George Town*, George Town World Heritage Incorporated, 2015.

Lim, P. Pui Huen, *Wong Ah Fook: Immigrant Builder and Entrepreneur*, Times Edition, 2012.

Lo, Dorothy, *Chinese Festivals in Malaya*, Singapore, Eastern Universities, 1958.

Loh, Wei Leng, Badriyah Haji Salleh, Mahani Musa, Wong Yee Tuan and Marcus Langdon, *Biographical Dictionary of Mercantile Personalities of Penang*, Kuala Lumpur: Think City/ MBRAS, 2013

Low, James, *The British Settlement of Penang*, Singapore: Oxford University Press, 1972.

Macgowan, J., *Men and Manners of Modern China*, London: T. Fisher Unwin, 1912.

Mackie, Jamie, 'Towkays and Tycoons: The Chinese in Indonesian Economic Life in the 1920s and 1980s', *Southeast Asia Program Publications*, Cornell University, 1991.

Mai Lin Tjoa-Bonatz, 'Ordering of Housing and the Urbanization Process: Shophouses in Colonial Penang', *Journal of the Malayan Branch of the Royal Asiatic Society*, vol. LXXI, no. 2, 1998.

Majlis Perbandaran George Town, *Penang information guide/compiled and issued by Municipal Commissioners of George Town, Penang by M. J. Thorpe, Penang*, The Municipal Commissioners of George Town, 1938.

Malay Peninsula: *Old Photograps of Malaya and Singapore by C.J. Kleingrothe, C. 1900 from the Collection of HRH Sultan Idris Shah of Selangor*, Jugra Publications, produced and designed by Editions Didier Millet, 2009.

Mamoru, Shinozaki, *Syonan – My Story. The Japanese Occupation of Singapore*, Singapore: Marshall Cavendish Editions, 1975

Martin, Montgomery R., *History of the British Possessions in the Indian & Atlantic Oceans*, London: Whittaker & Co.

McKeown, Adam, 'Chinese Emigration in Global Context, 1850-1940', *Journal of Global History*, London School of Economics and Political Science, 2010.

Moll-Murata, Christine, 'Chinese Guilds from the Seventeenth to the Twentieth Centuries: An Overview', *IRSH*, Internationaal Instituut voor Sociale Geschiedenis, 2008.

Morse, Hosea Ballou, *The Gilds of China*, New York: Longmans, Green & Co, 1909.

Morse, Hosea Ballou, *The Trade and Administration of the Chinese Empire*, New York: Longmans, Green & Co, 1908.

Moule, Arthur Evans, *The Chinese People, A Handbook on China*, London: Society For Promoting Christian Knowledge, 1914.

Oei, Hui-Lan with Isabella Taves, *No Feast Lasts Forever*, New York: Quadrangle, The New York Times Book Co., 1975.

Olson, Emma, *The Chinese of Malaya: A Study of an Immigrant Group as a Field for Mission Work*, Chicago: University of Chicago, 1932.

Onghokham, 'Chinese Capitalism in Dutch Java', *Southeast Asian Studies*, vol. 27, no. 2, 1989.

Ooi, Keat Gin, 'Domestic Servants Par Excellence: The Black & White Amahs of Malaya and Singapore with Special Reference to Penang', *Journal of the Malayan Branch of the Royal Asiatic Society*, vol. 65, 1992.

Pan, Lynn, *The Encyclopedia of the Chinese Overseas*, Singapore: Editions Didier Millet, 2nd ed., 2006.

Pickering, W.A., 'Chinese Secret Societies and their Origin', *Journal of the Malayan Branch of the Royal Asiatic Society*, no. 1, 1878.

Pitcher P.W., *In And About Amoy*, Shanghai & Foochow: The Methodist Publishing House in China, 1912.

Pitcher P.W., *Fifty Years in Amoy*, New York: Board of Publication Of The Reformed Church in America, 1893.

Purcell, Victor, *The Chinese in Malaya*, Kuala Lumpur: Oxford University Press, 1967.

Ross, John DD, *The Origin of the Chinese People*, Kuala Lumpur: Pelanduk Publications, 2001.

Ruskanda, Farid, Isa Ridwan, *Java Sugar Industry and Sugar Cane Engineering in Nineteenth Century*, Indonesia: Ruslitbang-Kim LIPI, 2013.

Saravanamuttu, Manicasothy, *The Sara Saga*, Penang: Areca Reprints, 2010.

Schlegel, Gustave, *The Hung-League or Heaven Earth League*, Singapore: Lange & Co, 1866.

Short, Brock K., 'Indigenous Banking in an Early Period of Development: The Straits Settlements, 1914-1940', *The Malayan Economic Review*, vol. XVI, no. 1, 1971.

Sing, Ging Su, *The Chinese Family System*, New York: Columbia University, 1922.

Smith, Arthur H., *Chinese Characteristics*, London: Oliphant, Anderson and Ferrier, 1900.

Smith, Arthur H., *Village Life in China*, London: Oliphant, Anderson and Ferrier, 1900.

Smyth, Montague, Kegan Paul, *Sidelights on Chinese Life*, Trench, Trubner & Co, 1907.

Stead, Alfred, *China and Her Mysteries*, London: Hood, Douglas & Howard, 1901.

Stockwell, A.J., 'The Crucible of The Malayan Nation: The University and the Making of a New Malaya. 1938-62', *Modern Asian Studies*, 2008.

Tan, Chee Beng, 'Chinese Religion in Malaysia: A General View', *Asian Folklore Studies*, vol. 42, 1983.

Tan, Chee Beng ed., *Chinese Transnational Networks*, London: Routledge, 2007.

Tan, Ee-Leong, 'The Chinese Banks Incorporated in Singapore & the Federation of Malaya', *Journal of the Malayan Branch of the Royal Asiatic Society*, vol. XXVI, no. 1, 1953.

Tan, Kim Hong, *The Chinese in Penang: A Pictorial History*, Penang: Areca Books, 2007.

Taylor, Isaac H., *Home Life in China*, London: Methuen & Co, 1914.

The Laws of the Straits Settlements Vol 1, 1835-1900, Rev. Ed., London: Waterlow & Sons Ltd, 1920.

The Laws of the Straits Settlements Vol 2, 1901-1907, Rev. Ed., London: Waterlow & Sons Ltd, 1920.

Tregonning K. G., *Straits Tin – A Brief Account of the First Seventy-Five Years of The Straits Trading Company*, Ltd, Singapore: The Straits Times Press, 1962.

Trocki, Carl A., 'A Drug on the Market: Opium and the Chinese in Southeast Asia, 1750-1880', A paper presented to the International Society for the Study of the Chinese Overseas, Elsinore, Denmark, 5-10 May 2004.

Trocki, Carl A., 'Chinese Revenue Farms and Borders in Southeast Asia', *Modern Asian Studies*, vol. 43, no. 1, 2009.

Tsu, Yu-Yue, *The Spirit of Chinese Philanthropy: A Study in Mutual Aid*, New York: Columbia Univeristy, 1912.

Turnbull, C.M., 'Penang's Changing Role in the Straits Settlements, 1826-1946', The Penang Story – International Conference 2002.

Wade, Geoff, 'An Early Age of Commerce in Southeast Asia, 900-1300 CE', *Journal of Southeast Asian Studies*, vol. 40, no. 2, 2009.

Wang Gungwu, *China and the Chinese Overseas*, Singapore: Eastern Universities Press, 2003.

Wang, Han, Jia Beishi, 'A Morphological Study of Traditional Shophouse in China and Southeast Asia', The University of Hong Kong, Hong Kong, 2014.

Westenra Sambon L., 'Acclimatization of Europeans in Tropical Countries', *The Geographical Journal*, vol. 12, no. 6, 1898.

Willmott, Donald Earl, *The Chinese of Semarang: A Changing Minority Community in Indonesia*, Ithaca, New York: Cornell University Press, 1960.

Wiseman, Roger, 'Three Crises: Management in the Colonial Java Sugar Industry 1880s-1930s', University of Adelaide, 2001.

Wong Hun Sum, *The Japanese Occupation of Malaya (Singapore) and its Currency*, Wong's Collection, 1996.

Wong, Yee Tuan, 'The Big Five Hokkien Families in Penang, 1830s-1890s', *Chinese Southern Diaspora Studies*, vol. 1, 2007.

Wright, Arnold & H.A. Cartwright, *Twentieth Century Impressions of British Malaya: Its History, People, Commerce, industries and Resources*, London: Lloyd's Greater Britain Publishing Company Ltd, 1908.

Wu, Ching-Chao, 'The Chinese Family: Organisation, Names and Kinship Terms', *American Anthropologist*, vol. 29, no. 3, 1927.

Wu, Xiao An, *Chinese Business in the Making of a Malay State, 1882-1941: Kedah and Penang*, London: Routledge Curzon, 2003.

Vaughan, J. D., *The Manners and Customs of The Chinese of The Straits Settlements*, Kuala Lumpur: Oxford University Press, Singapore, 1879.

Vlieland, C.A., 'The Population of the Malay Peninsula: A Study in Human Migration', *The Geographical Review*, vol. 24, no. 1, 1934.

Yen, Ching Hwang, *Community and Politics: The Chinese in Colonial Singapore and Malaysia*, Singapore: Times Academic Press, 1995.

Yen, Ching-Hwang, *The Chinese in Southeast Asia and Beyond*, Singapore: World Scientific, 2008.

Yen, Ching Hwang, *The Overseas Chinese and the 1911 Revolution: With Special Reference to Singapore and Malaya*, Kuala Lumpur: Oxford University Press, 1976.

Yeoh, Brenda S.A., *Contesting Space In Colonial Singapore: Power and relations and the urban built environment*, Singapore: Singapore University Press, 2003.

Zelin, Madeleine, 'Informal Law and The Firm in Early Modern China', Paper prepared for the First IERC Conference: The Economic Performance of Civilizations: Roles of Culture, Religion, and the Law, University of Southern California, Los Angeles, February 23-24, 2007.

Zhao, Youg Qing, 'The Company Law in China', *Indiana International & Comparative Law Review*, vol. 6, no. 2, 1996.

Zhou, Min, 'The Chinese Diaspora and International Migration', *Social Transformations in Chinese Studies*, vol. 1, no. 1, University of California, 2006.

Index